CW00523271

TRAVELS IN TREMBLING WATERS

To Frank & Margaret.

With best wishes

TRAVELS IN TREMBLING WATERS

THE DIARY OF
A TEA PLANTER'S WIFE

DOIREAN CAMPBELL

Doirean Campbell.

The Book Guild Ltd
Sussex, England.

To Piet

"The Tea Tree stands on the mountain but has its leaves in the valley".

Palaung Proverb.

The Book Guild Ltd
25 High Street
Lewes, Sussex
first Published 1989
© Doirean Campbell 1989
Set in Baskerville
Typeset by Hawks Phototypesetters Ltd
Copthorne, West Sussex
Printed in Great Britain by
Antony Rowe Ltd
Chippenham, Wilts

ISBN 0 86332 376 6

CONTENTS

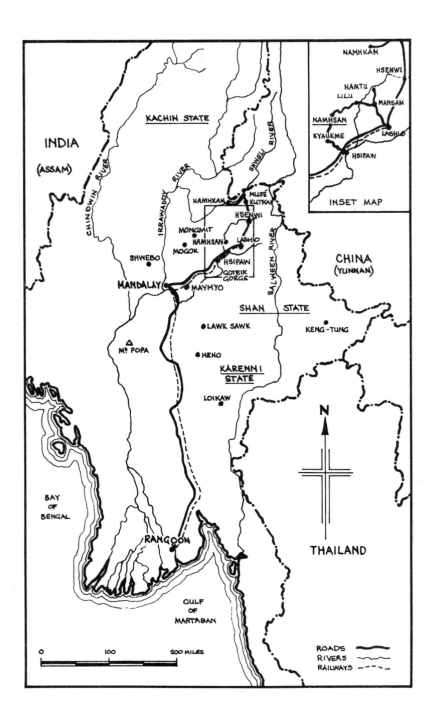

I

In Search of Thusan-ti's Garden

The soft warm night air caressed my face, dulling the senses with the cloying scent of Queen of the Night.

I settled back comfortably in the big car, watching the changing pattern of the myriad of flickering lights as we sped by settlements on the outskirts of Rangoon. Despite the late hour, Kit, our kind host, had come to Mingladon Airport to help us through the lengthy formalities and as we drove towards the city, he warned me not to fall asleep or I would miss the great pagoda. Here and there, amongst the clusters of small wooden houses, I saw smokey fires. Around some of them sat faceless figures huddled close in deep concentration. I wondered what they could be doing in that darkest hour before dawn. Gambling perhaps, or hatching some mischief? My thoughts strayed back to the beginning of this journey just a few short months before. It had all started one wet August evening in South India. I had married a tea planter and after two years was happily adjusted to life on the tea estates. Then, one evening, everything changed when the Group Manager called with the news that Piet was to be asked to take over the tea factory at Namhsan, North Shan States. It would only be for two years at the most, said Wyon, but I would have to do some serious thinking about the prospect. Could I face the isolation and loneliness it would mean?

Like most other tea planters we knew, Piet had served in the Indian Army, returning to the tea estates after the war. It was then that he had been sent to Burma to spend a few months in remote Tawngpeng, managing the Company's tea factory.

He had often spoken to me of that fabled forgotten land of mountains. It was a beautiful place he would say, like an enchanted garden perpetually full of lovely flowers, of exotic birds and animals which knew little fear of man for they were protected by the religious principles of the Palaungs, a quiet, gentle, fun-loving people who wore costumes of dazzling colours and talked in bated breath of Thusan-ti, their legendary Dragon Grandmother. Even so it was a daunting prospect. For a year at a stretch I would be lost in those lonely hills; in old Ohm Yah, the old Palaung name for the capital town, there were no other Europeans and few of the indigenous people spoke English. Unless I learned something of the local languages I would be unable to converse with anybody apart from my husband.

I knew he would be only too happy to return there and for my part I had devoured travel books from early childhood and longed to see all the far-away — places I had read about. I was not going to miss an opportunity such as this. After all, it would not be for ever, merely an interlude in my life like a teabreak in a long day. We had returned to England in the September for a short leave and in the New Year had set out in search of Thusan-ti's Enchanted Garden.

My reverie was suddenly shattered as we swept around a bend in the road by the sight of a great golden bell silhouetted against the midnight blue of the sky. The soft floodlighting and halo of silvery stars gave it an air of mysterious beauty, so different from the glittering daytime image I was to see. This was the best way to see the famous Shwé Dagon Pagoda for the first time, said Kit but I would judge for myself when I had seen the great pagoda in all its golden magnificence, with solid gold Plantain Bud and jewel-encrusted Hti on the pinnacle.

Surrounded by a forest of gilded mini pagodas and glittering temples, the great pagoda had slumbered there on top of Singaturra Hill for more than a thousand years, surviving conflicts and natural disasters.

We swept on into the residential area of the great city, past little houses, imposing residences in flower-filled gardens, vast concrete buildings of ultra modern design. Then we drew up under the lofty porch of a beautiful old house, built in the style of the Scottish Hunting Lodges and set in a wide expanse of green lawns and shady trees. It was almost dawn and I was too tired to appreciate the lovely old house; there would be time for that later. Kit suggested we took a shower before weariness finally overcame us, and that was to result in the first of the many surprises that Burma had in store for me.

As the luke-warm water gushed noisily out of the giant copper "rose" over my head, there was a piercing shriek outside the open bathroom window and to my horror, a ferocious-looking green dragon about three feet long, crawled in from the empty blackness framed by the window to march purposefully along the water pipe and sit on top of the shower rose over my head, screeching 'Tak-Too-oo-oo' whilst it stared fixedly at me with fierce yellow eyes.

I was completely mesmerised, quite certain that at any moment it would come and take a bite out of me. At last I plucked up the courage to turn off the shower and immediately the intruder began to retreat slowly along the water pipe to disappear into the dark world without, its protesting screech fading to a low groan, I breathed again, thankful I had had such a lucky escape.

The next morning, when I told Nina about my night visitor, she had laughed and said it was considered to be very auspicious to be greeted by a Tak-Too on arrival in Burma, especially if the giant lizard "called" seven times. Well, my small dragon had certainly done that and so I hoped it portended good things.

Apart from the Golden Pagoda and the Green Dragon, there were other things which over the years became treasured memories of a charming city. The Lakes, dotted with tiny tree-covered islands where Burmese and foreigners alike sailed their small boats. The great ocean-going ships on the Rangoon River and dodging in and out amongst these giants, the tiny high-prowed boats, with a single oarsman, who plied to and fro taking passengers and goods to the other side. There were the gardens, displays of art and industry and the many temples. On that first occasion, though, we had little time for frivolities, most of our days being taken up with the formalities of getting our Stay Permits and Foreigners' Registration Certificates, the F.R.C's which I was to find were the cause of much trouble and heartbreak for many of the non-Burmese inhabitants of the Shan Hills.

Our final destination was a long and tiring journey away, by land routes and by air. There was only one flight a week to the Northern States and so it was early one morning that we set out for Lashio, a journey that was to take us over the low-lying plains of the south to the rolling hills and eventually to the isolated mountains of the north.

We landed first for refuelling at Loikaw, capital of the Karenni State. As we left the aircraft to stretch our legs, we were rather surprised to see that a group of black-clad people who had been squatting by the boundary fence, had boarded the aircraft. Every seat was taken. Our alarm at the thought of being stranded for days on an empty airfield was allayed however when, refuelling finished, the black-clad strangers quietly filed out of the plane and returned to their places by the boundary fence.

Curious about these people and their odd behaviour, I asked who they were. They were Padaungs, I was told. They came each week to meet the plane and sit inside, as though about to take off, perhaps to dream of travelling the world. I had heard of the Giraffe Necked Women of Burma but had never expected to share my seat on the aircraft with one. The curious practice of stretching their necks with brass rings was said to have started as a protection against maurauding leopards and became a mark of beauty for the Padaung Women, although the practice is in decline.

Our next stop was at HeHo in the South Shan State, near Yaunghwe and Taungyi, and we stepped out into the fresh, cool air to see a vista of low rolling hills and just beyond, the beautiful Inlé Lake. We journeyed on to Mandalay, where our agent was waiting to welcome us, pressing us not to leave it too long before we visited the famous town.

After Mandalay the terrain became more mountainous and we flew low over deep wooded valleys and sharp, knife-like ridges. It was like a traditional Chinese painting. With mounting excitement I saw the town of Lashio below and a mile or so away, a green "pocket handkerchief" bordered by low jungle-covered hills. This was the airfield, which was to be our main lifeline with the outside world.

We were greeted by a genial Chinese who wore a brightly checked lumber-jacket against the chill air. This was Martin Tan, our Lashio agent. With him the driver from Namhsan who handed Piet a letter of welcome from the man we had come so far to replace. It sent a shiver of fear down my spine as I read that dacoits, armed robbers, were operating up to milepost thirteen but after that, our host had written, we need have no worries. The Land Rover was loaded up with a vast array of boxes and tins, our luggage was squeezed in and we drove on to have our first glimpse of Lashio. At first sight it seemed to be merely a sprawling collection of wooden houses and shops, dominated surprisingly by a gleaming white mosque. We made only a brief stop on that first visit, to meet the charming Mrs Tan and then we were on our way to remote and legendary Tawngpeng, taking between four and five hours to cover the eighty miles.

After travelling some way along the road, I remembered the letter and began to count the milestones. As we drove past No. 13 I breathed a sigh of relief and settled down to enjoy the journey, not realising that the danger of dacoity was with us until we had passed the thirteenth milestone from Namhsan, not Lashio. At least that first fascinating glimpse of my new world was not spoiled by fear of an ambush around each bend in the road.

This was a land of jungle-covered hills, precipitous ridges and deep valleys. The jungle on either side of the road seemed to flash and sparkle with a kaleidoscope of bright colours as exotic birds rose to our noisy passing. We disturbed great flocks of green parakeets feeding on fruits in the more open parts of the forest and had to hoot at the gaudy Hoopoes which strutted, in the road. A sudden streak of vivid scarlet crossed the windscreen and it was only later, after a friend had given me a long lecture on local birds, that I was able to satisfy my curiosity and learn something of the Scarlet Minivet, called "Prince Bird" in Burmese. In time I saw many other beautiful birds and they made all the little brown birds of the English countryside seem drab by comparison.

There was the dark elegance of the Racket Tailed Drongo, in contrast to the Paradise Flycatcher, which trailed long tailfeathers like wisps of white chiffon ribbon as it flew from tree to tree in a curious undulating flight. There were the Treepies, the bright turquoise of the Rollers, the red-and-orange plumaged Trogon, and the Great Coucal which looked like a great orange-backed crow. Loveliest of all perhaps was the Fairy Bluebird, settling with a sudden flash of sapphire blue on a tree, its scintillating blue sheen standing out against the dark green of the trees completed the magic of the scene for me, and time passed quickly with so much of interest to observe. The tall trees on either side of the road were a riot of colour, and I was to find that the "Flower Show" lasted throughout the year, each month having a special display.

The names of the few villages we passed through were fascinating. There was EeNi, where we stopped to buy eggs, and YayOh where the jungle suddenly opened out into a small flat plain enclosed by the surrounding hills, and where it seemed so hot and dry that my lips and eyes burned. The whole area was covered with spikey, purple flowers, which at a distance looked like heather and in March, just before the rains, that little plain seemed to burst into flame. When the small bushes dotted around the whole area blossomed, the bare stems so thickly encrusted with orange bell flowers that the bushes seemed to glow. Later, in August, the showy Scarlet Gingers would display their fiery flower spikes. As we left the YayOh Plain our eyes were caught by grotesque rock formations which formed the barrier enclosing the whole area. The odd-looking boulders might have been deliberately arranged to make fortifications, or, perhaps, the perfect spot for an ambush.

We drove on through heavier jungle and now the road wound steeply downhill. A Giant Iguana suddenly scuttled across the road and our driver told us the big lizard was lucky to have escaped the local hunters. If it ventured onto the road it would certainly be caught, for big lizards were considered to be a delicacy by some of the local people.

The jungle-covered hills rose steeply above the road as we approached the flying ferry at Lilu. the river formed a barrier which effectively separated the higher hills from the plains and foothills we had just crossed. Only when the ferry was working was it possible to cross the deep, swift-flowing River Namtu. We drove onto a wooden pontoon built on top of two old Army landing craft. A heavy cable had been stretched across the river between two giant trees and the ferry raft was attached to this by another stout cable and pulley. The boatman would set the giant rudder so that the bows of the raft's boats were turned away from the wire towards the opposite bank. The strong-flowing current on the sides of the boats set the pulley running across the cable and the raft would be taken swiftly and effortlessly across. We drove up a steep ramp to a tiny huddle of thatched bamboo huts with a tea shop, which we found was the main shopping centre and meeting house for both villagers and visitors alike.

NaPeng village was about a mile beyond the ferry, home of the fishermen who depended for their living on that beautiful "Fickle Jade", the River Namtu, which sometimes allowed them to prosper, giving her bounty generously, and at other times became a cruel monster, destroying them and everything they possessed in uncontrolled spate.

The road began to twist and rise steeply; it was not so many years since it had been carved out of the sheer hillsides. Indeed before the motor road was made there had been only a narrow track through the jungle and to reach Tawngpeng, or Loi Lung as the Palaungs of old had called their kindom of mountains, travellers had to face a long and arduous and often dangerous journey, either on foot or by pony.

I saw that the vegetation had changed on this side of the river. There were curious-looking tree ferns. The trees were giants with smooth, straight trunks and a canopy of foliage, high above which I was to find was festooned with flowering creepers for most of the year. One spread in drifts over the branches like fresh snow; another had velvety flowers of soft pink, similar to the lovely Congea. The Heavenly Blue wove a pattern of deep blue against the green canopy and here and there the undergrowth was splashed with patches of scarlet and yellow where the lovely Gloriosa Lilies twined their way towards the light. The spreading branches of the great trees were thickly encrusted with spikey ruffs which I decided must be orchid plants. What were then bare, burning, rock walls rising sheer above the road, were to become a cascade of sapphire blue with the first rains, when the trailing, stunted little shrubs which grew precariously from every crack and crevice in the rock face burst into blossom, covering everything with a bright blue mantle. They looked like the brooms which grew in my father's garden in England but I had never seen one in such a blue.

In places, springs oozed from the rocks, allowing a thick carpet of mosses to spread over everything. In such damp spots I was to find the lavender blue flowers similar to the Streptocarpus and the familiar Impatiens, which seemed to have spread everywhere, filling the drains and ditches with its candy pink flowers. The road hugged the rock face without wall or parapet to give protection. I looked over the edge of the sheer drop and saw that in places there were several hundred feet of jagged rocks down to the sparkling ribbon of the Nam Ko-Ai River, which followed its winding and rocky course far below in the depths of that lush green valley.

The hillside across that deep, narrow valley was scarred with bright green squares, the mark of the Tawng-Yah, as the hill rice was called. Small groups of nomadic rice growers cut down the jungle trees and after burning off the undergrowth, would plant up the area with rice and vegetables, leaving the charred forest giants where they had fallen. After two years they would move on, burning their wasteful way through the virgin jungle, destroying the natural habitat for both flora and fauna. In their wake followed the bamboos, for there was nobody responsible for replanting the timber.

We drove into a tiny valley where there was a small tea factory and a few acres of straggly tea bushes. The old milestone announced that it was mile thirteen. Dotted here and there amongst the fringe of jungle trees I saw some leafy giants festooned with jumbo-sized "candles" of white flowers, which looked remarkably like the horse chestnuts of the English countryside. Later, I was to meet the tea factory owner and I remembered the trees in his valley. Did they produce any nuts I wanted to know? He promised he would bring me a sample. Later that year, long after I had forgotten about the "chestnuts", Po Thein called to see me. He had brought a few of the nuts I had enquired about, he said, and I looked in surprise at the large knobbly sack he held out. With disbelief I stared at its contents. They were conkers all right but each nut was at least the size of a cricket ball, some even larger. Swinging on the end of a string those king-sized conkers would have made lethal weapons. Were they used for any purpose? I asked. He shook his head; it was only a jungle tree he explained.

Time had passed quickly and soon we were emerging onto the hill tops. The air was cooler and the views breathtaking. Across a deep wooded valley I caught my first glimpse of Namhsan, Ohm Yah in the Palaung language. On a long, knife-like ridge which nestled between the higher mountains was a sprawling collection of tall wooden houses and nearby, looming above the township on its own small hill, stood a large white building. This was the Haw said our driver, home of the Sawbwa, or Ruler, of Tawngpeng State. It was a modern building after the style of an elegant English country house, and built on the site of an old Haw which had been destroyed by incendiary bombs during the war years. It had been a Palace of great magnificence, I was told, with a central tower over the Hall of Audience and with the principal state rooms heavily ornamented and lavishly gilded.

My first impression of Namhsan was of a long narrow winding street shadowed by tall houses of mellow pine, by houses and shops which perched precariously on the very edge of the precipice, their rear walls supported by stilts. Brightening the shadowed streets and dim interiors of the shops were dazzling flashes of scarlet and I saw that the women were dressed in robes of brightest red with velvet or silk brocade blouses in every colour one might find in a child's paintbox. They stopped their parading to stare at the strangers and held in check the pink-cheeked smiling children.

The hillsides above the town were alight with pink where groves of lovely flowering cherries bordered the spreading tea fields. Then we were driving into a garden filled with English flowers, roses, dahlias, lilies and larkspur. Our long journey was over.

Built on a sheer hillside, the garden had a commanding view it would be hard to match. We were immediately taken over by a very friendly Labrador, Bess, a much-travelled dog whose globe trotting days were at an end and who was eventually to stay on with us. A tall, handsome man walked across the lawn to welcome us, a man who had spent the greater part of his life in the teak forests of Burma. During the war years he had escaped with the Bombay Burmah's work force of elephants in the face of the advancing Japanese, a story written about so vividly by another member of our Corporation.[†] It was late and the air was chilly; logs crackled in the great fireplace of polished teak, in a room that was long and low with walls of mellow pine; red and white chintz curtains framed the superb scenery, and, looking out, I saw that Thusan-ti's Garden was as beautiful as I had been led to believe. Thusan-ti, the Dragon Grandmother of Palaung legends, had hidden her kingdom well, and it lay secure in its mountain fortress, seemingly untouched by the passing of centuries and yet with the feeling of welcome, of belonging, all around us and I knew I would not regret going there.

Not everyone liked the isolation of Namhsan. The nearest European neighbours were at the Bawdwin Silver Mines, many hours journey away. H.L.B. though had enjoyed the lonely life of the teak forest manager. He had gone to

---

† Elephant Bill — Lt. Col. J. H. Williams O.B.E. — Hart Davis. & Bundoola

Namhsan to manage the tea factory to fill the gap left by others, and had stayed on for several years before finally retiring. That was when we became a part of the story and Thusan-ti and her Enchanted Garden were to cast their spell over us.

2

Loi Lung — The Land of Mountains

The next month was a flurry of activity at the factory with the handing over, our meetings with the staff, the tea growers, the townspeople and for myself, a time to explore the nearby hills. Farewell luncheons for H.L.B., the retiring manager, were given by many different sections of the community. He had been well-liked and I knew that it would not be easy for us to take his place.

I had already realised from that first intriguing glimpse of Tawngpeng, that I had ventured into a naturalist's paradise and the more I saw, the deeper the enchantment grew. I saw Silver Pheasant in silver and black plumage, with handsome scarlet head and black cockade. Lovely Green Peacock lived in the surrounding forests, Partridge, junglefowl and woodcock were plentiful on all the hills. Our host organised a shoot but those lovely birds were scarce that day and I was secretly glad, for it seemed a pity to kill such beauty. My scarlet pants, though, were blamed for the vanishing birds and I was forbidden to go out with the guns again until our baggage arrived from Rangoon and I was able to wear more suitable clothing.

Below the garden the hillside dropped steeply a thousand feet to a crystal stream and a tiny lake. Along the ridge top giant sunflowers nodded their gold heads around thickets of Pieris, bright with scarlet and pink leaves and dainty lily of the valley flowers. Everywhere I saw flowering cherries in random shades of pink and on the higher slopes, darkly-shaded patches of pine trees. Deeper in the sheltered valley grew the showy Pink Cassia, the Yellow Cassia, Bauhinias, with their strange cleft leaves and flowers like huge white scented orchids.

I was to find many other lovely flowers, shrubs, trees. One tree which grew in profusion there was the Persian Lilac. This was one of the sacred trees of the East. Of medium height, in March, it would be covered with panicles of pale lilac blossom, very much like the old-fashioned English Lilac and with a heavy lilac scent which drifted afar on the sun drenched air. I was to find many other flowers and orchids and my "wild garden" grew over the years, to the amusement of my Palaung and Chinese friends, who little realised that those weeds were looked upon as treasures by plant collectors of the Western World.

We were invited to the Haw for a farewell luncheon given for H.L.B. by the Sawbwa and, when I met the Mahadevi, or Queen Consort, who became a kind friend, I was relieved to find that I was not the only woman there who spoke English. She would laugh gently at my mistakes and put me right with the language and customs. Without her kind help my life would have been so much more difficult, for amongst the local people five languages were spoken, Palaung, Yunnanese, Shan, Burmese and Hindi, as well as the minor languages, such as Palay and Lishaw. The children would slip from one language to another without stopping to think about it. I decided to concentrate on Burmese as this had become the first language in the schools and was widely spoken by the younger generation. I could try the others later.

The people were friendly and helpful but they made it quite plain from the beginning that I was the odd one out; I must learn to fit in with their ways and religious beliefs. They studied and watched me with polite interest. At first it was the most difficult thing I have ever done, to sit back and keep my thoughts to myself when I wanted to shout aloud that my new friends were wrong, or when I saw them doing things which to me were the last word in cruelty. Yet over the years, I learned to accept that others had a right to their differing ways, and I am sure I became a kinder, gentler, more considerate person as a result of my efforts to please. I began to study the costumes worn by the women, realising that this was the only way to distinguish between the different "Clans" and it added to the interest to know which village was visiting the town on the Moon Days and Feast Days, when crowds of brilliantly attired women could be seen shopping or promenading. "Visiting" played a very important part in their lives and was almost a ritual. The women were shy at first and objected to our efforts to photograph them. Often on our walks we would meet groups of women walking into town or returning home to their villages with heavy bags of provisions, but when they saw strangers they would cover their faces with both hands, peeping shyly through their fingers. As they came to know us though they stopped behaving in this demure way and would greet us with broad black-toothed grins, calling out in Palaung, 'Me ka gyo, Ahn, Ahn?', the traditional greeting, 'Are you well?'.

The practice of betel chewing spoiled their beauty, for it not only blackened their teeth but made their lips an unnatural glutinous crimson. Their faces were round as the moon, their skins fair and their eyes dark and almond-shaped. Being hill people they were short and stocky, brimming with health from the clear fresh air of the mountains. The men would always walk on ahead of their womenfolk and the children. The men wore clothes of sombre black, or tan, which matched the sunbaked earth, on their heads a white or pink turban. The pants they wore were wide as 'Oxford Bags' and with the crotch at knee level, this enabled them to be hitched up almost to chin level, to become baggy flapping shorts if there was a river to ford or boggy ground to cross.

One feature of the district which intrigued me was the complicated system of bamboo water pipes, which irrigated the parched fields in the dry season, as well as providing the only drinking water for many isolated villages. Often the source of the water would be a clear spring or small stream high in the hills. The freshly-cut bamboos were first hollowed, then split in half lengthways and placed end to end on stilts of varying heights to maintain a steady flow of water, the top half being secured over the channels to prevent evaporation. From a distance these bamboo aquaducts looked like the the veins in a giant leaf as they spread out through the tea fields, and the water was always fresh and cool. They were maintained with care by all the tea growers and villages they supplied, so that even in the dryest season no-one was short of water. Tired wayfarers who knew the secret of those bamboo spiderwebs had no need to go thirsty.

During those first few weeks I learned much about my new friends: that it was impolite to question them, that they would tell me the things they felt I should know at some auspicious moment, and that I must be prepared for them to say strange and unusual things. On one occasion for instance the Treasury Minister and his wife came to tea. He was a nephew of the Sawbwa and spoke good English but his wife did not and the conversation became rather one-sided. Anxious to acquaint me with the ways of his people, he asked if I had noticed the costumes worn by the women of Zayangyi. When I said I thought they were exotically beautiful, he replied seriously, 'You know that our Grandmother was a Dragon and because of this our women wear the Dragon's Dress in her memory?' He spoke with quiet sincerity and I would not have dared to so much as smile. It was a strange remark that I felt needed an explanation, but it was not until some years later that I was told the full story of Thusan-ti, the Dragon Princess, legendary mother of the Egg Prince, whose son was to become the first of a long line of Sawbwas.

Beyond the garden wall the hillside fell sheer to the valley below, and on our first Moon Day we decided to explore the well-beaten track which snaked steeply downwards. I had never before seen a more precipitous highway, yet this was the main road to the villages below and was in constant use by people and pack animals. In places it was cut deep into the hill; in others it ran down the very edge of the knife-like ridge like a narrow ribbon, its surface beaten as hard as concrete over the centuries. Almost a thousand feet below the garden the track suddenly opened out into a wide green valley. Ahead we saw a small lake fed by numerous streams, which tumbled down the rocky hillside. This lake fed three rivers and we saw that each was spanned by an ancient wooden bridge with an ornamental roof, the timbers smooth and dark with age, the boards we trod pitted with countless hoof marks, Had we somehow strayed into a miniature Alpine Valley?

The waters of the lake were icy and the widest of the three rivers was spanned by a flimsy bamboo footbridge, which I was tempted to try. It was about a foot wide, the bamboos lashed together with rattan and the moment I was well out over the water the flimsy contraption began to shake and undulate as though it had a will of its own and was intent on pitching me into the water. By this time I had become a compulsive plant collector, and every walk brought me some new flower. Down there by the water's edge I spotted thick clumps of balsam, with curled shrimp-like flowers of an eye-catching orange and red.

It was a strange, quiet place, completely enclosed by the steep tea-covered hillsides and, as I was to discover later, it was the home of the pickled tea wells. It was a sobering thought as we began the slow steep climb homewards that whenever the women of the valley went shopping they had to toil up that tortuous track.

Everything in Tawngpeng was on a grand scale: the mountains and valleys and the Palaungs with their Grand Palaces and even grander festivals, but these paled into insignificence when compared with the displays put on by the elements at the onset of the rainy season. I had never seen such spectacular thunderstorms anywhere on my travels. The sky would darken behind the highest hill and a wild wind would sweep into the valley, bringing torrential rain. Then as though some unseen hand had suddenly drawn a black curtain across the sky, a midnight darkness would descend, whilst great flashes of lightning illumed the lost landscape. The thunderclaps bounced around the valley and hills, which amplified the sound as if some monstrous pop group was crashing out its deafening music. It was not surprising that the superstitious Palaungs of old had thought Thusan-ti was venting her anger on them.

Guests who came to stay at this season always seemed surprised and rather awed by the ferocity of the elements. One visiting author found it an inspiration for a new novel which he was writing. He was recovering from a bout of malaria and work on the book was at a standstill, when one of our more spectacular storms blew up at mid-morning. I took some coffee along to the guest room and as the door opened I stared with surprise to see the room in semi-darkness, the busy author prone on the floor with a typewriter under his nose, on either side of it, a guttering candle stuck onto the polished teak floor. His wife stopped me as I put out a hand to the light switch. 'Inspiration' she whispered, and I crept away quietly, not wanting to break the spell.

It was not only the storms which were on a grand scale; the sunsets of Tawngpeng were also rather awe-inspiring. One evening, whilst our author friend was busy working on his book, we took his wife up to Zayangyi to watch one of those sunsets. At first she had been amused, saying she thought such things were a bit old-fashioned, but the magnificence of the colour display had silenced her for a while.

On their last evening with us before their final departure from Burma they had walked together across the lawn into a glorious setting sun, through a drifting shower of lavender blue as the Jacaranda trees shed their flowers, against a screen of flaming oranges, reds and pinks, outlining the dark purple of the distant hills. What better inspiration did one need to set the pen embellishing the pages of romantic novels?

Not all our guests found inspiration in the elements, and a

less happy incident occured when a party of Americans, Christian Audio Visuals, invited themselves to stay. The heavenly "music" evidently did not please them and during the night's storm they abandoned their beds to walk around the house, opening all doors and windows. Next morning I found the houseboys standing in silent dismay, staring at the white Indian carpet which lay sodden beneath a deep layer of leaves and debris brought in by the whirlwind. The curtains had flapped soggily all night long against the newly-oiled wooden walls of the bungalow, and were permanently stained.

Dr Peel arrived for refreshments one stormy morning full of a strange tragedy he had been called to at Mankai village the day before. It had happened at about 11.30 am, as everyone sat around the hearth after their mid-day meal, waiting for the thunderstorm to abate. At a house in the centre of the village the family froze with fear as a ball of fire flew throught the open door, circled the group around the hearth and as though homing-in on a pre-selected victim, chose an eleven-year-old girl who sat beyond the fire facing the open door, striking her in the back and killing her instantly. The only sign of the injury, said the Doctor, was a round black spot about the size of a tennis ball where she had been struck and around it, a radiating mass of black lines like a giant spider's web.

The family were sure they had angered the Nats, and gave lavish ceremonies to appease the spirits. Exactly one week afterwards though, a fireball again struck at Mankai, felling the only may-man thi tree in the village and the elders called a meeting to decide what must be done to remove the curse which had descended upon them all.

Occasionally there would be violent hailstorms, which would spread a white carpet over the garden. This was always a great event, and our houseboys would abandon work to dash outside, gather handfulls, fill their bags, eat some of it, and rub some over their faces.

The first of the monsoon storms would generally result in the white ants swarming, a regular event which I came to dread. Just as darkness fell the insects would pour out of their nests in a great winged stream and from a wide area, would be lured by our lights. Once alerted to an approaching swarm the household would quickly put into action our defence plan. Not that it did any good. Despite tightly-closed doors, extinguished lights, towels stuffed under doors, the pests would find some crack or opening and invade us in relentless hordes, dropping into our soup, creeping into cupboards and corners in their search for a new home.

Once they reached the house they would shed their flimsy wings, which we would sweep up by the bucketful, and then scurry madly around the floor in small "crocodiles" of five or six, each holding onto the tail of its leader. Our ginger kitten, Tish, would chase them tirelessly, eating the succulent morsels until he was gorged, and if anyone was careless enough to step onto a small ant, as it hurried around the polished teak floor, the result would be a large oily stain which nothing would remove. The morning after a big swarm we would find the damp lawn "vandalised" by large circles, where every vestige of green had been torn away, and small craters literally gnawed into the earth by countless, pale biscuit-brown ants motivated by the urgent instinct to dig out their new nests before the sun was up.

Fortunately, the stormy period was short-lived and for most of the year the weather was as gentle, kind and predictable as the Palaungs themselves, who forgot the fireballs and fearsome rattling of the Heavens for a few months, fatalistically accepting that these awesome reminders of their own insignificance would appear again at the appointed time.

3

The Heavenly Lords

Before setting out for my new home I had tried to discover something about the peoples of the Shan Plateau, but there was little that would help me to understand my new neighbours.

The Shans had been driven out of China by the land-hungry Tartars sometime around the thirteenth century, and had swept into the eastern hills of Upper Burma, where they eventually settled in constant, internecine conflict. Each small group was led by a fierce warlike chief, the SaoPha or Sawbwa, a Heavenly Lord who would continually try to extend his boundaries at the expense of his neighbours, laying waste to land and habitation in the process, seeking plunder and hostages. In this turbulent way the Shan States came into being: thirty or so separate States, each of which paid annual tribute to the Sunrise King in his Golden City in Mandalay, but who otherwise were left to settle their differences by the sword, the Burmese taking no part in their quarrels.

They were persuaded to accept the protection of the British Flag after the defeat of King Thibaw, each of the old Heavenly Lords agreeing to give allegiance to the British Crown on the understanding that the British would protect their Rights and Privileges as Hereditary Princes for all time. I was there at the time of the Cession, when those Rights and Privileges were taken from them and I had no answer to their silent accusation. Some of those descendants of the old Heavenly Lords were heard to say rather bitterly that their trust in the "Understanding"[(i)] had been misplaced; they felt that their British "Brothers" had rather let them down.

In those early days the Administration was left in the hands of the Sawbwas, with British Officers of the Frontier Service posted to each of the larger states to advise and assist, to persuade them of the wisdom of living together peacefully rather than waste their resources in constant fighting amongst themselves, to draw them into the modern world as painlessly as possible. It was in 1922 that the States joined in a Federation with the Sawbwas holding council presided over by a Senior British Official. So the old Heavenly Lords gave up their warlike ways and met to discuss their differences in peace across the Council Table. The premier State was Hsipaw, followed by Hsenwi, Tawngpeng and Mongmit, which were perhaps the richest of the States, although the largest of the States was Kentung. There were many others, KoKang, Wa, YaungHwe, MongPawn, in all about thirty and some of the smaller States were ruled by the Myosa, minor Lords who generally paid tribute to one of their more powerful neighbours.

Not all of these States were peopled by the Shans. Tawngpeng was the traditional home of the Palaungs, gentle hardworking tea growers with their own language, arts and crafts, a people considered to be of Mongolian origin. The Khuns were the traditional ruling family of Kentung and they also were thought to be of Mongolian origin. It was only amongst a few of the older members of the Tribe that the Khun language was still used. Or so we were told. Kentung was one of the Opium States and many of the powerful traffickers were reluctant to give up this lucrative trade when the poppy was banned; it was not easy to enforce the law in those remote hills. There were other minority races to be found mingling with the Shans, small groups of Kachins, Palays and Lishaws all keeping their own identity, language, costumes and customs.

Most of these peoples were devout Buddhists and followed the custom of polygamy. Custom called for the Heavenly Lords to live in a Grand Palace, with three Queens and as many concubines as they wished. Each Sawbwa consequently would vie with his neighbours to display a Regalia which matched that of the Sunrise King, a rich collection which included a crown of gold, ornate swords with jewelled scabbards of silver or gold, racks of spears, white silk ceremonial umbrellas, ceremonial fly whisks, slippers of gold and richly-jewelled belts.

A Sawbwa's three Queens must not lack gold, silver and jewels and for all the grand State Occasions, the Heavenly Lord would display the rich caparisons for his horses or elephants, silk banners decorated with enlightening texts and finally, the ultimate emblem of regal dignity, flat, open umbrellas, with long slender handles, fashioned out of solid gold to gleam like the sun itself.

The local name for the palaces of those Heavenly Lords was 'Haw" and although these came in many differing sizes, they were all built to the same design as the Golden Palace at Mandalay. The older Haws were all of wood, often on stilts and over the Throne Room there would be a tall, tapering spire which would have up to eight diminishing roofs, for by law only the Sunrise King might have more roofs over his head. On either side of the Audience Chamber and Throne Room were single-storey wings with numerous rooms of all sizes, studies and bedrooms. Those old Palaces had been vast, rambling places, housing the large families and innumerable servants and bodyguards.

In 1937 the Senior Sawbwas travelled West. They attended the Coronation and were impressed by what they saw of England, each returning home determined to build a new Grand Haw in the English style. It was these I was to see, large elegant mansions which might have been transported from English country estates, complete with landscaped gardens, although they still retained one link with the past, a tall tower over the Throne Room.

The Audience Chamber was always a focal point and would be entered by wide-pillared doors which faced the throne. The lofty roof would be supported by a row of pillars down each side of the long room; in the old Haws these had been wooden columns lavishly ornamented and studded with coloured glass in the Mandalay style and, so the Mahadevi told me, the ceilings also were heavily embellished with gilded mouldings. The walls behind the pillars were used to display the Regalia and Relics, rows of spears and swords, great drums and gongs, plates and shields of gold and perhaps an impressive display of ancient muzzle-loading guns, all of which had to be surrendered to the Burmese Army as the insurrection grew.

The throne was always a traditional symbol and made in the form of two interlocking triangles one upon the other, signifying fire and water, the greatness and power, the virility of the Lord who sat upon it in the shade of four white silk umbrellas. The magnificent throne of the Sawbwa of Tawng-peng had been fashioned out of silver but was destroyed when the old Haw was burnt down by incendiary bombs dropped by the Americans during the Japanese occupation. When Piet had first visited Tawngpeng the Sawbwa and his vast family had been living in a temporary residence built of bamboo, whilst the new Haw was being built and it was this great mansion which I first saw gleaming white against the distant hills.

The garden had been carefully landscaped, with formal flower beds, shrubs and tall flowering trees; the Palaungs loved flowers. A great pool glinted with the gold of fish, and the Sawbwa's famous white fantail doves coo'ed and preened in an ornamental dovecote. The Palace Guard no longer dressed in the ornate costumes of olden days but were well-trained members of the State Police and armed with modern rifles instead of the spears and swords of their ancestors.

There was one link with the outside world, a small radio transmitting and receiving station, which enabled the Sawbwa and his Ministers, as well as the townspeople, to communicate with Rangoon.

When we last heard of that Grand Palace it was being used as a rice store, the Sawbwa and his family no longer in residence.

FOOTNOTE:

(i) LORDS OF THE SUNSET. Maurice Collis 1936. Faber & Faber.
From his chapter **The Shans.**- "After the fall of Mandalay Sir George Scott and others negotiated with the Shans, inducing them to pay homage to the British Crown on the understanding that their rights and priviliges as hereditary Princes of the Shan were secured to them forever".

Mr Collis spent one night in Namhsan as guest of the Sawbwa of Tawngpeng and he likened the town to a "lamasery in the wastes of Tibet. the solitude was overwhelming," he said.

4

Ka-Tur — Tribe of Palaung

The Palaungs are a peaceful, gentle people. Secure in their secret Kingdom of Tawngpeng they had missed the upheavals which beset the warring Shans, Chinese and Burmese. This isolation and the mountainous terrain, also cut them off from one another and accounts for the separate groups within the Tribe, not unlike the Scottish Clans said Mahadevi, each having its own individual costume and dialect.

They seem to have originated from the border areas with China, and the theory that they were of Mongolian origin was perhaps borne out by the legend of the Egg Prince, a story which also features in Mongolian legends. Whatever their beginnings, they have lived secure and happy in their beautiful mountain Kingdom, ruled in a fatherly fashion by their Sawbwas and somehow forgotten by fleeting time.

The sense of timelessness intrigued me from the first. It was tantalising to feel the invisible barrier which surrounded them and to know I might never get through it to find a mutual understanding. They looked with interest on the outside world but showed little desire to join the sophisticated city dwellers. They were ready to make use of those few things which they considered would improve their health and happiness and were only too pleased when that indifferent world left them to their own devices.

Namhsan, capital of Tawngeng State, was called OhmYah in the Palaung language and it meant "Trembling Waters". It was given this unusual name because the ground on which the town was built trembled and became a quaking marsh in the rainy season, with a great torrent of water gushing out of the rocky ground. Now the land has been drained and no longer lives up to its name.

In the old days, when a Palaung Sawbwa first entered his Haw, tradition demanded that his people should come to him and in a lavish ceremony, bring him a Drum, a Sword, a Spear and a beautiful girl to be his wife. The Sawbwa was the "father" figure and although his word was final on all matters of policy and justice, his people had the right to go to him for advice on all matters. The State was divided into NEH, large Districts each governed by a Nehbaing or Senior Headman. These districts were sub-divided into TIK, the Circles, each a hundredth part of the larger District, and each with an elected Tik--Thugyi or Headman. All Headmen were elected by the elders and if they proved to be weak or corrupt would soon be replaced. This was also the case with the Sawbwas and although a ruling Sawbwa would name one of his sons to succeed him, the new Sawbwa would soon have to prove that he was worthy or risk being deposed by the elders, with one of his brothers being elected in his place.

Once a year the Sawbwa would visit his people and tour each Neh, occasions which were an excuse for great ceremony and feasting. For all important religious festivals the people would go to the Haw in vast colourful processions, with music and dancing and bearing gifts. The Sawbwa would be seated on his throne, and the crowds would file past him, paying their respects in deep obeisance to their Religious Leader.

Though born and brought up to rigid traditions, he did much to modernise his State, encouraging the tea growers to cultivate and prune the tea gardens. Tawngpeng's only industry, though, was locked deep in those old traditions, the people suspicious of change.

The Sawbwa was a typical Palaung, stockily built with broad, fair-skinned face and twinkling slant eyes, which could snap in anger, silencing even the boldest of those around him. He had a ready sense of humour and enjoyed life to the full, his vast family calling him affectionately, "The Travelling Sawbwa". Even in his later years he was active and athletic. Calling at the Haw one morning I was met at the entrance by Mahadevi, who pointed at the roof. The Sawbwa had insisted on climbing up the ladder onto the roof to see how the repair work was progressing. 'I wish he would remember he is no longer a boy,' she said.

Of his five wives the first two had died in childbirth, but they had lived together quite amicably at the Haw, unlike the three wives who succeeded them. The Palaung Lady was his first wife and he had eloped with her according to Palaung tradition. The second he married to please his father and because of her rank the Princess from Lawksawk became his first Mahadevi. The second Mahadevi was charming and beautiful, the mother of four sons and eight daughters. He also married a handsome Shan and this Sao Nang and her children lived at the Lesser Haw, a rambling wooden palace built in traditional style on the hillside just below the Hawgyi. His fifth and last wife was known as The Chinese Lady, and she lived in seclusion at Payagyi with her only son, and kept apart from the "cold war" between her senior "Sisters" of the two Haws.

Meeting the Sawbwa in Darjeeling on one occasion, Piet had asked how many children he had, only to receive the answer 'Now is it thirty three or thirty four?' In the end the Sawbwa called over his Equerry to settle the matter. If, however, you asked that same question in Namhsan you would promote a lengthy argument as it was generally accepted that the children "recognised" by that last of the old Heavenly Lords numbered more than a hundred, if the gossips could be believed.

The Mahadevi and the Sao Nang were both women of spirit and in order to have peaceful household, he wisely kept them apart. I soon learned that it was not tactful to mention the Sao Nang when talking to Mahadevi for the atmosphere would become noticeably cooler and the subject of the conversation would be politely but firmly changed.

I would sometimes see a small stately procession of ladies, bejewelled and dressed in their finest clothes, and chattering loudly as they walked one behind the other in order of seniority on their way to the Lesser Haw, where the Sao Nang would be waiting to escort them to the Hawgyi, or Grand Haw, to pay their respects to Mahadevi. Generally however these two wives kept well apart, each leading a separate existence with their joint husband.

I was told that in former days, if approached by any member of his family for financial help, the Sawbwa would follow the custom of granting them the "contract" for the next Pwé. This would then be sold to a Contractor, a professional organiser who would run the gambling festival as a business, the value of each "contract" varying with the more auspicious and popular dates. In this way the Princes and Princesses were kept in funds without the State Purse or the Sawbwa's pocket suffering any loss; the Palaungs, being compulsive gamblers, were only too happy with the system, for the Pwé was the only form of light entertainment in Tawngpeng.

When a young American couple wrote to us asking if we could arrange for them to live in one of the remote villages, where they could study the Palaungs and their customs, we consulted the Sawbwa and he seemed pleased and ready to offer every assistance. Perhaps at last someone would tell the world about his people, he said, and he seemed genuinely disappointed when the Americans were refused visas.

During the last year we were in Tawngpeng the troubles brought by increasing insurrection kept Mahadevi in Rangoon with her family. So the Sao Nang came into her own and was able to move more freely once her senior "sister" was no longer to be considered. The Palaungs saw less of their Sawbwa as the troubled times kept him away from his homeland. He died in Rangoon in August 1975, after a long illness, and his passing brought the end of an era, the end of a long line of colourful, autocratic, romantic Rulers whose powers had been unquestioned, with traditions and life-style which no longer fitted into the modern concept of government gradually overtaking Burma. His sons, no longer allowed to use their former titles, have gone out into the world, following widely differing professions, for today there is no place in Burma for such men as their father. Perhaps the world is a poorer place for their passing.

The son of the Palaung Lady became Heir Apparent, taking the title of Kyemaing. He was as tall as his father and very popular amongst his people. he and his younger brother, son of the Princess from Lawksawk, had been sent to school in England but on the outbreak of war the eldest Prince returned to Tawngpeng to help his father with State Affairs. The younger brother joined the R.A.F., only to be shot down and killed on active service soon afterwards.

The young Kyemaing had been betrothed to a Shan Princess, as custom demanded, but as he grew to manhood he fell in love with a beautiful Palaung girl and, following the custom, persuaded the lady to elope with him. As this was an accepted part of the Palaung wedding ceremony the Sawbwa had little choice but to welcome his new daughter-in-law. The Shan Princess saw things differently. She felt she had been jilted, and refused to marry into a polygamous household, even though this custom was still accepted and her rank would have made her the senior wife.

This broken engagement perhaps signified a change of attitudes in the younger generation towards polygamy. The Kyemaing took only the one wife and I found her a most attractive, lively personality and a very astute businesswoman. She managed her husband's tea estates and factory whilst he joined the central administration as Resident.

One bright, sunny morning the Haw Land Rover drew up outside and the Mahadevi hurried up to the door, all smiles and excitement.

'I had to come and tell you A----- has eloped', she said.

I was at a loss for words, particularly as she seemed so delighted. Having just come from India, where any girl who had behaved in such a way would have been in disgrace and her family far from pleased, I was puzzled by the Mahadevi's obvious pleasure over the affair.

'And what does Sawbwagyi think about it?' I asked her, but her reply only puzzled me further.

'Oh! He is delighted and has sent for the PanJan.' She said.

I was more than confounded but to question would have been impolite. She went on to give me the arrangements she was making for the wedding, which was to be held in Rangoon.

Shortly after this I had an unexpected visit from a nephew of the Sawbwa. He greeted me with the happiest of smiles.

'I had to come and tell you the good news. My brother has eloped and is to be married soon.' He said, and with raised eyebrows I listened to the details of the impending wedding.

But that was not to be the end of this rash of elopements. Soon afterwards my bungalow staff brought me the news that Maung Nyunt, the youngest Houseboy, had eloped with a girl from a neighbouring village, then changed his mind. After much trouble he had withdrawn from the engagement, having paid K100/- to the girl's father to release him from the Contract. I began to think it was like the measles; everyone was catching the complaint. It was not until some considerable time afterwards that I learned the meaning of this odd behaviour.

In each community a man and a woman are chosen to be the Great Pak-Ké's and it is their duty to teach the Palaung customs, the language and rhymes of courtship and song, to boys and girls who have reached the age of fourteen years. The Pak-Ké's choose two people to help them, the Vai Ra-Lyang, or Older Brother, and the Vai Ra-Pya, or Older Sister. In August each year the young people who have been chosen for the Prüh, or "Taming of the Sons", are called by the Great Pak-Ké's and for three months are taught the Language of Courtship, traditional rhymes and set speeches which form the art of courtship in Palaung society.

The Prüs must give up their wild ways, learn to be polite and useful citizens and must be tattoo'd if a boy. An equal number of boys and girls are chosen each year and each boy draws the name of one of the girls in this mock matrimonial lottery. This girl will be his partner, and for three months he must visit her house and court her using the rhymes and speeches he has learned, so absorbing the Palaung traditions and culture and preparing himself for the day when with pretty speeches and old-world courtesy he may wish to win the lady of his choice.

At the Full Moon in October there will be a big party and each couple must enact the Courtship, reciting all they have learned before the Great Pak-Ké's and an invited audience. After this they may give up the partnership, though often marriages result from this student courtship. The "Passing Out" ceremony is held at the Zayangyi Pongyi Kyaung and is an occasion for feasting. The boys wear two hoods around their waist, given to them by the girl partner, one in front and one behind, fastened by a tassled girdle. The men and boys make a large circle around the Orchestra and follow each other round and round, waving their arms and contorting their bodies. They roll up one leg of their baggy pants and tuck a handkerchief into the back of their girdle. The girls follow in an outer circle and try to snatch the handkerchief from their partner. At dawn, after a night of dancing and feasting, they will return home.

The Prühs are now no longer children and the boys may

wear the dah in their belt; to be seen wearing the short sword
or fighting knife is a sign of maturity. From the age of eleven
years boys may be tattoo'd and no boy is allowed to dance in
the "Taming" ceremony unless he can show the tattoo mark.
This is done mainly to impress the girls, and at one time a
man had to cover his entire body with blue lacy patterning in
order to be fashionable.

This has now fallen into disfavour and three dots of blue on
each temple is the only visible sign of the old custom to be
seen on most boys.

Before a Palaung man may ask for a girl's hand in marriage
he must first persuade her to elope with him. He will visit her
house and from the place of honour around the fire, which is
always kept in readiness for guests, he must bring into use the
rhymes and traditional speeches learned during the Taming
Ceremony. Without her father's knowledge he must then take
her to the house of an elderly female relation. There she will
remain throughout the night, accompanied by six girl friends
whilst the lovelorn swain sits outside on the doorstep, awaiting
the girl's father, who will arrive at dawn to take his daughter
home. The lovers must then elope again, three times in all. On
the third occasion, if the girl wishes to marry, she will refuse to
return to her father's house and the man must send his friends
to ask officially for her hand in marriage. At first her father
will refuse and seem angry, but in the end he will be
persuaded and send for the Pan-Jan.

The Pan-Jan is the professional marriage arranger and does
not "match make" as in some countries. After many long
speeches and many meetings, which may take several days, the
marriage is agreed. On the day of the wedding there is a great
feast and the Bridegroom appears before the Elders and asks
for a blessing. To the Pan-Jan and the Bride's father he must
pay the Bride-Price, which is always made in tobacco and
from the Bride's father he will receive a new suit of clothes and
a turban. The man and all his friends go to the Bride's house
in happy, noisy procession, accompanied by an orchestra and
taking with them a round, lacquered wedding tray on which
rice and flowers have been arranged and which the Elders and
parents touch to bless the marriage. After this the feasting
begins and the traditional Palaung singing.

The singer will stand on a table and sway and bend from

side to side to the rhythm of the throbbing drums. Holding his head on one side and with the little finger in his ear, he sings up the scale until a certain note vibrates in his head. Then in incredible high-pitched, glottal, throbbing sounds he will sing the praises of the Bride and Groom, their parents and all the guests, making up witty stories and putting them into song until he tires. Another singer will then take up the challenge, and another and so on for at least two days without a break in the merrymaking and song.

The men sit on one side of the room with the women opposite and they will feast for as long as there is someone willing to sing. Traditionally they should then go in procession to the Haw and ask the Sawbwa for his blessing. After this the Bride, accompanied by her six attendants carrying her belongings in trunks and suitcases, followed by an orchestra and all her relations and friends, go in triumphal procession to the Bridegroom's house, where another feast awaits them.

On such occasions all the unmarried girls will wear lovely new costumes and display all their silver and gold ornaments, for these are a part of each girl's dowry and she may be hoping to catch the eye of one of the eligible bachelors. February and March are considered the two most auspicious months for weddings.

After marrying it was traditional for a girl to shave her head, but modern Palaung Misses are reluctant to lose their long black tresses and the custom is maintained only by a few older women.

Palaung children are given names by the Sayadaw when they are one month old, the name depending on the day of the week and month in which the child is born. Palaungs love and spoil children, treat them with the greatest kindness and never chastise them.

When a baby's hair is first cut the father will take the hair to a distant, lonely spot and bury it in the ground, preferably in a rat or mouse hole; when a grown person has a haircut, however the hair will be taken and secretly hidden high up in a roof or a tree top, to prevent it being stepped on, or used as a charm to work spells. No Palaung would ever wear the clothing of others, or pass underneath clothing hanging out to dry which belonged to another, particularly to a woman, for the bad characteristics of the last wearer of that clothing might descend on them. As with other Eastern peoples it was considered wrong to touch the head or turban of another and no Palaung would ever lay his hands on the shoulders, or step on the shadow of a Pongyi, the Sawbwa, or an old person.

The Elders are held in great respect; they are consulted on all matters and their wishes carried out; the oldest woman in a family was always the most respected member of it. Indeed Tawngpeng was something of an ideal society, for there was a place at the hearth for all the older members of the family, no matter how distant the relationship and they would be treated with loving care to the end. No child was ever unwanted or abandoned, as all were part of the family unit and a place would be found for them around the hearth, no matter how poor that family might be.

When a house was to be built the Soothsayer would be called in to divine the place and the direction the house should face, and the day when building should commence. All Palaung houses are built above ground on stilts and the steps up to the door must be of an even number. When the chief post for the house is set up it is considered lucky if sparrows immediately sit on it but should a hawk or jungle bird perch on it first the site would be abandoned.

Whenever the Sawbwa builds a new Haw the width of the doorway must traditionally be five times the length of his foot. Lizards in the house are considered a good omen and it is especially lucky if one falls onto a person sitting below. Bees swarming in the roof are thought to be lucky but find them under the floor and they must be driven out. The most feared thing to bring ill-luck on a house is for a dove to fly into it or a snake to cross the threshold; one must not kill the creatures but drive them out as quickly as possible.

Inside the House the main room will have a central open fire and around this each member of the family has a place traditionally allocated according to age and no-one must ever sit in another's seat even after that person has died. The dead are treated with great reverence and are always placed along the length of a house with the head towards the door. They would be laid out in great state and in their finest clothes. For four days everybody comes to pay respects and the family of the dead person provide a continuous feast for all comers. The body would then be taken to a high place and burned on a pyre. I have seen elderly Palaungs and small children sorting through the ashes of a funeral pyre on Zayangyi Hill looking for relics of the departed, a bone, perhaps a tooth, or a fingernail. Seven days after the death the family give another feast and for a week there will be gambling and feasting in honour of the dead person. No-one mourns the dead because they hope to have gone on to a better life and eventually Neikban, but had one not led a good life and done enough Acts of Merit one might descend to a more lowly form of life and for this reason no Palaung will kill or harm any living creature no matter how small or lowly.

A Palaung man might have more than one wife and a number of mistresses and his womenfolk would accept this but theirs was a Matriarchal society. The voice of the women was very powerful, the oldest woman in a family having the final say on all matters affecting the home and family business. It was to the Grandmother that everyone took their problems. The women "masterminded" the business world of the Palaungs. They ran their husbands, tea gardens and factories and built up their own businesses with expertise and efficency whilst their menfolk did the talking, arranged the contracts, the buying, but only after first discussing such matters with their womenfolk.

It was not unusual for women to be moneylenders, a business they carried on with ruthless efficency. The husband of one such lady was often to be seen with expensive cameras, radios and on one occasion a bus, which he explained was a bad debt his wife had collected.

At public functions the sexes would be separated, the men sitting on one side of the room, the women and children on the other. A woman would never be seen publicly disagreeing with her husband; their differences were always settled around the hearth.

Life in a Palaung village was simple. The young and active members of the community tended the tea fields, weeding, cultivating, plucking the leaf during the season. The older men, women and the children remained in the village tending livestock, growing vegetables, cooking, weaving, dressmaking. During the "off season" when no leaf grew on the bushes, there was firewood to be collected from distant hillsides. All the more accessible timber had been taken over the years and as the population grew and thrived, the felling bit deeper each year into the fast diminishing forests. Sometimes they cut a few feet above ground level leaving the stump to produce new growth, often they took only the large side branches leaving the main trunk for they believed that the spirit of the tree rested there and so the hillsides deprived of the jungle cover became ever more arid and windswept

The timber felled would be cut into three foot lengths and then split into manageable pieces to be carried back to the village where everyone had a share to stack around their house, for wood was the only source of fuel and a year's supply had to be collected. Everyone from the oldest to the youngest had a part to play, no matter how small, in the day to day running of the village. When work was done they would gather around the hearth and with wit and much laughter would tell stories old and new, throughout the night if there was someone willing to sing to them. There was a gentle happiness in their way of life that I came to admire and I hoped they would not have too many changes forced on them by the outside world.

Their Ruler tried to draw them into the modern world without destroying their simple way of life. The Sawbwa's main interest was in farming and he and his family owned large tea gardens with well tended and pruned bushes and modern factories. At the lower elevations of Tawngpeng State around Panglong, the Sawbwa had large fruit orchards where he experimented with improved varieties of oranges, grapefruit and pineapples and there also he had plantations of tung trees grown for the wood oil contained in the kernels. He would talk with much enthusiasm about his latest projects and each year as October drew near he would call on us to enquire casually if the young avocado tree in our orchard was showing signs of bearing fruit. His trees would fruit before ours he would say with a twinkle in his eye and one day he called on us, obviously happy, though modest, about the gift of ripe avocados he had brought us.

Later the Burmese Government was to decide to widen the scope of horticulture in Tawngpeng and the Palaungs were ordered to grow apples. Each village was supplied with young trees and under the strict supervision of the Burmese Army the people formed corvées to prepare suitable ground and to plant the new apple orchards around each village. Whether this experiment was a success or not we never knew as we had to leave Tawngpeng before the trees matured.

Piet and I had our own conservation scheme and with the diminishing fuel supplies in mind, we began to plant up the scrub jungle below our garden with pine seedlings. Each year the diminishing pine woods on the higher slopes were devastated by fire and few of the tiny seedlings survived the holocaust. We began to dedicate our Moon Day holidays to saving the pines and would collect a few of the doomed seedlings each year, planting them to replace some of the forest giants which had been felled for firewood. Over the years our small forest flourished and we tried to persuade our Palaung friends to follow our example having proved how easy it would be for them to lay down fuel reserves for the next generation.

5

Ohm Yah — The Valley of Trembling Waters

Namhsan, as Ohm Yah is now officially called, sprawled along the top of a knife-like ridge which nestled between the two higher mountain ranges as if nature wished to shelter and hide this lovely place. Tall houses built of mellow wood lined either side of the long street. Most of these were shops with living quarters above.

You could buy almost anything in those Bazaar shops, pottery, cloth, shoes, groceries, fancy foods, sweets, even such luxuries as gold, silver and tins of chocolates, but I soon learned to shop with care, for on close inspection the small tins of toothpaste bore the name "Gills", and the pancake make-up looked much like the compacts I bought at home but the name "Max Facer" was confusing — things were not always what they seemed at first glance. There were Tea Shops with displays of highly coloured buns and fancy biscuits. At either end of the main street was a busy Restaurant festooned with plucked chickens and strings of sausages for customers to choose from.

The dentist displayed a painted sign of an enormous set of false teeth and extractions and fillings were done before an interested crowd of onlookers who would gather around the open-fronted surgery. Mr Liang Yem Chang's shop was always fascinating, there were rows of jars containing curious and mysterious objects. Such things as antlers, rhinoceros horn, ginseng, snakes blood pills and other strange medicines sharing the shelves with phials of penicillin and other antibiotics. Mr Chang owned the restaurants and was one of the senior members of the community. His wife was a pretty woman with a ready smile and a charming manner, she loved children and had a large family. If we needed any advice or information on local customs we could be sure of their help.

Just beyond Mr Chang's shop on a small hill above the road stood the tiny hospital where Dr Peel and his Karen wife lived. An Indian who had served as Medical Officer with the British Army during the forty-one years he had lived in Burma, he had neglected to take out Burmese Nationality although it had always been his intention to do so and it was to cost him his job as Namhsan's Medical Officer when the new Regime decreed that only Burmese Citizens could hold such important positions. He tried to carry on a private practice but eventually gave up the uneven struggle and emigrated to Australia. Throughout the troubles which gradually beset the peace loving Palaungs, Dr Peel would often drop in at 11 am. hoping for a dish of tea and he would unburden himself to us. In this way we were kept in touch with both Bazaar rumour and reality in a situation which was to become like some nightmarish film with the people around us the unwilling actors.

A little way up the street was Dr Lu's house which was Surgery and Baptist Church in one. There was yet another Doctor who lived in the Bazaar Quarter, Dr Dat who practised Homeopathic Medicine, and we would see him striding over the hills to distant villages.

The one link with the outer world was the tiny Cinema; always packed to capacity, it showed mainly Chinese and Japanese films. At the end of the street was a dark and sinister building with a wide, carved wooden entrance over which hung a large notice written both in English and Chinese — "Licensed to Sell Liquor and Opium" — it was the downfall of many of Namhsan's citizens for addicts were all too common.

The Police Station and Township Office occupied a large compound bounded by a steep precipice on the edge of which stood the "Lock-up". No fortress could have been more impregnable than that dreadful wooden cage into which all wrong-doers and drunks alike were pushed headlong through a tiny door about three feet above ground level. There was no chance of "rushing" the guards and it seemed more suited to wild animals, open to the elements and without even the minimum necessities of life nor any pretence at comfort. But there was no uproar, no protest at such conditions and I think that Namhsan must have had the lowest crime-rate and the emptiest of Eastern prisons.

The town was proud of its Fire Service and justifiably so. The bright red fire tender was kept filled from static tanks placed at strategic points around the town. It proved its readiness and efficiency on the day the houses occupied by two of our Drivers went up in flames. It was on the spot within five minutes, the sudden pall of smoke having caught the eye of the ever vigilant fire watchers at the Station.

The Zayangyi Quarter was one of the oldest parts of the town. The ancient wooden houses were not so big and prosperous looking as in the newer areas and there were many small ill-made houses with thatched roofs, occupied mainly by poor Chinese working for the muleteers. Here the women made To Fu, small creamy white "cakes" like blocks of soft cheese which they made from bean curd. The beans were first mashed in home made wooden mincing machines, the purée fermented and then, using their own secret recipes, they fashioned the "curd" into the small white blocks which were placed on slatted wooden frames and dried in the sun. When the To Fu season came round the streets would be lined on both sides with racks of the delicacy which could be eaten fried, or pickled in big jars. Preserved in oils, spiced with chilli, herbs and garlic it looked, tasted and smelt remarkably like ripe Camembert cheese. I acquired quite a taste for this savoury To Fu but found the little white cakes tasteless and insipid although the local people considered the To Fu-Kyauk a great delicacy.

Around the big Mule Depots there was always activity with packs and saddlery to be repaired whilst the mules rested between journeys. There always seemed to be groups of laughing children busy helping the grown-ups. Fluffy Chow dogs dozed guardedly in the sun whilst flocks of the odd looking Chinese Geese got in everyone's way. Most evenings we would take a short cut up the hillside to Zayangyi when we exercised the dogs. A small mischievous Palaung boy aged about three years befriended us. He would run up to us chanting something in Palaung and then dash away laughing. His mother would apologise and we would tell her what a fine boy he was. Soon his little friends joined in the fun and we would be followed by a dozen or more toddlers who called after us "Yah Bo, Dah Bo dah Yah Bo, hmor me loch Yah Bo?" or something which sounded like that. Curious to know what they were saying I asked about it at the Haw one day when having lunch with the Sawbwa and Mahadevi. They both laughed and said I might not be very pleased but they would lend me an old book which gave some English/Palaung vocabulary.

What those mischievous children were saying was "Big Grandmother, where are you going to, Big Grandfather and Big Grandmother?" I decided to tease those children and from the old book I would learn a phrase to answer their questions. They were surprised and amused and it became a game of which they never tired whilst I learned to make simple conversation with them. There were three tones in Palaung which was spoken in a harsh high pitched voice from the back of the throat and full of glottal stops which gave it an ugly sound compared with the more soft sensuous sounding Burmese language.

I tried out my new language one evening when walking up a steep track above Zayangyi. An old woman stood on the path petrified with fear as the two Alsatians bounded up to her. I rushed forward to restrain the dogs and using my newly aquired Palaung made polite conversation. She stared, broke into a huge smile displaying black betel-stained teeth, thrust into my arms the biggest cabbage I have ever seen and dashed off down the hill shouting aloud that the foreigner had spoken to her in Palaung. I was stuck with that outsize in cabbages for the rest of my evening walk for I had to return through Zayangyi and I could not have hurt her feelings by seeming to spurn her gift. But the language game had pleased the parents as well as amusing the children. From that day on Piet and I became Dah Bo and Yah Bo, the Big Grandfather and Big Grandmother and were no longer The Foreigners.

There were three schools in Namhsan. the High School was directly across the valley and each morning at 9.0 am. I would hear the children singing the National Anthem. Education was free at this State School and I would see children of all ages and nationalities walking in, often many miles from outlying villages in all weathers. The girls wore blue cotton tamein and white blouses whilst the uniform for the boys was tan Shan pants and white shirt. The Overseas Chinese School stood on a small hill overlooking the town centre and was attended by most of the Chinese children although a small fee was charged. They wore neat navy and white uniforms and each day they marched through the town to school in a long well ordered crocodile. The smallest school catered for the Muslim children and throughout the day one would hear them chanting their lessons in an upstairs room above their Mosque.

An early morning walk along the main street was always interesting. There would be a small procession of monks in saffron robes each carrying a large black begging bowl and led by a small boy who carried a bell-shaped brass gong which he banged noisily to warn householders who would bring out their daily offerings of rice. Perhaps a woman would be seated on her door step combing waist-length shiny black hair or a small baby sitting in a huge enamel basin having a bath on the pavement watched by a knot of gaily dressed toddlers, lovely children with pink cheeks as fair as any English child. But the one thing which always amused our English and American visitors was to see the small Chinese children in their slit trousers. Nappies were unheard of and the babies wore trousers to suit the custom, two separate legs in bright cotton material held together by the elastic waistband leaving a huge slit from navel to the back of the waist, draughty no doubt but convenient. The tiny babies were always strapped onto someone's back; if the mother was busy then an older sister or brother would be called upon but no baby was ever left alone for even a few minutes. It was usual to see quite small children playing happily with their friends despite the quilted cocoon on their backs.

In that stronghold of Buddhism there were two big Pongyi Kyaungs, one near the Haw and the other at Zayangyi, and these Monasteries were the hub of existence for the Palaungs whose lives revolved around the four great annual festivals. The first of these, Thingyan, fell in April. This was the Water Festival and was based on ancient rites for the New Year. At a time when water was most scarce and precious the whole country seemed to go crazy and for three days at least no-one was safe from getting a soaking. In July the full Moon of Wazo brought in Lent which lasted for three months, the fasting broken only by a week of "visiting" at the middle of the long fast which ended with the Full Moon of Taddingyut, the Festival of Lights, perhaps the most spectacular of the four festivals and a time when the people showed their joy after the long months of self denial by lighting the dark nights, by feasting and celebrations. In Namhsan at this time they also celebrated the Mya Tha Peik and later in November the Full Moon of Tazaungmon gave them an excuse for renewing the feasting with Tazaungdaing and the weaving of the Yellow Robe and with Katheins when the people displayed their annual gifts to the Monks. The last of the annual celebrations was given by the Palaungs of Zayangyi to honour the memory of the legendary King Mani Saytu Min. To express their gratitude for his gift of a Tea Seed the silver statue of the old King was processed through the town in great splendour.

The site for old Ohm Yah had been well chosen by those Palaungs of old and although the town no longer trembles, I saw little evidence of any great changes brought by the passing centuries except perhaps that the "Tea Seed" had brought prosperity to the gentle Palaungs as the old King was said to have predicted.

6

The Legend of the Dragon Grandmother

In the beginnings of time the Earth had many strange creatures prowling through its swamps, forests and over the hills, but said the old Palaung legends, deep inside the Earth the Nāgās, or Dragon Spirit People, had made their home.

Thusan-ti, their Princess inhabited a lake high in the mountains of Upper Burma. Her greatest pleasure was to take the form of a lovely maiden and to sing and dance in the sunshine on the banks of her lake. Her joy and grace attracted the young Sun Prince who had come down to Earth seeking adventure. They fell in love and were secretly married. Their happiness made the whole earth bright with sunshine and song and it was not long before their secret came to the ears of the old Sun Queen. She was not happy about her new daughter-in-law and so she persuaded her son to go to his wife's bedside at midnight and look upon her face by torchlight. What the love-lorn Prince saw was not the beautiful face of his young bride but the hooded, scaly head of a dragon — the Sun Prince fled.

The deserted Thusan-ti was inconsolable and for days the Earth was darkened and shook and trembled with her cries. The Sun Prince was unhappy also and so he sent her a gift, a costly jewel in a gold casket. Two golden parrots were ordered to carry the precious gift to Thusan-ti but although they flew swiftly far and wide the unhappy Thusan-ti was hard to find. The tired parrots hung the casket in the branches of a tree overhanging a stream and thinking it would be safe there flew off to feed with a flock of ordinary parrots in a nearby wood.

Each day of his life an old fisherman had trawled the stream with his net and on this morning he stopped with surprise, for just when it seemed he had been lucky enough to catch a

48

gleaming golden fish he found his net was empty. Then he saw the glittering reflection of the gold casket in the water. There was no-one about, the casket seemed abandoned, he was poor and his large family hungry. Tempted, the fisherman peeped inside and in a flash he had substituted a worthless pebble in place of the sparkling jewel and gone on his way trawling the stream as though nothing had happened.

The two golden messengers returned at last for the casket and, unaware of the theft, they delivered the gift to Thusan-ti. She was delighted with the lovely casket, with the fond message from her absent lover, but when she saw the contents her anger knew no bounds. Mere neglect was hard to bear but an insult such as this was unforgivable.

Storms, floods, cyclones and tremors ravaged the earth as the jilted Princess gave vent to her fury. It seemed as though a great flash of lightning tore the heavens asunder as she flung her gold hairpin high into the air. The superstitious villagers watched and wondered as three golden comets streaked across the sky not knowing they were Thusan-ti's three golden eggs which, with all the ferocity of her anger and misery, she had hurled far into the night.

The hairpin fell in Wa country and even today the Wa people still find gold dust where it shattered. The first golden egg crashed with a thunderous roar in a rocky valley called Keer-Tawng staining all the rocks blood red and to this day rubies still abound in that valley near Mogok. The second egg was found by a villager who had gone down to the nearby river for water. He rescued the lovely gold egg from the riverbed and happy that his luck had changed he hurried home to show the treasure to his wife. They both watched over it for a week and then to their great surprise and joy it hatched into a beautiful baby boy who grew up to be handsome, strong, brave and wise.

With the help of a magic bow given to him by his father, the Sun Prince, he saved the people of Pagan from the ravages of four wild beasts which attacked the town daily, one from the north, another from the south and the other two from the east and west. In concerted attack they besieged the town. The Pig, the Frog, the Cock and the Snake, immortalised by the game of Ley-Gon-Gyn, were finally vanquished by Hpyu Sawti Min who married the local Princess and ruled the kingdom wisely.

The third egg fell near the Shweli River and was found by a farmer after the floods had abated. As he scraped away the mud he stared in disbelief, but his wife was delighted and she watched over the great gold egg until one day to her astonishment a baby boy hatched out. This Egg Prince was also brave and bold and he married a Princess of Se Lan. To remind him of his origins he had the gold eggshell mounted on top of a tall tower but this angered a powerful neighbour, a Prince of Yunnan who coveted the glittering dome. A long and bitter war resulted which was waged for many years. In the end the Egg Prince vanquished his enemies and peace and prosperity returned to Se Lan.

One of his sons he sent to rule over the Kingdom of Yunnan. Another son of the Egg Prince was weak and sickly and his father sent him to the Highlands of Loi Lung where, in the pure air of the Valley of Trembling Waters he grew to be as strong and brave as his father. He stayed on in Ohm Yah to rule the Palaung People, the first Sawbwa.

Thusan-ti had married a Năgá but she was unhappy, she could not forget those three golden eggs.† Her desire to know what had happened to them decided her to send her young daughter up to the surface as a lovely young girl to seek for news of the lost eggs. As the young Princess, Nang Shwe Ke, stepped into the outer world at Bawdwin the grains of sand in the stream turned to silver as her feet touched them. The ever watchful Sun Prince knew at once who she was and sent his grandson Min Shwethi to meet her.

Inevitably they fell in love and married to live happily in the Valley of Trembling Waters until the day that Nang Shwe Ke forgot that she must not immerse herself in water on any seventh anniversary of taking human form or she would have to return to the underworld of the Nagás for ever. This was the seventh year and as she dived into the ice cold waters of a lake one hot day she felt herself becoming a Nagá again. Min Shwethi sent his little daughter to look for her mother but the frightened girl found only a dragon who begged her to promise that in her mother's memory she would always wear clothes

---

† Golden Earth — Norman Lewis — Jonathan Cape — 1952. Chapter 12 — Page 157 — Lines 10 to 28 — the egg born Prince legend.

like the skin of a dragon. Of red with nine colours upon it, with silver and gold, a jewelled hood upon her head like the hood of a dragon and with a red stripe across her breast. The Palaung women of Zayangyi, all descendants of the Sawbwas, have kept that promise made to Nang Shwe Ke by her little daughter and in return Thusan-ti watches over their fate and fortunes

The Legend of Thusan-ti was a very real part of the lives of the Palaungs and they believed that she still watches over them and will fly over the town to warn them of danger and impending troubles.

I would not have openly scoffed at their beliefs but my doubts were rather shaken one day during lunch when a strange happening occurred which sent Aik Sai trembling under the Matey Room table. Ba Than Gyaw had dashed outside and returned to ask if I would come and see for myself. Everything had stopped he said. Puzzled, I went into the garden and found he was right. It was as though someone had waved a magic wand and time had stopped for a few moments. The perpetual breeze was no longer rustling through the trees, not a bird, bee nor butterfly was to be seen and an uncanny stillness had fallen over everything.

An ear piercing whine was growing louder. It sounded like a jet plane screaming just over the rooftop but the sky was an empty blue. The only aeroplane which ever passed our way was an old Dakota which buzzed over perhaps two or three times a year but this was a different kind of noise. Then high overhead I saw a wispy grey shadow, or was it a cloud, or what? It was moving at great speed overhead and as it passed out of sight over the hill the noise died away. At once the garden came to life again, the cherry trees swayed and rustled once more as the soft breeze caressed them, the birds twittered noisily and I saw that the butterflies and bees were flitting busily around the flowers as though nothing had occurred. If I had not seen it I would not have believed it, yet for those few moments the garden had been stilled.

The Palaungs believe firmly that such happenings are the work of the Dragon Grandmother and certainly if such visitations were an ill-omen they had plenty of trouble from that day on as the Insurrection grew throughout the Shan States and the peaceful hardworking gentle Palaungs found

themselves increasingly at the mercy of both the Shan Army
and the Burmese Army. Wanting only to be left in peace to
enjoy their Festivals they became involved in a quarrel which
was not of their seeking, their quiet paradise torn apart by the
two warring factions.

I suppose there must have been some rational explanation
for that strange phenomenon but whatever the cause, for a few
moments in each generation of Palaungs, time will stand still
and they are firm believers in Thusan-ti.

We had been having difficulty in getting photographs of the
Dragon costume. The Palaung women were shy and disliked
being treated as curiosities by visitors from the outside world.
When we mentioned this to the Minister one day he suggested
that we might like to photograph his two young daughters
wearing their ceremonial costumes, and a few days later his
wife and two lovely daughters had come to have their pictures
taken and bringing an extra costume for me to wear. Until
that morning I had not understood the meaning of the various
parts of the Dragons Dress and the connection with the
Dragon Grandmother. Each of the nine separate pieces of the
dress had to be put on in the correct sequence if it was to fit in
any way. The Princess was a small woman and her robes did
not fit me anywhere, the underskirt was much too short and I
had to make do with a red tablecloth borrowed from the Cook
which caused a great deal of merriment.

Velvet gaiters of black or navy blue were secured with long
ropes of plaited silver which were coiled around the legs. Over
the long red underskirt they tied a red apron with the dragon's
stripe across its centre and over all these a heavy overskirt, in
red flannel for everyday, or costly silk brocade for ceremonial
occasions. This was open at the front to display the apron and
it was weighted at the corners by bunches of bobbles made of
coloured wool on stems of silver wire. All were carefully
arranged to display the silver at their ankles and the blocks of
brightly coloured material which edged all the various parts of
the dress. These coloured blocks formed a part of the nine
colours spoken of in the Legend and were all intricately
stitched with traditional geometrical patterns. A white lace
cloth across the hips displayed the lovely and costly silver
girdle. This was composed of many layers of silver chains from
which dangled hundreds of small silver ornaments usually fish

or small animals each carefully fashioned and beautifully engraved.

They wore a loose fitting blouse of linen for everyday but the finest silk brocade in gleaming jewel colours for special days. This was edged with red and had a red stripe across the breast which again was heavily stitched, and detachable sleeves in bright contrasting colours tied above the elbows.

On their head they wore a black velvet pillbox hat encrusted with coiled silver wire and if the girl was rich it would have on the crown a disc of heavy embossed silver. Draped over the hat went the final piece of the costume, a flowing peaked hood of red, edged and banded with the stitched blocks of colour, across its back the dragons stripe and peak of heavy embroidery encrusted with jewels and silver.

As if this was not enough to catch the eye these descendants of the Dragon Princess adorned themselves with delicate gold necklaces and in their ears dangled giant "tin-lids" of heavy gold in which they fastened jungle fowl feathers or fresh flowers. Across the front of the blouse they pinned large silver butterflies and peacock medallions of heavy silver were sewn onto the front edge of the hood. This wealth of silver and gold was part of a girl's dowry and unmarried girls would display all their worldly wealth in this way whenever there was a Festival.

Wearing the costume made me realise why every Palaung woman walked with the air of a fairytale princess. In order to keep all the various parts in place they needed to hold their heads high and walk with a supple grace. This lovely scarlet dress was worn only by the women of Zayangyi, all descendants of Thusan-ti's grandaughter, but there were five other clans each with their own distinctive dress.

The women of KonHai, the Kyemaing's village, wore long dirndl skirts of coarse handwoven cotton of black, flecked with yellow and white, the hem edged with narrow blocks of brightly coloured velvet. The long sleeved blouse was of purple cotton with a deep "V" neckline edged with narrow bands of red and black braid and with two wide bands of orange and green around the waist and on their heads white turbans decorated with pink silk tassels.

The Tawngma costume had a more Mongolian touch. An ankle length black velvet "dressing gown" with high mandarin collar and long side slits. This elegant dress was entirely edged with narrow blocks of brightest coloured velvets, dark velvet gaiters peeped through a bright pink silk underskirt and a heavy silver belt encircled the waist, on their heads a small folded turban of pink silk with bands of bright colours across the front.

Kyaukhpu villagers wore handwoven cotton skirts of raspberry pink striped around with bands of blue and lines of yellow and black. Over this an open fronted overskirt and apron of white, striped and flecked in black. Their jackets were of plain navy edged with red and on their heads a white turban decorated with red and orange stripes across the front, on their legs the black gaiters held in place by silver cords.

A different style of dress was worn by the Aram Palaungs. This was a sarong of fine cotton in wide horizontal bands of black and red, which fastened under the arms and had no visible means of support. Resting on their hips was a three inch wide hoop of heavy silver. They wore loose jackets of navy, black or purple edged with red and on their heads a white turban decorated with a black stripe and rows of coloured bobbles, on their legs the black velvet gaiters.

The women of Manlom wore a dress very similar to that of the Aram ladies but the sarong was of bright green and purple bands and their jacket, a brief white bolero edged with coloured bobbles. Their gaiters were white and fastened with a row of coloured bobbles whilst around their hips they wore two heavy silver hoops and on their heads a small folded turban of white banded with the coloured bobbles.

These were the six "Clans" of Palaungs and whenever a village "visited" Namhsan one knew at once by the dress of the women where they had come from.

There were the Palays in sombre black edged with red and the Lishaws in their blue tunics braided with red and blue, wool tassels dangling almost to their heels and their distinctive "cartwheel" turbans often almost three feeet in diameter. They wore curious earrings with long chains which framed the chin and believed stubbornly that the camera would steal their soul and so we never managed to get a photograph.

Most of the cloth for these lovely colourful costumes was made by the women of each Clan or Group. It was handwoven and hand dyed with their own secret dyes just as their mothers and grandmothers had done for generations. Most houses would have a small wooden loom set up in the main room and many of these women would spin as they walked along the tracks over the hills using a wooden bobbin which turned and twisted up and down like a yo-yo.

Although colourful Burmese and imported cloth was readily available in all the Bazaar shops each group clung stubbornly to the traditions behind the dress and showed little desire for change.

7

Moon Days and Festivities

I was soon to discover that life in Namhsan was governed absolutely by the Moon Days. All important festivals took place at the Full Moon and the use of the Lunar Calendar was confusing to say the least. I lost all track of the days and weeks. Towards the end of the dry season we would see many small ceremonies to propitiate the Nats and bring the rains.

Driving towards Hsipaw after a picnic lunch by the River Namhsin one hot dry April day we heard the sounds of music coming from the river and to our surprise saw an orchestra floating by. In the centre of a long bamboo raft, a tiny spired pagoda had been built of gold paper. Huge gold paper fish sported playfully along each side of the raft amongst waves of colourful paper streamers. The Musicians, dressed in their finest clothes, sat on stools at the front of the craft playing a merry tune whilst the boatman at the rear played a long be-ribboned pole. Zan Lyn told us that these fishermen from the river villages made such a pilgrimage each year, taking offerings to a large pagoda some distance down river where they would pray for a successful fishing season. Zan Lyn, our Driver, had appointed himself our guide.

The Water Festival was the first grand religious festival of the year and took place at the Full Moon of Thingyan. After months of drought the air would be thick with smoke from fires which smouldered on all the tinder dry jungle slopes. The people prayed for rain but at the same time those few precious drops of water still left would be thrown over friends and enemies alike

Our first tea season there opened on April 7th and four days later our first guests arrived. Katie and Colin wanted to see for

themselves the Tawngpeng of the old legends and the Water
Festival holiday had seemed a good time to come.

The flight from Rangoon followed by the long drive over the
jungle and hill roads was tiring enough under normal
circumstances but at this season after six months of drought
the jungles were often ablaze with spectacular fires and if these
were raging on both sides of the road, it seemed as though one
drove through an avenue of flames. The air would be hot and
dry, filled with choking smoke and wood ash which stung the
eyes whilst one's hair crackled with the heat. White hot rocks
would crash down the hillside scattering onto the road and I
always hoped they would miss the petrol tank. The flames
would engulf whole trees to their topmost branches and before
this great wall of flames the jungle creatures fled together:
Deer, Leopard Cat, Bear, packs of Red Dog, one of the fiercest
of the forest animals, and many others, their natural enmity
forgotten as they searched for a safe refuge.

In the heart of the fire the green bamboos exploded keeping
up a fusillade and overhead flocks of Giant Hornbill would
flap noisily to safety, their weird honking giving a warning to
all the small creatures below. It was very spectacular and a
journey through such an inferno was not easily forgotten. How
one welcomed the cool fresh air of the hills as the road neared
Namhsan.

There had been a particularly bad fire on the day that our
guests arrived and Katie was unnerved as well as exhausted,
but there were more unnerving experiences to be faced in
Namhsan which was under siege from gangs of water throwers
who roamed the streets looking for targets. The least one could
expect was to be squirted with a bicycle pump and the worst,
to have them turn on the town's fire hose. It all had to be
taken with a smile and was done in a friendly manner.

The next morning we were invaded by a wedding party. It
had become the custom for the wedding photographs to be
taken in our garden and the guests would spend an hour or
more admiring the flowers and fish, picking the fruit and
playing games. It was open house every day and the uninvited
guests expected me to join in their celebrations. Katie was
scandalised to hear that this was a regular occurrence and
considered it an invasion of privacy but that word meant
nothing to the local people who felt that a garden was a place

to be enjoyed by everyone and they would have thought me
very unkind and unfriendly had I closed the gates.

Colin and Katie's visit coincided with the main Pwé of the
year. This gambling festival always lasted for at least a week
and if the money was still flowing freely the Contractor would
apply to the Sawbwa for an extension. The Palaungs were
compulsive gamblers and could not have enough of the Pwés.
Mr Chang had invited us all to join him at the Pwé and as we
climbed the long rickety staircase up to the Pwé ground we
found ourselves stepping into a scene which might have been
an English Country Fair with the spectators all in fancy dress.
The ground was ablaze of lights, coloured flags and balloons,
marquees of all sizes and stalls which catered for every possible
gambling taste. There were giant dice which rolled down a
sloping board, spinning wheels to bet on, dice and draughts
boards by the dozen.

At one end of the Pwé were a number of tea shops and a
restaurant all of which did a roaring trade and the pi dogs
gathered to snap up the scraps. The noise was unbelievable
with loudspeakers blaring out Chinese and Burmese music
non-stop. In the centre of the Pwé stood the main attraction,
Ley Gon Gyn, the Four Animals Game. A dice game for
serious gamblers, it had lost its origins in the mists of time but
annually the peoples of the Shan States did battle with the
four beasts and as the Legend foretold it was generally the
Four Animals which carried off the booty.

Mr Chang took us to a raised platform at the back of the
marquee which was railed off from the crowds and we could
see down onto the long table. Either side of the Banker the
table was marked out in squares and triangles with the
diagonals marking the territory of each of the four "Animals",
the Pig, the Frog, the Cock and the Snake which as in the old
legends controlled the north, the south, the east and the west.
You could place a straight bet or cover your chances
depending on which square, triangle or line you placed your
money. The Banker spun a top-like dice which was marked on
the four sides with the animal symbols. He covered the
spinning dice with a large silver bowl and only when the dice
was heard to drop would he call for bets, the hush would
become hubbub for the few minutes before he uncovered the
lucky animal.

There was no limit on the stakes and in general the Banker seemed to have all the luck, but on one unforgettable occasion I saw the Bank broken. If the Banker gave a pre-arranged signal to his Assistants and the two burly guards it passed unnoticed, suddenly I saw him fling the dice into the silver bowl, snap down the lid of his money box and before anyone realised what had happened he was running across the Pwé Ground closely followed by his associates. The crowd was momentarily shocked into silence, then with a roar of fury they leap to their feet and chased after the luckless Banker giving tongue to their feelings.

There was also a lottery with thirty-six "Animals" to choose from. Astrologers would be consulted, chance meetings, dreams, all would be taken into consideration before choosing one of the tickets and at 9 pm. each evening the "Animal" drawn would be placed on top of a tall pole for everyone to see.

At the far end of this bright scene there was always a dimly lit marquee into which furtive looking figures would slip from time to time, no Pwé would nave been complete without the Opium Den. Katie was fascinated and insisted that we must peep inside. Quietly we slid through the flap door and looked around. It seemed strangely quiet after the commotion without. In the centre of the bare earth floor one tiny oil wick burned smokily in an earthenware pot throwing dim shadows around the marquee. The air was heavy with the sickly smell from the opium pipes and in the dim light we could see shadowy figures reclining on wooden forms which were set out end to end around the sides of the marquee. Some of the faceless silhouettes lay propped on an elbow smoking odd looking long pipes, others reclined, motionless, staring into space, and a few lay sprawled on their backs lost to this world in some pipe dream. There was a silent sad emptiness about the place which gave it a sinister air and we slipped out thankful that no-one had accosted us and wondering why anyone could wish to waste time in such empty squalor when outside all was light and gaiety.

I think that perhaps the invitation to lunch at the Haw was the highlight of the visit for Katie. The Haw gardens were at their best. The bejewelled Mahadevi was a delightful Hostess and the Sawbwa a good conversationalist as well as a charming and amusing Host.

Katie had been avoiding the town because of the water throwing gangs but on our way home she decided she must have a souvenir of this occasion so we stopped in the Bazaar near some suitable shops. Being a canny Scot she was not content to buy the first thing she saw and enthusiasm getting the better of caution led us into trouble. As we rounded a corner we found ourselves facing a gang of about thirty youths armed with syringes, buckets and bowls. When they began to sprinkle us with water we retreated into one of the Indian shops but they followed ignoring the panic stricken shopkeeper who with despairing gesticulations begged us to go away. Realising that the water throwers would spoil all the goods on display I stepped outside, calling to Katie to follow but she slipped into the living quarters behind the shop whilst I got a bucketful of water down the back of my neck. I was surrounded by the now happy crowd to be squirted, sprinkled and soaked to the skin before I was allowed to go and they turned to search for Katie, besieging the frantic shopkeeper who was doing his best to protect his wares. Piet and Colin, realising what had happened, were reversing the Land Rover with horn blaring, Katie made a dash for it but was no match for the jubilant crowd. They surrounded the Land Rover and drenched us all enjoying every minute of our discomfiture; what a sorry sight we must have looked but our tormenters expected happy smiles and banter from their victims and it all had to be taken in good spirit.

The next morning Katie and I walked up to Zayangyi with the dogs and as we crossed the "Airstrip", a name we had given the flat hill top, a train of mules came jingling towards us, the big "leader" mule festooned with red wool tassels, a cockade of jungle fowl feathers nodding between its ears. They belonged to an aged Chinese whose sad old face was lined and wrinkled with toil and trouble and perhaps a hint of suspicion and fear. It was the impassive face of old China. He had two sons, the elder a surly sinister looking fellow who never spoke to us and a younger boy who had become a firm friend. He must have been about twelve years old and was quite the fiercest, most villainous looking child I had ever met. He might have stepped straight out of an epic film about the Mongol hordes. This particular morning he marched up to Katie, poked his dah into her chest and in the hissing sibilant Yunnanese language snarled 'What is your name?'

Katie was convinced that we were in the hands of some blood thirsty bandit, she clung to my arm and whispered 'What can we do?'. I introduced her to my friend and assured her that he was quite harmless and merely interested to know who the stranger was but she was not really convinced and could not get away fast enough. We were to meet this sinister family in the most out of the way places and decidedly suspicious circumstances and I am sure that it was only our good relations with the younger boy which saved us from considerable danger on more than one occasion.

On their last evening we took our guests up to Zayangyi to see one of the glorious sunsets from that vantage point. As we walked amongst the cluster of tiny pagodas which surrounded the big shrine, six fat puppies emerged from a niche, playfully glad to see us.

Katie was enchanted, 'I'll have this one which are you having?' she said picking up a fat wriggling bundle after hearing that they had been abandoned there, given as an offering to the pagoda.

We looked at her in silence for a minute then I said 'You can't take them Katie, they're an offering' and I walked on towards the Land Rover. She could not believe she had heard aright. 'How could you be so cruel' she raged, and certainly it was hard to excuse the custom. The Palaungs would not take life and this was one way in which they tried to keep down the dog population. Devotees would take regular offerings of rice to even the most distant shrines so the abandoned puppies could find food and if they survived the cold and the marauding panthers they might find their way down to a village where they would be fed and cared for. It was one of the local customs which I disliked intensely but had to accept if I was to remain a friend of those people. My explanations sounded hollow even to me and Katie would not be comforted. The week she had spent in Namhsan would not be easily forgotten for a number of reasons.

8

Domestic Incidents

After H.L.B. had left on his final journey to Rangoon and retirement, his cook and butler refused to stay on. They had never worked for a woman and had no intention of trying the experience. Trained servants were reluctant to come to such a remote place as Namhsan particularly if they could find work in Rangoon or Mandalay. However a Burman named Kyaw Khin and a Chinese Cook, Lusit Ching, were willing to try us, with eventual disastrous results. The pair loathed each other and the experiment ended in a fight, Kyaw Khin attacking Ching with a chopper, though possibly not without some provocation for Ching could be very infuriating at times. They had chased one another around the dining table during one Sunday Lunch, each trying to shout his grievances above the other as they brandished their weapons, quite spoiling our roast beef and Yorkshire pudding. The butler had been sent back to Mandalay the next day, Ching left shortly afterwards.

I took on another Burman Aye Pé, and decided to train local boys for other duties. Aye Pé was a good cook but unfortunately he became addicted to the locally brewed liquor and in the end he too had to be sent away for his own good and Ching descended on us asking for his old job back. Realising that I would never find a better cook I decided to put up with his temperamental ways and he ruled us all tyrannically for the rest of our stay in the Shan States.

Eastern kitchens are not exactly a magazine image of luxury and convenience but in retrospect the kitchens in the Indian Bungalows seemed to have been a modern delight compared with the dark greasy corrugated iron shed which served as a kitchen at Namhsan. I ordered a complete "spring clean" and re-decoration and a small army of people worked on it for days. I was asked to view the transformed kitchen. The ceiling and walls had been whitewashed, the wooden bench scrubbed until it gleamed and the floor was spotless. The bow-legged iron cooking stove had been scraped clean and blackleaded and the roof high pile of long pieces of split tree trunks which were fed whole into the fire had vanished to a neat woodpile outside. It almost looked like a kitchen.

The cook opened the wire gauze doors of the cupboard to show me the tidy well scrubbed shelves when I saw something scuttle behind the drawer. Thinking it was a mouse, I pulled out the drawer and looked cautiously inside. Several hundred pairs of gleaming little red eyes stared back at me through a sea of waving antennae. There were cockroaches in such numbers that they sat two and three deep, one on top of another. I picked up the Flit gun and gave them a good burst of spray then as an afterthought sprayed the whole kitchen. It was as though I had let loose a horde of maddened demons. Thousands of long-legged "beasties" appeared from every crack and cranny to dash madly around the room. Brown ones, ginger and ghastly white, they swarmed everywhere, ran up my legs dropped onto my head from the ceiling, the more I sprayed them the wilder became their mad dance whilst I dashed around the room stamping on all I could reach screaming 'Kill them'.

The whole Bungalow Staff stood in a silent disapproving group by the door watching me with shocked pitying eyes. As Buddhists they could not believe that anyone would indulge in wholesale slaughter even of cockroaches. Suddenly I realised that their religious principles were something I was going to have to learn to live with, but I was certainly not going to accept that it meant I would have to put up with those filthy little insects without a struggle. I flung the Flit gun at the boys almost snarling 'clean up this mess' and stormed off to the top of a nearby hill to think things over. Something had to be done but losing my temper would not help, eventually I came to the conclusion that I must persuade the cockroaches to commit suicide and I returned home remembering childhood days and jammy wasp traps. I was going to invent an infallible cockroach trap. I sent out a call for old beer bottles and into each I poured a small quantity of a potion which I hoped would be irresistible. These traps were left at strategic points around the kitchen and Matey Room and were an instant success. The next morning Law Htan appeared at the breakfast table all smiles and bearing a silver salver with twenty or so corpses on it, the night's "bag". The boys were quite happy to set these traps and the cockroaches could hardly wait to sample the nectar. This way it seemed that we did not infringe any Buddhist principles and everyone was happy including any sozzled cockroaches.

Over the months the traps certainly decimated the pests although I was never to completely eliminate them. They would pop up at the most awkward moments to embarrass me. Breakfasting in the Summer House one fine morning with visitors from Rangoon, as I poured out the coffee I saw something large and black plop into one of the cups. To my horror a cockroach floated to the surface and my instant reaction was to flick the offending body into the nearest plantpot. I could only hope that our guests were too busy talking "shop" with Piet to have noticed. Sickened by the thought of sipping stewed cockroaches, I picked up the steaming pot and announced firmly to the astonished men that the coffee was cold and hurried away to the kitchen to make sure that no more of my "friends" took a hot bath in the next brew. Had I been asked to name a list of Seven Horrors of the East, cockroaches would undoubtedly have headed my list at that particular moment.

H.L.B. had warned me that the local people looked upon the garden as their own and I had already experienced the wedding parties but it was not unusual to find strangers wandering around admiring the flowers and the gold-fish and most days the children came by the dozen.

At first I felt rather disconcerted when Sunday lunch had to be eaten before a row of spectators at the dining room window. I eventually convinced myself that they meant no harm and were merely curious to see how the foreigners behaved and we would joke about it being feeding time at the Zoo.

The Gurkha Mali, Ram, was a handsome old man. His great joy was the hosepipe and he would play with it all day unless I gave him a work schedule. He objected to the uninvited visitors and would shoo them away quite rudely on the flimsiest of pretexts. Hearing shouts of 'go back to the Bazaar' coming from the gates one morning whilst breakfasting in the Summer House, I dashed over to rescue two charming ladies, visiting Professors from Rangoon, but Ram was quite unrepentant.

We were able to grow most English vegetables and flowers as well as peaches, pineapples, lemons, bananas, plums, and for about nine months of the year, strawberries which were quite the most deliciously flavoured ones I had ever tasted.

One morning Ram was waiting for me, a worried frown on his handsome face. Bad spirits were devouring the broccoli he said and there was nothing he could do about it. I went down to the vegetable garden to see the culprits, to find the all too familiar hairy caterpillars. Why was he so worried I asked him, surely he had dealt with such pests before? He shook his head and insisted that this was bad magic, each morning he had sent these beings away but by nightfall they were back again bigger and stronger than ever. I knew he was an opium addict and decided that it must be affecting his reasoning so I suggested he tried again. It would be alright if I was there. Immediately he produced chopsticks and gently picked up each caterpillar to put it carefully on the ground as he told it to go away, it must not eat Takin Ma's broccoli. Naturally as fast as he put them down they began to crawl aloft again to continue their interrupted feed. Poor Ram, I knew it was no good showing anger, but perhaps a bit of psychology would be a match for magic and I filled a shallow tin with insecticide adding some red colouring to make it look dangerous. I told Ram that it was a strong magic powder, he had only to put each bad spirit into it before releasing it on the ground to banish them for ever. He was not convinced but agreed to give the powder a trial and the next morning he was waiting for me, anxious to have more of the magic powder, it was so powerful he said that all the bad spirits had vanished just as I had predicted. He could not do enough to please me and I wondered if perhaps he was afraid I might put a spell on him if he displeased me.

'Bad magic' was again to rear its ugly head when the milk suddenly turned a transparent bluish colour. I waylaid the milkman, a tough wiry Gurkha who along with about a dozen of his kinsmen walked into Namhsan each morning carrying two large milk cans each half full on a yoke made of a long whippy bamboo pole which rested across one shoulder. They walked in single file their cans bobbing rhythmically to their curious trotting gait. Later I walked to their village on a high ridge just below the highest hill in the district and I felt he deserved every kyat he earned.

The women, older men and children stayed in the settlement tending the herds of buffalo and growing maize and vegetables whilst the younger men made the daily trek into town to sell the milk. My milkman left the main party and took the shortcut down the hill at Zayangyi stopping at my garden tap to fill his cans to the brim with water before measuring out the milk. I had objected to this well established custom but as milk was always in short supply we had an agreement that I paid him double the town rate for a measure taken before the water was added.

Realising that he had been up to his tricks again I asked for an explanation. He told me a sorry tale of magic. Some bad spirit had taken all the goodness out of the grass and the milk was wasting away. Nothing could be done about it he said, but I was ready for him having bought a lactometer on my last home leave. I asked him to watch carefully whilst my magic stick tried to discover what was wrong with the milk. He scratched his head and frowned fiercely when I showed him the results, it was more than half water. Gently I suggested that there must be something he could do to put things right. As though fascinated he stared at the lactometer, he shook his head and muttered to himself. At last he said he thought there might be a cure but he would have to consult the Elders. They would try to appease the bad spirits, it might take two or three days he added.

Well, each following day the milk improved in appearance until on the fourth day he asked to see me. He was all smiles, everything was alright he said. I asked if he would like to see what my magic stick predicted and he was suitably impressed when it confirmed that the milk was normal once more.

This little game was played out at regular intervals throughout my stay in Tawngpeng. No-one laughed and no tempers were lost, but it was a serious game. He would not have respected me had I let him get away with it, but to have accused him of adding water to the milk would have offended his dignity and I would have found that he was unable to supply any milk at all. By playing this strange game with him I won his respect and for most of the year, got what I wanted.

Regretfully Ram had been pensioned off and sent back to his village. His addiction to opium had seriously affected his health and Dr Peel thought he should be cared for by his relations.

Padmal, the new Mali, was an extremely handsome Nepali, a good and willing worker, but his one fault was his weakness for the forbidden liquor brewed secretly in most of the villages. Two of our Chinese workers had been making the stuff in their houses: they lived in the workers settlement just beyond our garden and one morning they were tipped off about an impending police raid. The police arrived to find the path swilling with fermenting rice wine but as there was none to be found in any of the houses they could not arrest the culprits.

They had all been severely reprimanded by Piet. If they were caught again illegally brewing they would have to be dismissed but that had not stopped them from secretly buying the forbidden spirits from the stills to be found in most villages and selling it to their friends.

At least once a week Padmal would get well and truly "stoned", pick on one of the staff wives and serenade her all night long with ribald Gurkhali army songs.

Tearful wives complained that their husbands accused them of encouraging the fellow and angry husbands demanded that the Mali must go or blood would be let whilst I was playing a cool hand hoping that things would blow over.

So, it was with this situation in the background, that the peace of one bright sunny morning was rudely shattered at 11.05 am. The mid-day break was taken from 11.00 am. to noon, a tray of drinks would be left on the verandah for me and the houseboys would go home for their dinner, I would be entirely alone until Piet came down to join me.

On this particular morning all hell broke loose at five minutes past the hour. A woman screamed and bloodcurdling shouts and roars disturbed the usual peace. The next moment the Mali was charging wildly across the lawn brandishing a kukri and screaming 'Sher, Sher' — Tiger. He saluted smartly and announced that there was a panther at the bottom of the

garden which looked like a tiger and he had just chopped off
its head. My heart sank, obviously the fellow had been on the
bottle all morning and was seeing pink tigers. Eyeing the kukri
nervously the thought occurred to me, that unless I kept cool,
calm and collected he might possibly have my head off as well.
I tried to think of a few soothing words. Of course I would go
along and view the remains but first I must finish my
elevenses, meanwhile why not go and tell Thakin all about it.
It worked. He jumped to attention, saluted again and charged
off across the lawn making bloodthirsty noises and I hoped
Piet would know how to deal with him. As it turned out I was
misjudging Padmal, there really had been a panther at the
bottom of the garden. It had tree'd an old Palaung woman
who had come to gather aromatic leaves and her screams had
brought Padmal at the double and two of our Karens who
were going home for dinner. The three of them had attacked
the beast and with one mighty swipe the Mali had chopped off
its head, Set upon by three such formidable hunters the big cat
had little chance of escaping their sharp dahs. By the time Piet
reached the scene the panther was skinned and the excited
crowd was drawing lots for the prize joints, the paws and other
unmentionable organs. They believed that to eat such a
powerful beast would give them all its strength, the paws for
physical strength and the sex organs for virility.

When I realised that it was a rare Clouded Leopard, I felt
rather sorry it had been destroyed. It was smaller than the
ordinary leopard, was buff in colour with a white belly and
down each side parallel to the ribs were elongated smudgy
blotches edged with black which at a distance looked like
stripes. On the head, legs and tail it had the usual spots. This
threatened species lives in jungle areas up to 7,500 feet
elevation in Upper Burma.

On reflection I began to wonder what would have happened
had I come face to face with that great cat at the bottom of
my garden, especially if it had had designs on me. would I
have been able to shin up a tree as nimbly as the old woman
had done? She was seventy years if a day. Sadly I came to the
conclusion that I would most probably have ended up inside
the beast and it might be a good thing that it was dead.
Ordinary panther, were fairly plentiful but they were shy
creatures and did little damage. I saw one being chased by

three men one evening whilst out with the dogs and was glad it was occupied, for dog is a favourite dish of the panther. One took shelter in a small hut used by the tea pluckers; when the women went inside at mid-day it gave them a nasty shock as it bolted for the door knocking the terrified women off their feet.

I was always more afraid of the bear than the panther; these were the Himalayan Black Bear, fluffy black "Teddy Bears" with deadly claws. We often heard them whistling at dusk in the jungle below the garden and there was always the chance that the dogs might stumble onto one when we were out on our walks, the danger being that the bear would attack ferociously in self defence. On one occasion we were held up for ten minutes or so when a big black brute stood in the middle of the road refusing to give way. Eventually it turned away from us to climb up a steep bank and vanish in the long grass. Most of the game had little interest in us except to keep out of our way and as it was against the religious principles of the Palaungs to kill any amimal, Tawngpeng was something of a nature reserve.

Burma, like so many countries, is the home of beautiful and rare animals, many of which are threatened species. The Clouded Leopard was only one of these but I was told that there were a number of other little known animals still fighting a losing battle for existence.

There was the strange and little known Takin, or Tharmin in Burmese. My Kachin Mali told me that it looked rather like an ungainly cow with a short hairy tail and very heavy legs. Despite its heavy build this shy mountain animal is very agile and is found only in some of the more remote parts of the Kachin State and in China. Another of Burma's rare animals is the Two Horned Rhinoceros, or Wet Kyan. This is small and its tough armour-plated body bristles with short hairs. It still survives in small numbers in suitable terrain around the major rivers. Other threatened species are the Tapir, the Brow Antlered Deer and the Banteng, or Saing. The greatest danger to these fast diminishing species is the ignorance of their rarity amongst the farmers in the more remote regions. After all when a poor hardworking peasant farmer sees his crops trampled or eaten by wild cattle, or his stock killed by leopard, one cannot blame him for taking action to protect his property, often his very existence, a fact which played a large part in the slow but sure extermination of these rare wild animals.

My brother Charles had come to stay. He lived in Malaya and whilst returning home on leave he had broken his journey at Rangoon and caught the Lashio plane. I had last seen him in India some years before and we had a lot of family news to catch up on.

It was May and that was the mushroom season. Each year I had seen the short almost lawn-like grass which covered a flat hilltop near Zayangyi thick with delicious looking pink button mushrooms and I asked Chas for his opinion; were they edible? Generally we found they had been trampled and squashed but on this occasion they looked fresh, exactly like the English field mushrooms and they smelled inviting, so we took a few home to experiment with. Perhaps fortunately, the kitchen was locked by the time we returned home and so we put the mushrooms into a spare bathroom. We would try some tests on them later but we forgot them until the following morning or the story might have had a very different ending.

Next day, remembering our find we took them across to the kitchen passing TanYin, the Palaung girl who did all the things for me which custom would not allow a man to do. As she caught sight of the mushrooms she gave a gasp of horror, dropped her iron and caught my arm begging me to throw away the "bad ones". As we entered the kitchen there was a cry of dismay from Ching, and the houseboys all took up TanYins cry, 'Thei mé — you'll die' they all said. The innocent looking little mushrooms had passed all the tests we had tried on them but in the face of such genuine concern we decided to put them into the dustbin without further ado. Chas was later told by a doctor friend that those particular mushrooms found in the hills af Asia are extremely poisonous. To eat even the smallest portion would result in paralysis of the respiratory system and at Namhsan, with the nearest hospital five hours journey away, we would have had little chance of recovery.

This incident rather put me off trying any other indigenous fungi. The Bazaars were full of odd looking toadstools of every shape and size at this time of the year, but I was not keen to try any of them. About a week after Chas had left us to resume his journey home to England, Ba Than Gyaw brought me a message from the cook. Could he see me? A few moments later Ching had bounced into the room brandishing a large basketful of truly cartoon-land style toadstools announcing his intention of serving them for dinner that night, only to get rather a cool reception.

They had shiny glutinous crimson caps about three inches diameter and with ghastly white gills and stems, they looked more than poisonous.

'We're not eating those' I said and Ching bristled; these were not like the Zayangyi mushrooms, these were good ones and he had picked them himself he informed me with dignity, so I suggested that he should eat them all himself. He brandished the basket under my nose again insisting that these mushrooms were very good to eat and I shoo'd him away refusing to accept his gift.

At dinner that night there was a sudden commotion in the Matey room, I could hear Ching shouting angrily at being refused entry to the dining room. Then suddenly the door burst open and the cook stormed into the room sweeping all the other boys aside with a large dish of stewed toadstools. He placed the dish in front of me with a bang, pointed a finger at me and bellowed 'You eat or I resign'.

I stared at him for a minute wondering how best to handle the situation without him losing face or he certainly would resign.

'First you eat' I said firmly and served him up a plateful. He promptly sat down with us at the table and to disapproving clucks from Ba Than Gyaw, he polished off the lot. I watched him closely, half expecting to see him curl up screaming with pain or fall across the table unconscious but no, he looked infuriatingly fit and had obviously enjoyed the feast. In the end I had to apologise for having doubted him and sampled some myself. After that there was no stopping him. We were served with a variety of the most deadly looking toadstools for the next few months until the novelty wore off and Ching began to persecute the townspeople with bread, but there lies another story.

During Chas's visit we went down to Lilu for our usual weekend outing. In Mankai village we found a group of boys waiting hopefully. They never missed a chance to accompany us and would spend the whole day swimming. They would pile into the back of the Land Rover and PoSein would produce a home made flute, Aye Gyaw and Aik Buint would start to beat out a rhythm with sticks and so they would make music all the way down to the river. We had no boat at that time and had to cross the water at the Lilu Ferry, then walk along a track on the opposite bank of the river, coming eventually to a small clearing where we had built a Shan House.

That hot sunny day in May we found our path bordered with giant Arum lilies. The huge flowers were of a delicate creamy apricot colour, the spadix of deepest orange thick with pollen. We thought they were lovely and decided to dig up one corm and try growing it at home. We found it had a corm the size of a dinner plate. I had never before seen one of such a size.

Our day was very successful and Chas caught a large fish at the first cast. I tried fishing there for years and never had a single bite, but we cooked this fish for our supper and it tasted like trout. As we boarded the ferry on our way home, the Shan Boatman, whom I had decided to call Ghengis because of his marked resemblance to that fierce looking warrior, noticed our lily. A look of horror came over his expressive face and he asked what we intended to do with it.

'Throw it overboard' he shouted clutching his throat and heaving realistically over the side but we refused to be put off insisting that such beauty could not be as nasty as he suggested.

We put our lily in the back of the Land Rover with the boys and though we noticed that they were rather subdued on the return journey and that their goodbyes were not as effusive as usual, we thought nothing of it. Deciding that it was too late to plant the arum we left it on the Matey room verandah for the night and forgot all about it. In Namhsan it was always dark very early in the evening because we nestled beneath the high ridges which brought a sudden nightfall. It would be quite dark by 7 pm. at the very latest throughout the year and the evenings were always cool. The houseboys liked to finish their work early because of the long cold nights and it was the custom for families to sit close around the fire listening to the storytellers, and so in deference to this custom we always had an early dinner and they would leave before 8.30 pm.

On this particular evening it must have been about 9 pm.

when I noticed the objectionable odour. I searched the whole house and found nothing, yet still the nauseating smell spread through the house as though some unkind person had dumped a rotting carcase on our doorstep.

The two men joined be in the search and it was then that we discovered the culprit. We saw our lovely lily was crawling with black beetles of every kind and size, attracted by the awful smell. We had brought home a carrion lily!

At least it explained something which had puzzled me on a number of occasions when driving along the jungle roads during April and May. At certain spots there was always a strong scent of carrion and seeing that the vegetation was crawling with beetles and flies we had jumped to the conclusion that some wild animal lay dead there. Now we would know better. If in the future we came across that ghastly aroma, we would know that in some dark corner not far away there would be a flower of unbelieveable loveliness and noisome habits.

Gambling had been banned at the factory after a rather sensational fight over a gambling debt.

The cook had chosen that week to rush down to Mandalay at a moment's notice, having heard a rumour that his wife had won the State Lottery. We were managing with the help of Law Htan, one of the Chinese houseboys who seemed to cope very well but the added responsibility rather went to his head. On being told that the ban also covered his activities and he must cease to run gambling parties in his house each night, he promptly organised a strike and the whole bungalow staff walked out. I found the kitchen deserted, lunch half cooked, a batch of bread left to its fate in the dying stove and I decided I must show them that I could get on very well without them or they would have a formidable weapon to use against me in the future. All went well until mid-afternoon when the bath boiler had to be lit. It was a pot-bellied iron monster which lurked in a tiny smoke blackened room behind the bathrooms. I had watched the boys light it. They would stuff three foot long billets of wood through the small hole on top, a few wood chips below, pour kerosene over the lot and apply a match below, whereupon it would blaze away merrily. I found it was not as easy as it looked and my efforts failed dismally in clouds of choking smoke. All I succeeded in doing was to singe my eyelashes and very nearly blow the whole thing apart. The stinging smoke brought copious tears to my eyes. I was covered with soot and fuming with frustration as I dashed off to the sitting room in search of another box of matches.

As I burst into the room I found myself face to face with two intruders who were carrying off the new transistor radio. I recognised a former houseboy who must have heard of the strike and knowing the ways of the household guessed that I would be occupied with the reluctant bath boiler at that time in the afternoon. A look of horror spread over their faces, they dropped the radio and with a howl of apparent fear they leaped out of the open window and ran across the lawn towards a path which led down to the jungle below. Without stopping to think I gave a shriek of rage. This was the last straw in an impossible day! I was out of the window and after them in a trice shouting every abuse I could think of in the five local languages.

I had chased them at least a hundred yards down the jungle path before I came to my senses and remembered that they were well armed and that if I did catch them that they would probably have panicked and attacked me with their dahs. I returned hastily to the garden above and as I approached the house I caught sight of my reflection in one of the windows. Like some Ancient Briton painted with woad my face was a horrifying mask streaked into strange patterns with soot and tears. I collapsed onto the lawn helpless with laughter at the awful vision. No wonder the intruders had fled, they probably thought that I was an avenging Nat especially as there had been stories that the bungalow was haunted, and after seeing such a frightening apparition no intruder would face the household ghosts a second time. We had no more unwelcome visitors. The story spread quickly on the Bazaar grapevine and the houseboys had an excuse to return to work without loss of face which was so very important to those people. I decided it was best to forget about the strike and so all ended happily.

Ba Than Gyaw had been pestering me for some weeks to buy him a bottle of Mandalay rum. He was a Karen and had been brought up by a Baptist Missionary. He spoke beautiful old fashioned "Oxford" English and when new guests called the butler, putting their requests in stilted phrases, it always amused me to see the surprise on their faces when he replied. I asked why he was so anxious to have the rum. Was he throwing a party? He explained that it was for his wife who was about to have her first baby. In Namhsan babies were brought into the world without modern aids, no hospitals, no anaesthetics nor analgesics and Ba Than Gyaw said, more often than not, no Midwife. Babies have a habit of choosing the middle of the night to be born and unless the distraught father could provide transport and give the midwife a handsome present she would not turn out after dark. The unhappy husband would have to walk to town or sometimes outlying villages to try and find some old woman accustomed to helping on such occasions.

Ba Than Gyaw said he would give the rum to his wife and when the labour pains told her that her time was near she would drink the whole bottleful to be so drunk she would know little about the event. This was the only form of anaesthetic available to the women, he said. I was shocked, it made Western women seem pampered by comparison. I knew that our company donated a generous annual contribution towards medical expenses for the factory staff and workers and that it was supposed to include the services of the midwife. I had made a firm rule never to interfere with company business and local politics but I felt that this was different. Those women needed help and I was not going to rest with an easy conscience if I made no effort on their behalf. I explained all the facts to Piet who was as concerned as I was and he lost no time in passing on our concern to the highest authority.

Eventually changes took place and I was told that the new midwife was a kindly woman who answered emergency calls, no matter what the hour.

Soon after this incident I had called on our agent in Lashio to be told that his wife was in hospital for a minor operation. It seemed that a girl from Namhsan, Ranie, had decided that she wished to be a doctor and her father, an enlightened man, had given her every help and encouragement. Now Ranie had qualified and was at the hospital in Lashio. Rather to everyones, surprise, she was an astounding success. If she could have made each day 48 hours long it would still not have been enough for her to attend to the growing queue of women who wanted to consult her. It had been a shock our agent said, to find that his own wife had covered up her pain and ill-health

knowing that he would have insisted on taking her to see the
doctor, but she could not bring herself to talk of such intimate
problems to a man. Death would have been preferable to that.
It was not only his wife, said our friend, but all the ladies in
the district were the same. Later I talked to his wife about the
problem of the lack of women doctors and her words showed
me that it went deeper than just shyness with a male doctor.

'I was happy to talk to Ranie quite freely of my symptoms'
she said 'you see she is one of us, not a foreigner from other
districts who would not have understood how we felt about so
many things'

The new doctor had the advantage not only of being a
woman but also of being a local girl whom they all knew and
trusted, and how they had needed her.

Piet and I had visited the famous hospital at Namhkam to
meet Dr Seagrave. He told us of the early struggles to found
the first hospital there, how he and a few helpers had gathered
from the river all the smooth, rounded stones which formed
the walls of the old building. Now there was a large modern
hospital but the old walls would always remind them of their
beginnings, he had said. He still worked each day at that time
but no longer operated because his hands were too unsteady
and we smiled at his words, for when shaking hands with the
stocky, massive shouldered, silver haired Doctor we had both
winced under his iron grip. He spoke with feeling of his
endeavours to help the people he loved. So many isolated
village communities were without trained medical aides he said
and he told us of some of his training schemes, both past and
present. I could imagine the difficulties he might have had in
persuading girls from isolated communities to train for any
career, tradition was against it, but judging by the efficient,
neatly uniformed nurses I had seen quietly at work on the
wards, his training schemes had met with a great deal of
success. From the beginning the Sawbwas had backed his
training schemes, he told us, but not all the States had
responded immediately as some of those he approached wanted
to be sure that any girl sent to Namhkam would not be under
any pressure to change her religion, for the hospital was also a
Mission School, and the doctor had smiled to himself as he
recounted his efforts.

I heard of few Palaung girls being encouraged to take up

nursing or any other career which would have taken them away from their homeland. Most of the women in the Tawngpeng State seemed content with the old way of life, remaining in their villages tending the tea gardens, their only ambition to be a wife and mother.

The fresh clear mountain air of Tawngpeng was famous, praised even in the legends of old. Perhaps this was why the Palaungs, who all smoked heavily from an early age, suffered no ill effects. Those who did not fall to an assassin's dah or bullet would generally live to a great age and most of them fit and active to the last, although like so many mountain peoples, they were often plagued by goitre.

I talked to Dr Peel on this subject one morning when he dropped in for a dish of tea. How was it, I asked, that there were no cripples, spastics or mentally retarded, and his reply was the last thing I had expected to hear. Any baby born less than perfect never survived for more than a few days he said. It was not that they actually harmed such a baby, they would not take life, but they would also make no attempt to prolong such a life. They considered there was something abnormal about multiple births and few twins survived.

The doctor told me that over the years he had been called many times to attend most of the Sawbwa's large family and on several occasions in the early days he had been puzzled by an unusual ceremony. At frequent intervals a servant had brought in a small cup filled with a clear liquid. This would be presented to the Sawbwa and after his nod of approval it would them be offered to the patient who would sip the potion. The doctor felt he should know what was in this medicine he had not prescribed but his queries always brought only a smile and the reply 'To give them strength'.

On one occasion when the Doctor had returned home he had received a summons from the old Mahadevi who was anxious for news of a patient and the Doctor took the opportunity to ask her about the ceremony of the drink which had so puzzled him.

The great lady had laughed, 'Oh, we all get that' she said 'to give us strength you know'.

Seeing the perplexed look on the doctor's face she had relented and explained that it was only water, water that had first been poured over the hands of the Sawbwa. As he was a holy person, it was thought that his strength would flow into the water and benefit all those who drank it. Things are different now, said the doctor. Faith healing is forgotten and antibiotics the only medicine the Palaungs believe in.

During my first few months in Burma everyone had offered me good advice but it was Gerard's witty tale which lingered longest in my mind. He had enjoyed his self-imposed isolation he told me, and invitations to visit his hill-top home were rarely given. His attitude to visitors had hardened he said after a rather trying incident at the hands of the small son of a young couple who appeared on his doorstep, uninvited, one evening.

Within the hour, said our friend, he was regretting his rash decision to take them in. The fond parents were devout disciples of Dr Spock and their mischievous young son could do no wrong in their eyes. He had managed to do no more than voice his disapproval over some of his young guest's pranks but when he awoke the next morning to see his tormentor tip-toeing across the bedroom carrying off the tooth glass his patience deserted him. He had reached the garden just in time to see the whole lot, glass, teeth and all being thrown over the precipice to the jungle below. Momentarily stunned then consumed with fury, he had told his guests just what he would do to their precious son if he caught him and the fond parents departed with more haste than dignity. For days the jungle had been searched for the missing teeth without success. Our friend could only cable his dentist in London and try to survive on mince and milk puddings instead of his usual diet of local game. He advised me to follow his strict rule. Since that dreadful day he had never opened his doors to enyone except close friends and carefully scrutinised V.I.P's.

I could see his point. We were going to live in one of the worlds beauty spots and the tourists would pour in given the chance, but I was to find that when one lived in complete isolation amongst an alien people a friendly face from the outer world was hard to resist and I would always forget that well meant advice.

Our guests were of many differing nationalities, frequently uninvited and although I had my doubts about one or two of them, they made an interesting diversion during our annual exile.

Had I known Gerard better I might have spotted that he was dropping a few hints about the sort of nocturnal diversions the houseboys might be tempted to indulge in without actually putting it into so many words but I was slow to get the point of his story until many months later, being wise after the event.

The story he told me of his days in the Forestry Service and of the favourite Ayah who had sold a peep-hole in the Ladies' bath tent to the men down at the logging camp had sounded very funny as an after dinner diversion and I forgot about it until months afterwards when I began to feel that I was being watched as I splashed and soaped in the bath each evening. Piet was amused and insisted I must be imagining things but a few days later, soft footfalls and whispering without, convinced me I was right.

The bungalow was built of wood with an inner skin of pine to keep out the cold winter winds and my late night stroll around the garden was a revelation. From each bathroom pencil shafts of light stabbed the dark night and from each carefully selected hole there was a clear view of everything within. I was furious and announced that I intended to reprimand the whole staff later that evening. For a man to be publicly reprimanded by a woman was condsidered to be a serious loss of face, no man would touch my shoes, wash my clothes or iron them and soon after my arrival I had to have the washing line re-sited so that no man need walk underneath my clothing. Had I carried out my threat it would have meant a total "walk-out" of the whole bungalow staff.

The thought of the disruption this would mean spurred Piet to action and he "read the riot act", and that we thought would be an end to the affair. A few days later as we returned from our evening walk a strange sight met our eyes. Across the lawn marched one of our senior drivers, his face contorted with anger as he frogmarched one of the erring houseboys up to us. He stood to attention, saluted smartly, kicked his young brother sharply on the shin as a reminder that he also must stand to attention and began to apologise. His brother's behaviour had brought shame on his whole family he said, ThakinMa had only to say the word and he would give the young scoundrel the beating he deserved. I could only insist that the matter must be forgotten and that I did not really blame him as I was sure the peep-holes had been handed down over several "generations" of houseboys and had one of them not forgotten to replace the corks I might never have known about them.

Regular travellers to far-away-places were usually aware that a peek into the Embassy "book" could provide them with a list of expatriates living "up-country" and whether casual callers might get a welcome or a cool reception. What was said of us was to lead to a succession of visitors of all nationalities who punctuated our isolation with numerous bright spots, although I often felt that our houseboys were not so happy about the intrusion.

One morning I had found Ba Than Gyaw standing in front of the guest bedroom door motionless, a ferocious scowl on an unusually red face. Was something wrong I asked and he turned slowly to stare at me for a moment before replying in his old fashioned English, 'Madam, I might have expected a Burmese gentleman to behave in that way but not an English gentleman', and he turned away without further explanation leaving me mystified and rather intrigued. Just what had my uninvited guests been up to?

One favourite family worked for the British council in Mandalay. The first time they had written asking if they might come to stay I had replied by return cable 'Delighted to have you, bring a dozen eggs'. As Lisa handed me a box of eggs she said that neither she nor her husband ate them and we had stared at each other for a moment until I explained that all chickens had died of cholera and in Namhsan eggs were off the market. They laughed, it was the same in Mandalay said our new friends but thinking that perhaps this obviously eccentric hostess might not allow them to cross the doorstep if they arrived without the eggy pass, they had searched the district before finding any.

A friend in Rangoon had written asking if we would take in an Australian author and his wife who were in Rangoon and with a visa for only three weeks. They were seeking inspiration for a book, would we give them some local colour he wanted to know. At that time we were suffering the culinary arts of a local lad and strange and embarrassing things were liable to occur. I had cabled a reply 'Send them up if they can stand the cooking' and they had accepted at once, intrigued to discover what lay behind the unusual invitation. They had driven up late one evening more impressed than they had expected to be by the magnificent scenery and surprised by the chill of the evening air. They had enjoyed a hot bath and were relaxing in front of a blazing log fire having a drink before dinner when the peace was shattered as the door burst open and a wild figure fell into the room brandishing a tattered umbrella. With some unease and disbelief they had stared at the intruder who shouted and gesticulated, his shirt flapping open revealing a gleaming tattoo'd chest, his baggy pants slit and torn displaying knobbly knees and a battered trilby pulled low over a face which was streaked with strange black hieroglyphics, obviously the work of sooty fingers. I explained to their great relief that it was only the cook, Aik Hti, who had come to tell me he had spilled the soup.

The next morning, as I was checking that breakfast would not be a disaster, the author appeared at the kitchen door and on being asked if they had enjoyed a peaceful night he replied that it had been perfect until the bed collapsed. To my embarrassment I found he was not joking and I found his wife standing in silent contemplation over the crumbled ruins of the bed. Ahoy, the carpenter was called and we were alarmed to find that the white ants had also consumed the two main floor joists. Our guests were lucky that the whole floor had not given way.

One fine morning a party of Germans drove up to the door and under the misguided information that there was an "English Wallah Hotel" in the hills they drove up to the door and demanded a room with a view across the valley. Their embarrassed faces on learning the truth were so comical that I forgave them and took them in.

We always had breakfast and tea in the Summer House except on the very worst of the monsoon days and it was there that our visitors would generally find us.

One wet afternoon we had been marooned outside over our afternoon tea by an unexpected storm when a lone Englishman representing Glaxo had suddenly appeared out of the blanket of rain and mist to find us busy catching the drips from the leaky roof in empty tea cups and bowls. He must have had doubts about our mental state and we were intrigued to know what had brought him to Namhsan.

At breakfast one day a six foot lanky American woman bounded in announcing in a voice to match her size that she was "Mary Ann" and she laughed delightedly when we said we had already heard of her. We had seen a notice on the Visitors' Board at the Lashio Circuit House that the Reverend and Mrs ---X and Mary Ann would be staying there. We had pictured a precocious small child travelling with her parents. They were only friends she said and it had never occured to her to add her surname, everyone knew her as just Mary Ann, and we were to find she was right; she and the other members of the Fulbright Team were known to almost everyone we met. Diplomats, engineers, missionaries, tourists, our guests were interesting and kept us in touch with reality until the day the Central Government in Rangoon made an order forbidding foreigners to leave Rangoon without special permission. After that we saw few travellers.

After all our troubles with domestic staff, it was quite a relief when Ching suddenly returned to the fold. His gold dentures gleamed as he explained he was now free to take up his old job again and I decided that it was better to suffer his eccentricities than alcoholics and bad cooks.

Ching had aquired a new skill during his absence. He baked delicious, feather light, bread. Daily I would praise his new accomplishment and that was to lead to a great deal of trouble. Some months after the cook's return I was met one evening by a deputation of prominent citizens from the town. They all looked a picture of embarrassment as they explained that much as they admired and respected me they had come to ask me to release them from the burden of buying bread from my cook. They did not eat bread, they explained, and it was all being wasted. I could scarcely believe what I was hearing. It seemed that Ching had called on each prominent family in the town and told them that as his bread was so good TakinMa insisted that they should buy it from him. Out of respect for me they said they had felt obliged to take one small loaf, even though they none of them ate bread, but that had not satisfied the cook who increased his sales by doubling and trebling the orders and then sending threatening demands for payment. The situation was getting out of hand they said.

I sent for the cook and told him forcibly just what I thought of his behaviour and that he must never again pester people with his wares and certainly not use my name to promote his sales. Ching sulked for days. He considered he had lost face over the affair and that it was entirely my fault, but nothing could keep him quiet for long and he was soon devising new schemes to make his fortune but for a while he had time to concentrate on cooking for us and I had learned how to counter his capricious exploits. For me to reprimand him meant "loss of face" but if I called in one of the senior members of the factory staff and asked him to translate my complaints into Yunnanese, no feelings were offended and we managed to cover our differences with a veneer of Eastern politeness.

In all the years I lived in that remote little kingdom I suffered only one serious illness and that was rather a mystery; luckily whatever bug had laid me low was to cure itself as suddenly as it struck me down. It began with excruciating headaches. Soon any movement became agonising pain and I took to my bed convinced I was about to die. Dr Peel shook his head over me and admitted he did not know what was wrong with me but after the third day he decided I must eat and he vanished into the kitchen. That evening the cook had appeared at my bedside with a small bowl of soup. If I took every drop I would be well again the very next day he insisted and sure enough he was right. I never knew what the doctor had put in that tiny bowl of soup, but it banished my mystery illness for ever.

The local people believed that such unaccountable illnesses were the result of spells cast on them by some enemy and they took every precaution against such an eventuality. It was not wise to scoff at such ideas.

Piet escaped any serious ills except for one summer when he caught jaundice, perhaps through swimming in the polluted river, and it seemed months before his skin lost its yellow tinge.

Our flock of young houseboys never quite grew up and we came to accept their pranks as a matter of course. YuHsung and AikSiye would play whilst they worked and devise dreadful practical jokes to play on each other and dare one another to take the most hair-raising risks, while boring tasks such as bed-making would be enlivened by noisy games of "Cowboys and Indians'. Eventually I gave up trying to turn them into conventional houseboys. Had all the fun been taken out of their daily routine they would have deserted us. We had a long list of boys "in training", each waiting for a vacancy in the house. They would work in the garden for four days and on leave days would help inside. In this way we were never short of trained help if someone failed to turn up. Their main interest was to find out how the foreigners lived and behaved and so long as we treated them as personal friends, took an interest in their families and included them in our expeditions and outings, they responded with a good will and we learned a lot from them about the local people and customs.

YuHsung was typical of so many of the townspeople, of mixed parentage, intelligent and industrious if he had work to do. Unlike most of them, at the tender age of fifteen years he was sole supporter of a family of five. His father had an incapacitating souvenir of his escape across the border from China, a bullet in the stomach, and he was a semi-invalid. The mother worked hard to feed her family and as soon as YuHsung was old enough he also had to find work. I had viewed him with some doubts when he first came to ask for work saying he was too young and too small, but his reply had amused me. He was a dwarf he said, and so I took him on. I never saw him smile, that boy with a burden, and his grim young face already showed the scars of a responsibility far beyond his years, but he had a determination to succeed and I admired his loyalty to his family.

9

Tea

Tea was the sole reason for my being in that remote enchanted land. Having come from the tea estates of South India I thought I knew all about tea, the tea gardens and factories, but I was in for a few surprises. Nothing could have been more different than the tea gardens of Tawngpeng. The unpruned bushes were tall and straggly, every branch hung with moss and lichen making grotesque groves on the steep hillsides quite unlike anything I had ever seen in India. The Palaungs believed that powerful Nats lived in the tops of the bushes and to prune them would be to invite disaster. The Sawbwa and his family had led the way by pruning and cultivating their own gardens using the latest methods and the growers were impressed by the higher yields but still not prepared to risk offending those Nats. Bombay Burmah kept a demonstration plot of land and each year would hold pruning demonstrations all to no avail, the growers were not going to change their ways.

The origins of tea in Tawngpeng were lost in the mists of time but legend said that many centuries ago a Burmese King called Mani Saytu Min had returned from his travels in China and rested a while in Namhsan. He saw that the Palaungs were poor and they told him this was not due to their lack of industry but that nothing would grow on those precipitous hillsides. The King gave them one tea seed saying that if they tended it carefully they would prosper.

At Loi Seng Pagoda they made a shrine containing a life-size tableau depicting that momentous occasion which was to change their lives. Fashioned in stone, the benign King for ever holds out the precious seed and at his feet kneel three

Nehbaing, one of them holding our his right hand to take it showing all future generations his ignorance and ill-manners, for there, one must always give or receive a gift with two hands the left one clasping the right wrist, and so that precious gift came to be called Let-Ta-Hpet, One Hand, and eventually it was to become simply La-Hpet. Perhaps there is some truth in the story for Tawngpeng's tea is pale in colour and had the distinctive smokey flavour to be found in the high grown China teas. We were told yet another version of the Legend of the Tea Seed in which it was the Buddha who sent the Palaungs that precious gift in the beak of a Cuckoo and even today none of the tea growers will allow a single leaf to be plucked until the cuckoo has called over Loi Seng Hill.

Whatever the origins of the tea bush the Palaungs owe their prosperity to it and over the centuries the industry has grown with small factories to be seen near most villages. The unpruned bushes are so tall that the pluckers have to use ladders to reach the tender young leaves. Each "Flush" has a special name, the first and most prized being the Shwé Pi, and the factory owners have to compete for it with the manufacturers of pickled tea and green tea. Local pluckers could not cope with the sudden flush of leaf and so the on-set of the Shwé Pi was a signal for the migration of pluckers who would come annually from as far away as Mandalay and Shwebo. In the old days they would walk up to the hills, but we would see them come by the lorry load, often as many as fifty or sixty people, sitting on the roof, hanging onto every available inch of space. And when they left after at least a month's work with their pockets heavy with silver, the dacoits would be waiting to pounce on the unlucky ones who would return home empty handed.

The technicalities of tea production are best left to the experts, but our Namhsan Factory was large by local standards and produced good quality tea with a hint of the smokey flavour. The small local factories used a system developed from the rice pounders which had been in use for many centuries. these pounder type factories were often quite large with two batteries of pounders, some of them tiny with only one or two pounders. The pounder beams were made of wood and in a battery were raised in turn by cams on a drive shaft turned by a small engine. A projecting wooden cylinder near the end of each beam dropped by gravity into a small well in the concrete floor. A woman would sit cross-legged in front of each well, feeding the green leaf into it between the strokes, a dangerous job which often resulted in nasty injuries, but effectively broke up the leaf. The pounded leaf would be squeezed in mechanically operated presses to remove the surplus moisture after which it would be spread out on a tiled fermenting floor and later dried by stirring it on long iron sheets heated by wood fires.

The main disadvantage of this ingenious method was that if the leaf was not sufficiently well dried the tea would quickly go mouldy and if it was overdone it would have a burnt taste. We considered that all the locally made teas had this underlying burnt taste no matter how carefully prepared and this certainly distinguished it from the conventionally dried teas. Despite this the tea shops did a roaring trade. It was cheap to produce and sales were good. A factory with ten pounders could produce a maximum of about 150,000 lbs. of tea in a season. They were easy to build and maintain, production and labour costs were low and thus they became the thriving industry we found there. Often these low-grade teas would be blended with tea made in the conventional factories and the results of that were rather more palatable than the pure "pounder" teas.

There was yet another type of tea made only in the deep valleys of Tawngpeng, this was the pickled tea. 'The tree stands on the mountain but has its leaves in the valley' says an old Palaung proverb, and this was a reference to the ancient industry of pickled tea manufacture. Rich speculators would buy young tender green leaf from the Shwé Pi crop and transport it down to the "wells" in the valleys. Apparently the pickled tea would not mature properly if processed at the higher elevations. The wells were often twelve feet deep and five feet wide, lined first with fresh cow dung them a layer of thick green banana leaves which made an insulating barrier. The tender young tea leaves would first be steamed then rolled on bamboo mats until they were twisted and curled. These hand rolled leaves were then stored in the deep wells with a wooden lid on top weighted with stones to act as a press. A rich man might have several of these wells but it would be a year before he would get any return on his investment.

There was also the "Poor Man's Well", a four foot diameter wicker basket on the surface of the ground. This also was lined with cow dung and leaves and the tea leaf would be stored inside it and pressed with a weighted lid, but the quality of the pickled tea made by this method did not compare with that produced underground. After about a year the tea would be lifted, worked by rubbing it through the hands and then it would be packed into bamboo baskets. These curiously shaped baskets were lined with cow dung and leaves in the same way as the wells, and after filling they would be slotted onto the wooden saddle frames to be transported by pack bullock. The heavy ponderous bullocks would slowly wend their way up the steep tracks to the depots on the main road. I saw them many times, the leader bullock wearing a felt mask decorated with flowers and between its horns a cockade of silver pheasant feathers.

There was a "Wet Tea" depot quite near to our factory and I would stop to watch the processing. The baskets would be emptied onto a long wooden table. By now the leaf had an acrid vinegary smell which caught the nostrils as one walked close by and in no way resembled the black tea produced for drinking. The old Palaung man who ran the depot, his wife, daughters and perhaps a half dozen young men would spend several hours working the moist yellowish leaf between their hands, rolling it on the table until it became soft and pliable. Once more it would be packed into the curiously shaped baskets, each newly lined with cow dung and leaves and then loaded onto lorries to be sent to the various markets all over Burma.

This pickled tea was served as a dessert and the housewife would mix it with gingelly oil, garlic, spices to her own secret recipes and it was a favourite dish to serve at weddings and important festivals or if giving a Soonkway.

Another form of tea for drinking was made by the people of Zayangyi. This was the green tea which everyone sipped from tiny bowls endlessly throughout the day. Some took it with salt which to me was nauseating but without the salt, it made a refreshing drink and the pale green hot tea was served on every possible occasion.

For this green tea only the tenderest of green leaves would be used. There was a depot in Zayangyi where I would see the women and girls sitting cross-legged in front of huge wicker trays on which were piles of steamed leaves. These were hand rolled in the same way as those for pickled tea but then the rolled, twisted leaves would be spread out on the flat round bamboo mats and dried in the sun.

It needed only one generous pinch of this sun-dried tea in a tiny pot which would be filled and re-filled to keep the family and guests refreshed all morning.

The Kyemaing had built a new tea factory at KonHai and had installed all the latest tea machinery, Piet was keen to see new competitor and compare it with our own factory and so readily accepted the invitation to attend the official opening. The Astrologer had decided that April 23rd was the best day and he divined the most auspicious time to be 9.0 am. This meant a very early start for us. Although KonHai was only three hours walk away there was no direct road and it took three hours of hard driving over rough dust laden roads to reach the village in the Land Rover. We set out at 5.0 am. that morning and although everything in the valley was still in darkness I saw that the strip of sky framed by the high ridges had already turned to royal blue. Suddenly a shaft of gold pierced the semi-darkness and all at once the valley "lit-up" and we were bathed in sunshine, the birds were in full song and I saw that the villagers were already out and about on their way to the tea fields.

We reached the summit of the ridge just before 8.0 am. and there near the village of Omason we had breakfast under a remarkable umbrella shaped tree. It was the only one along the whole length of the ridge top and we had seen it standing out starkly against the skyline from our side of the valley. It was interesting to look back at Namhsan almost hidden beneath the towering ridges which were shaped rather like the crenellated walls of some medieval castle. Already we could see a thick cloud of dust on the road behind us as more guests began to arrive and we drove on down the ridge to the new bungalow. There we found a large crowd of guests already assembled and a big family gathering to support the Kyemaing. The Press was well represented and the photographers were busy.

I stopped by a small table which was covered with magic symbols and curious instruments and piled high with charts, the Astrologer was divining the exact moment when the Princess should cut the silken ribbon and declare the Myat Oon Tea Factory open. We were all ushered inside the big factory building where the huge Marshall Drier was about to be started up for the first time. The tea maker applied a flaming torch to the burners and there was an almighty bang as though a giant gas ring had plopped out; again he applied the torch fumbling in his anxiety not to ruin the auspicious moment and the giant machine gave an ominous roar. Piet whispered in my ear 'get back, it will blow up if he treats it like this' and he went forward to assist the embarrassed tea maker who succeeded at the third attempt. The Kyemaing fed the first leaf into the drier and production was under way. The great crowd of guests began to surge towards the house where a sumptuous feast was set out on long tables in the marquee and although it was only 10.30 am. everyone seemed to have good appetites.

The guests were entertained for the rest of the day with a Concert Party performing inside the factory and at night there was to be a Pwé in the garden.

About a month later we decided to try walking to KonHai. We would call on the Kyemaing's wife and see how things were going. We drove to Se-Ton-Hung village and set off walking down a precipitous track, so steep that it was difficult to stop ourselves from breaking into a run which would have been disastrous on that slippery track which countless feet and hooves had worn into deep ruts over the centuries.

It took us one and a half hours to reach the little river at the bottom of the valley and we found that it was spanned by one of the ancient wooden bridges with a pointed carved wooden roof. These bridges were a feature of the district and must have been standing there over many centuries. For an hour we climbed up a steep track on the other side. The hillside there was cultivated and the gaunt untidy looking tea bushes stretched as far as we could see. We picnicked near a cluster of ruined pagodas and not far from that place we came to KonHai village. The Myat Oon Tea Factory could be seen ablaze with lights at the far end of the village and beside it a sparkling new pagoda which had been re-built by the Kyemaing and his wife. We found the Princess in charge and the factory in full production. She was an astute businesswoman and ran the factory with smooth efficiency whilst her husband attended to affairs of state. She took us round, gave us refreshments and then we had to leave. With the prospect of that long tiring walk home in front of us we did not dare to linger, for no sensible travellers were ever found on those tracks after nightfall if they valued their safety. Only a few days before two traders had been murdered near KonHai and one could not forget the added danger of bear or panther being on the prowl.

The return journey up that precipitous hillside seemed endless and it was with relief that we saw the Land Rover ahead. Our walk had taken six hours, exactly the same time as the motor journey which must have covered many times the distance we had done on foot.

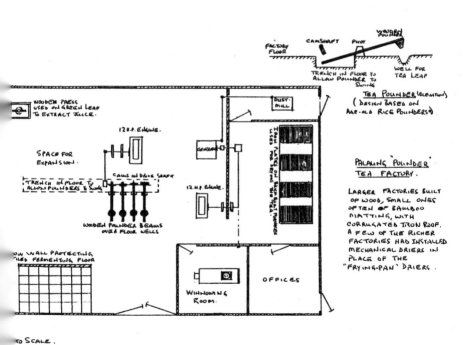

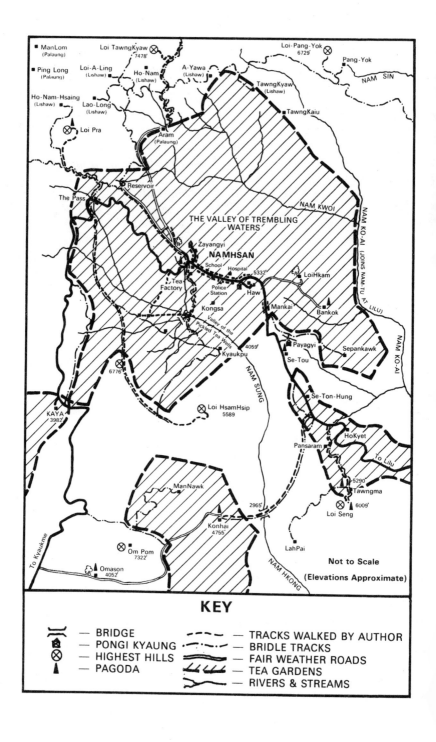

■ ManLom
(Palaung)

Loi TawngKyaw ⊗
7478'

Loi-Pang-Yok ⊗
6729'

Pang-Yok ■

■ Ping Long
(Palaung)

Loi-A-Ling ■
(Lishaw)

Ho-Nam ■
(Lishaw)

A-Yawa ■
(Lishaw)

NAM SIN

TawngKyaw ■
(Lishaw)

Ho-Nam-Hsaing ■
(Lishaw)

Lao-Long ■
(Lishaw)

TawngKaiu ■

⊗ Loi Pra

Aram ■
(Palaung)

Reservoir

The Pass

NAM KWOI

NAM KO-AI
(JOINS NAM-TU AT LILU)

THE VALLEY OF TREMBLING
WATERS

Zayangyi
NAMHSAN
School   Hospital
5332'

LoiHkam

NAM KO-AI

Tea
Factory

Police
Station

Haw

Kongsa

Mankai

Bankok

Valley of the
Pickled Tea Wells

Payagyi

Sepankawk

Kyaukpu   4059'

Se-Tou

⊗
6776'

Se-Ton-Hung

⊗ Loi HsamHsip
5589

KAYA
3982'

HoKyet

Pansaram

To Lilu

5290'

ManNawk

2965'

Tawngma

⊗   ▲ 6009'
Loi Seng

Konhai
4755'

To Kyaukme

LahPai

Not to Scale

(Elevations Approximate)

⊗ Om Pom
7322'

NAM HKONG

▲ Omason
4052'

KEY

— BRIDGE

— PONGI KYAUNG

⊗ — HIGHEST HILLS

▲ — PAGODA

– – – — TRACKS WALKED BY AUTHOR

·–·–· — BRIDLE TRACKS

— FAIR WEATHER ROADS

— TEA GARDENS

— RIVERS & STREAMS

10

Lashio

My first glimpse of Lashio had been brief and rather disappointing as it had seemed to be just a collection of wooden houses and shops. If one looked closer at the tree lined avenues on the outskirts however there were many large solid looking houses which were a legacy from the days when many British residents, (members of the old Frontier Service) had lived there. In the newer parts of the fast gowing town, modern luxury bungalows were springing up. Lashio had become a thriving State capital and its prosperous citizens liked Western style comforts.

Once a month we would emerge from our eyrie, as friends called our rather inaccessible bungalow, and we would drive down to Lashio to meet the weekly mail plane. This meant that we had to stop overnight and as we did not wish to advertise our movements for security reasons, we had to chance getting a room at the Circuit House, and this was to land us in some odd situations on several occasions.

The Circuit House was a typical Eastern rest house, a long single storey building with a central dining room and four or five bedrooms each with its own bathroom on either side forming a "U" shaped block, and as always, it was surrounded by a garden full of flowers, the dahlias being a speciality. There was a resident cook-butler who took a great delight in serving porridge. No matter how hot the weather it was sure to be on the menu.

We would often find the place full of tourists from Rangoon who would arrive on the weekly plane to return by road and rail via Mandalay. Generally they would be diplomats taking a brief holiday or sometimes visiting businessmen taking the

opportunity of seeing the Northern States. The cook suppli-
mented his salary by catering for these visitors. On one
occasion we sat down to breakfast with a visiting Ambassador
and unfortunately I was the first to try the toast and
marmalade, I almost swallowed a large chunk of glass;
someone had evidently dropped the marmalade pot and then
scraped up the contents hoping that no-one would notice. We
prodded the sticky preserve to find it was full of slivers of glass.
The cook was full of excuses. His profits were small, he could
not afford to throw away a whole pot of preserves he said. But
what if his guests became ill, or worse, I asked?

On our next visit we looked suspiciously at an all too familiar
pot of marmalade, the large bits of glass were gone but under
Piet's spoon minute invisible slivers of glass crunched
ominously. I called the cook and offered him the price of a
new jar in exchange for the pot of ground glass which I took
out into the garden. The Mali dug a deep hole amongst his
prize dahlias and we buried it furtively hoping the cook was
not watching us. How many unsuspecting guests had gone
home with the tummy ache or worse I wondered and hoped
that the cook would be more careful in future.

We had a new agent in Lashio, a former Assistant Resident
in British days and a man of considerable presence and
character. We would generally find him holding "court",
surrounded by a respectful group of friends and relations.
The youngest member of the family was not his daughter he
explained, but it was the custom for rich families to adopt girls
from poor families. They would be brought up as their own
daughters and in return these girls would help with the
housework.

When the "daughter" was of marriageable age she would be
free to leave if she wished. Her "family" would find her a
husband and give her all she needed to make a happy wedding
and then look for another suitable candidate to adopt.

Uncle, as everyone called our agent, insisted that we must
join the North Shan States Club, once the favourite haunt of
the British residents, and he would take us along there in the
evenings. Little had changed in the intervening years, the click
of the billiard balls, the strong scent of the cheroots, laughter
and tall stories still told in perfect English, only the ladies were
missing, the only other lady member I met there was the third

wife of the Sawbwa who was a keen tennis player.

Uncle arranged for us to "call" on the Head of State, at that time the Sawbwa of Hsenwi. One September morning at eleven o'clock we drove up to the pillared entrance of the Haw, a huge mansion set in lovely mature gardens. The great palace was silent, the shuttered windows stood out darkly against the gleaming white walls, and a silent footed servant led us to a shady verandah where presently the Head of State joined us. He was one of the elder statesmen of the Shan States, much respected and very wise. We talked of his garden and out of the corner of my eye I saw a servant creeping towards us, crouching so that his head was never higher than that of his Sawbwa. He placed tiny dishes of tea on small ornamental tables and moving awkwardly on bent knees, he crept silently away. I sipped the tea and almost choked, it was heavily salted and like nasty medicine I swallowed it quickly. To my dismay a silent crouching form appeared from nowhere and refilled my dish, and I had to sip the repulsive drink trying not to show my distaste. I heard soft whispering behind the shutters but it seemed that the princesses did not join such interviews. The great man was interested in us, in our work and in news from the western world, we talked of many things in friendly informal fashion. Afterwards I asked a friend why it was that this Sawbwa and his three wives lived together harmoniously in his Haw whilst the Tawngpeng Sawbwa kept a separate establishment for each of his three wives. Well, said my friend, the Hsenwi Sawbwa was an old fashioned man and took steps to make sure that his wives did not dominate him, or create disharmony in his life, whilst the Tawngpeng Sawbwa had more progressive views and allowed his wives more self-expression, thus he paid the price of his liberal attitudes.

Two of the young Hsenwi princes were at school in Australia and we just happened to be waiting at Lashio airport on the day they arrived home after a long absence. As they stepped off the plane the equerry whispered into the ear of the elder boy and immediately the two young schoolboys went down on their knees on the tarmac to make a deep obeisance to their father as he approached. After only a brief word he turned to walk back to his car and they followed him in silence, pausing briefly beside another car to make a polite bow to their mothers. There would be no public demonstrations of welcome. The contrast between the two worlds those boys knew must have been bewildering.

There was great competition amongst our bungalow boys to be the one chosen to accompany us on those Lashio visits. To them, Lashio was civilisation, the big city, and the main attraction was the cinema where they could see all the latest American films. The seats were always filled to capacity but it was an orderly crowd, perhaps because at the end of every other row of seats there would be a policeman armed with rifle or sten gun, fully loaded and ready for use in case of trouble.

The interval was quite a social occasion and one could be sure of meeting friends in the quadrangle where stalls and shops served refreshments under the stars.

Uncle often took us to meet his friends and to parties which had an air of Victorian Evenings of yester year. I remember with pleasure P.T. and his charming wife. He was a great mountain of a man looking more like a huge Tibetan bear than a Shan gentleman, for the Shans were usually small and of slight build. They would gather around the piano and P.T., who was a great fan of Grace Kelly, would play and sing True Love and there was a charm and quiet enjoyment about their simple pleasures.

When the Burmese Army took over the Government a large force was sent up to the Shan State to keep the peace, for dissatisfaction and unrest were beginning to show. They began to take a prominent part in local affairs, and the first thing they did was to create a golf course out of the jungle, a move which was to give us considerable pleasure on our monthly visits. They moved in heavy plant and cleared a large tract of scrub jungle, laying out a nine hole course. We stared with surprise at the transformation which took place in four short weeks. At first it was quite the most appallingly bad course I had ever played on, with tree stumps and great clumps of weeds in the fairways and cows lying immoveable, chewing their cud on the browns. The Lashio businessmen suddenly became keen golfers and the Bazaar shops were filled with golf gear. Within a year the course had been improved out of all recognition, and most business deals were clinched at dawn out on the golf course.

Resistance Day was celebrated on March 27th and we went

down to Lashio for a mammoth celebration given by the
Burmese Army. The Circuit House was almost fully occupied
by a party of Americans, come to try out the nightspots. One
of them asked if he might accompany us to the Resistance
Celebrations and thinking that perhaps he was interested in
local culture we took him along. He was a typical loquacious
American and met us at 7.00 p.m. dressed in Burmese style
with lungyi and gaungbaung. He always tried to fit in with the
local scene he told us In the Memorial Park we found a huge
crowd already gathered around the Independence Monument,
a large white concrete "rocket" which dominated the small
park. The trees were hung with fairy lights which threw
jewelled reflections onto the surface of the tiny lake. There was
music and dancing, a large stage had been set up at one end of
the park and the crowds cheered and jeered the contestants in
a Judo display. The Burmese Boxing held its audience
spellbound in a display in which fists, feet and teeth were all
put to good use.

The epic drama was performed by soldiers and told of
Thibaws last stand, a struggle by the Burmese Resistance
Fighters who had eventually put to flight the puny unloved
British. We watched with some amusement as they twisted and
manipulated history. We had been brought up on a rather
different interpretation of past events, but would not have
dared to argue.

After about half an hour our new friend had excused
himself. He must find some refreshments he said. We stayed on
watching the traditional dancing and sword dances until 10
p.m., when our American friend suddenly re-appeared saying
he had been nearby but unable to reach us in the crush. The
following morning we found the Americans already at
breakfast and it seemed that all was not as it should be. They
had returned late at night to find their rooms had been broken
into and searched. Nothing was missing but documents and
files lay scattered everywhere. One tall fair haired man seemed
particularly upset and in a near hysterical voice he turned on
our companion of the previous evening accusing him of being
behind the break-in. Smoothly, with practised charm our
"friend" gave us as his alibi, had he not spent the entire
evening in our company, and he went on to tease his
companions about their pleasures of the previous evening. I

felt a sharp kick on my ankle, a warning from Piet to keep out
of the unpleasant affair. We had no proof that our friend had
returned to the Circuit House, but he was gone a long time
and dressed like all the fashionable Burmese to be seen by the
dozen at the Pwé, he would have been unrecognisable. We left
them to their arguments and their suggestion that they would
enjoy a visit to Namhsan received a cool reception. Someone
we decided, had a guilty secret and we were going to have no
part in it.

In the Namhsan Bazaar shops we could buy groceries, fruit,
vegetables, tinned foods, cloth, shoes, sweets, almost everything
that was needed for the simple way of life, with one exception:
meat. Each year when the meat licence came up for auction it
was bought by the Sawbwa and as a staunch Buddhist he
would not allow it to be used to slaughter cattle. The Moslem
community were allowed to slaughter a few sheep for their
own consumption and the Chinese kept pigs, but if we wanted
beef we had to go to Old Lashio. The Burmese Army liked
their beef and showed no sentiment, although all cattle
slaughtered had to be more than twelve years old. Old Lashio
was not far from the airfield and in a corner of the Bazaar
there stood a small wooden hut with wire gauze over door and
windows, this was the butcher's shop as the hum of flies and
sickening smell of stale blood proclaimed. I ventured inside
only once. The smell was nauseating and I stared at the
strange objects which hung limply from hooks in the ceiling. I
had never seen such horrors in any butcher's shop at home
and found it hard to believe that people would eat such things.
But it was the maggots which put me off the place; the
benches and floor crawled with them. I made my excuses and
hurried out leaving ZanLyn to make the purchases. I would
never again have enjoyed my roast beef for lunch if I had first
seen it surrounded by the things which lurked in that dreadful
shop.

I always enjoyed a stroll around the big Bazaar at Lashio,
people sold such fascinating things. Apart from the usual stalls
to be seen in every Bazaar, there was a little old Shan woman
who squatted over a tiny basket of flowers which she had
gathered in the jungle, the sweet scented bauhinia flowers were
like large white orchids and women would buy them to flavour
sweetmeats. Later in the year she would have a basketful of

the sweet ginger flowers. Sometimes I would see a Lishaw woman patiently waiting for a customer beside a square of banana leaf on which a few succulent white grubs wriggled helplessly, or perhaps a tiny section of comb from a hornet's nest. In July and August they would bring trays of mushrooms quite unlike anything I had seen before, delicate spindly ones, some like the chanterelle, dark crimson ones and tiny feathery fairy parasols, they all looked quite deadly but were snapped up by smiling housewives.

Twice a year the potter would bring a great pile of bowls, pots, vases, oil jars in a green salt glaze, and "Ali Baba" jars of all sizes in a dark brown pottery decorated with an orange motif which resembled strands of seaweed.

The flower women always made a colourful display as they squatted by their baskets of gladioli, dahlias or asters, whichever was in season.

We would patronise most of the tea shops and restaurants in the interests of tea sales for the company and there we met some strange looking characters, old men with leathery, lined, careworn faces which creased into delighted smiles when we joined them for we were no longer looked upon as strangers to be distrusted. Bright eyed children would follow us and offer advice about our purchases. One of the favourite meeting houses for the citizens of Lashio was the Chinese tea shop on the main street. It was always packed to capacity. Some would be sampling the delicious hot dumplings filled with spicy meat, or the fancy cakes and new bread from the display cases, but many came just to meet their friends and sip endless cups of the sweet, sickly tea.

We were always haunted by two crazy men. Both had been soldiers and the war years had left them with very disturbed minds although they were quite harmless. One would follow us around brandishing letters written in English and he talked endless gibberish, part English, part Burmese. He would only quieten down if we read his letters. The other was dressed only in a loin cloth, his body would be garishly painted and wreaths of flowers adorned his hair. He would follow us silently around the town taking every opportunity to kneel at my feet and offer me flowers. After the second Army Coup both men vanished as they were an embarrassment to the Burmese Army. I hoped that they were being cared for in some kind home, but the traders of Lashio were delighted to be rid of the nuisances.

I remember a monstrous bit of carpentry which stood in brooding silence at the bottom of the garden behind the P.W.D. bungalow in Lashio. New fangled designs from the West had not penetrated as far as those premises and the hut was one of those necessities of life which had long been forgotten by the more progressive architects of the Western world. The rough hewn timbers seemed to have been carefully fixed to exclude even the tiniest shaft of light in that awful windowless box. The door was stout enough to resist any battering ram and it was hinged so that it swung quietly out of reach the moment anyone stepped inside.

Until the day I encountered that masterpiece, which surely must have been the origin of the term "A Rude Hut", it had never occurred to me that my early morning stroll down to the lavatory could possibly have been so fraught with danger. The story could have been just like the magician's magic box: the lady was seen to step inside and immediately vanished. I found myself on two slippery planks placed strategically over a deep wide stinking pit in which the maggots, vicious as piranha, heaved expectantly and no wonder. The slightest movement set up an alarming wobble of my flimsy foothold, there was no room to turn around even had I dared to try, any careless move could have plunged me down into the pit and oblivion. It was then I realised that the door had swung open behind me silently revealing my plight to the battery of windows in the Rest House, each with its occupant going through his morning ablutions. Perhaps someone would come to my rescue I thought, but no-one moved. There was only one thing I could do, I took a gigantic backwards leap to land safe but bruised in the sweet corn patch nearby. I steeled myself for a new approach, holding onto the elusive door I gingerly felt my way onto the shaky perch over that noisome pit in the semi darkness. The thought that every time I needed to "spend a penny" I would have to face that awful contraption spurred me to action, at all costs I had to find some means of controlling that elusive door. We bought a hammer, nails and a length of rope and devised a pulley which at least enabled us to step safely onto the planks with maximum light. I promptly put that unlovely hut on my list of "Horrors of the East", although in time, experience bred a more casual approach.

Each of the bedrooms in the Rest House boasted a private bathroom and these also had to be approached with caution. It was like setting foot on an ice-rink, my feet shot from under me and I skidded across the floor on my back to finish with one foot in a large hole in the wall which served as a plughole. I was very relieved that the walls were stoutly built or I might have shot straight through into space. An old zinc tub stood in a corner on a low wooden stool. If you paid the Gurkha Dewan handsomely he would bring a pailful of boiling water to mix with the green stagnant water in the tub. There was a ladle to pour the pea soup over one's soaped body and it swilled over the floor and out through the hole in the wall. The Circuit House would have rated a few more stars, each bathroom boasted one tap and a modern water closet, but no water. Water was a very precious commodity in Lashio and the general supply was turned off during the day. At night it came through as a tiny trickle and had to be used with the greatest care; there was no more until night. Although there was no water there was also no rude hut at the bottom of the garden and the stench from those lavatories was unbelievable. Well, I had wanted to discover how the other half of the world lived, and I found that it was not always to my liking.

II

The Last Grand Occasion

We had been invited to Lashio's Wedding of the Year. The daughter of one of the Kentung Princes was to marry the young Sao Phalong of Mong Pawn and, unlike most of the marriages amongst the Shan ruling families, this was a love match. They had met at University and to the satisfaction of their elders had fallen in love.

Uncle had asked us to go to his house to dress for the occasion and he escorted us to the ceremony, explaining the programme and pointing out guests of importance.

At 10.00 a.m. the Head of State would leave the Residency where parents and relations of both Bride and Groom would be assembled to pay homage to him. First the Bridegroom would arrive to pay homage, later the Bride, and the two young people had to pay homage, or kadaw, twelve times before their elders after which they would go in procession to the Grand Hall where the Head of State would be waiting for them.

We found in the hall a gathering as glittering and exotic as peacocks and butterflies. Most of the men wore brightly coloured silk lungyis or Shan suits with the baggy pants and Mandarin style jackets with their heads adorned by gaily coloured gaungbaung tied in a knot at one side and often pinned with a flashing jewel. The women were always elegantly dressed but on such occasions as this they would bring out all their jewellery and finest silks. The tightly wrapped tamein flattered their slender figures, the aingyi, or blouse, of finest chiffon would be covered with a long scarf of sheerest silk or sometimes they wore a brief jacket of filmy white. Their blouses fastened with jewelled buttons which matched their bracelets, rings, necklaces, their hair would be piled high in elaborate styles held in place with gold combs and they would pin fresh flowers at the side.

At one corner of the long room, a small latticed pavilion had been erected and it was decorated with hundreds of orchids.

Within the Pavilion the Head of State sat upon a gilded throne. In front of him was a long low gilded couch with vermilion velvet cushions on which sat the two young people, cross-legged and facing each other. There was a lengthy ceremony in which they were fed with rice after which they knelt before the Head of State making a deep obeisance, returning to their places on the couch. Throughout the fifty five minute ceremony a Pongyi beat a giant gong at regular intervals and another intoned prayers.

At last the Head of State rose to his feet and accompanied by his attendants, walked slowly through the vast concourse of bowing guests, followed by a dozen girls each carrying a large silver bowl containing rice and money which they scattered amongst the guests who smilingly ducked to avoid the flying coins. The Sao Phalong and his new Mahadevi paused in the doorway for photographs and I thought she looked just like the portraits of her mother painted by Sir Gerald Kelly many years before. Her tamein of white brocade shimmered with heavy gold and silver embroideries and clung to her slender figure. Across her shoulders, over a sheer white aingyi she had draped a long scarf of filmy white silk. Her hair was dressed in the wedding style, a heavily lacquered cylinder of hair on top of her head and her long black tresses flowed from it held in place by a hair ornament which formed a cascade of gold and silver orchids sparkling with jewels. In her hand she carried a Western style bouquet of flowers. The tall young bridegroom had become Ruler of Mong Pawn as a small child when his father was assassinated with Aung San and the whole council on that fateful day in 1947. He wore a long coat of gold silk over white Shan pants and his head was swathed in gauzy gold silk glittering with gold thread. Two attendants dressed in white held aloft the silk umbrellas, each with three tiers of white silk frills signifying the high rank of the couple. Four guards in black and white uniforms with bright pink turbans each carried a seven foot spear, the decorated haft encased in silver and with a long pink scarf tied beneath the blade to signify the peaceful intentions. The parents, relations and principal guests followed in glittering array, and it was mid afternoon before all the guests departed. Many would return that night for a lavish entertainment to be given by the Bride's father and five marquees had been erected in the garden to provide shelter for those guests who would be staying the night.

The father of the Bride, resplendent in the finest white silk, told me that I was lucky to witness this last grand occasion the Shan States would see. Sadly his jesting prophecy became reality for with the cession of the Sawbwas the insurrection was to spread and in the fateful Second Coup most of the Sawbwas were arrested, the young Bridegroom amongst them, to remain in detention at the pleasure of the Burmese Government, political pawns with no say in their destiny nor any chance to move in their own defence.

After all the glitter and ceremony there was a stark change of scene for us. Two of our Chinese workers were awaiting deportation; their F.R.C's had been wrongly dated when they had entered Burma as children, making them invalid. Their appeal for a stay of the deportation order was to be heard that same afternoon and Piet left the wedding reception to attend the Court, hoping to be allowed to bail them out. They were good loyal workers who had been employed by the company for many years. Both had married local girls and had young families from whom they would be separated if the appeal was refused. They were luckier than some of the other Chinese in Court that day and bail was granted but their troubles were not over and perhaps never would be resolved.

12

Christmas Parties

The most important member of the factory staff was the teamaker, a post originally held by an Indian. That first Christmas he suggested that it might be a good idea to give a party for the whole labour force and that the 21st. December was considered to be an auspicious date. The staff enjoyed organising lavish entertainments and it only needed a nod to start them arranging a gigantic picnic at the hot springs at Mansam on that next Moon Day.

We set out early on the two hour drive that morning and about half a mile from Mansam village, we turned onto a rough earth track through the jungle. We seemed to have been driving for an age when the track opened out into a large clearing, flat and grassy, and at the far end a bubbling stream of steaming spa water gushed out of a rocky grotto, to be caught in a large concrete tank. The water in the tank was too hot to bathe in but the little stream was a popular hot bath and used by all the villagers. We found a large crowd already assembled. Uncle had come over from Lashio, some of the Sawbwa's nephews and a number of businessmen, and a few friends who just happened to have heard that there was to be a picnic were also there. The curry and rice were already bubbling over glowing fires and busy groups of men were fashioning the "glasses". They cut long green leaves from wild banana trees, washed them in the hot stream and laid these out on the grass to form a tablecloth. For the glasses they cut long lengths of green bamboo which when cut into sections with a piece left as a handle looked rather like old fashioned milk ladles and made instant disposable crockery. The food was piled onto the banana leaves, crates of Mandalay beer appeared as if by magic and the hungry crowd had finished up the mountains of food almost before I had sampled a mouthful.

It was Pwé time at Mansam and a visiting troupe of dancers had been asked to join us. Their enthusiasm and natural gaiety made the dances a pleasure to watch. This was not the serious stuff for traditionalists but very entertaining. We left at dusk but the crowd of picnickers went on to the Pwé and would not return home until all gambling had ceased.

One fact had emerged from my travels around Burma. The Pwé was ever present, almost a national institution, and added to their love of colourful clothes gave a happy party atmosphere wherever one went. Except during the rainy season there would be a Pwé of some sort most days even in the smallest villages. Perhaps there would be a new pagoda to dedicate, an ear boring ceremony for a favourite daughter, the initiation of a young son, a wedding, a win on the State Lottery, every excuse was an opportunity.

The Zat Pwés were lengthy plays with themes from Buddhist lore. The Anyein Pwé was a light, happy affair full of clowning and repartee, dancing and singing to modern music. The Yein Pwés were more serious, group dancing and traditional song, a mixture of Opera and Ballet which demanded considerable training and team work. But always, whether traditional style or modern or even just good fun, music dancing and song went together.

At harvest time villagers would celebrate with the Ozi Dances when the performer played the elongated drum whilst posturing and dancing with the cumbersome instrument.

Every dance group had its own orchestra, no matter how small. It might only support a drum, clackers and flute or violin. On the other hand a large prosperous group might carry a big orchestra with a wide variety of strange looking instruments. The Pat-saing was a series of cylindrical drums, usually twenty one, mounted on a circular gilded frame of wood and rattan. The Kyi-waing had a series of eighteen bell metal gongs arranged circlewise like the Pat-saing and played two handed with round padded hammers. The elegant looking Burmese Harp, the Saunggauk, took its shape from a Burmese boat with graceful curving prow and the polished wood bowl was covered with deer hide. It had thirteen strings of spun silk which were tied with red cords and ended in dangling red tassels. There was a Zither shaped rather like a crocodile with three strings, and a Clarion of black wood with seven finger holes and one for the thumb, the mouthpiece being made of palm leaves, which was possibly the most ancient of the Burmese musical instruments. The Pattala or Xylophone was a set of twenty four well seasoned graduated bamboo slats mounted on a decorated semi-circular soundbox of black and gold. There were simpler instruments: the bamboo flute which had holes like the clarion but was blown through the side hole and a violin with a small trumpet at the back which was always held upright whilst being played. Then there were the timekeepers, the bamboo clappers and cup shaped bells. The choice was wide and by convention there was traditional music to go with those strange instruments.

There were special tunes and songs for set themes, fighting music, weeping songs, sleeping and flying tunes, music which portrayed certain types of people such as kings, ministers or priests. The moment they heard the music the audience knew exactly which characters would appear and what those characters would be doing. For the modern music, songs relevant to each important occasion would be composed and the dancers would be inspired by the music to interpret individually what they felt.

The dancers were always dressed in the brightest of colours, bedecked with beads and jewels and with their faces heavily made-up. They were adept at improvising and would compose witty songs about their audience at a moment's notice.

The gambling Pwés of the Shan States were different; there was no singing or dancing and the gamblers, intent on the dice, would scarcely notice the modern music blaring out over the loudspeakers. These Gambling Pwés were later to be banned by the Central Government and all protests and appeals to retain this type of Pwé came to nothing.

Our picnic had been a huge success but the following year I decided to give them a taste of an old fashioned English Garden Party; it would be our personal New Year gift. The staff were interested when I outlined the idea but doubtful of the wisdom of trying something new.

Before long I saw skittles and a bean board someone had made in his spare time, and a painted mule without a tail, the children were excited about the strange new games and could scarcely wait for the day to arrive. This garden party was not concerned with fund raising, just fun for everyone. There were races of every kind for the children and tea for everyone. Although some would be lucky enough to win prizes no child must go home empty handed and so we had balloons and gobstoppers for them all. The houseboys helped me count the sweets, exactly twenty for each child in brightly coloured cellophane bags, we had to be sure no-one was favoured with more than his friends.

I need not have wondered if anyone would support the event for by 2 p.m. on the appointed day our Pwé ground was packed. As it was a Moon Day, the Palaungs were massing in town and many stopped to watch the fun, their scarlet costumes brightening the banks around the volley ball and tennis courts. We had treasure hunts, bowling for a chicken and the smash hit of the afternoon, the Aunt Sally. Piet had volunteered to be the first target and, wearing a stove-pipe hat of red and white striped cardboard he bounced around behind stout protecting nets, the object of the game being to knock off his hat as many times as possible. They loved it, taking pot-shots at Takin and senior members of the staff was something they had never expected to have the opportunity to enjoy. Whenever a direct hit was scored a cheer went up from the Palaung spectators watching from the wings and the queue waiting to try this new sport never dwindled. At 4 p.m. the children's races became the great excitement and most of the games were new to them. Three-legged races were the funniest thing they had ever seen. There were egg and spoon races, obstacle races and each child was determined to win by hook or by crook.

At 5 p.m. everyone gathered in the Club Room for tea and iced buns. I smiled as I approached the doorway, there chalked in huge letters I read the legend "Zor Wyn The Big", the young son of our chief clerk had rather let his English and his prizes go to his head.

The experiment was a great success. Previously the Christmas parties had catered only for the men and including the families had created a happy atmosphere.

We had a small group of Karens on the permanent work force and being Christians they always made much of Christmas. They would call at the Bungalow on Christmas Eve bringing a variety of musical instruments and would entertain us with carols and songs.

There was a flourishing Baptist Church in Namhsan run by the Chinese, and we were invited to a play which was to be given in the Church on Christmas Eve. We found the big room above Dr Lu's surgery filled to overflowing. Everyone seemed to be there regardless of his or her Religious beliefs. We squeezed onto a wooden bench between some Palaung children and looked around the room, It was gaily decorated with stalls along each side selling soft drinks, tea and food. The jostling and chatter suddenly subsided as the curtains slowly opened to reveal a homely room such as one could find in any village house. Speaking in Burmese the actors told the story of the Prodigal Son, a Headman's son from a small village who, influenced by bad friends from the town, roistered and gambled away his wordly wealth despite his father's pleading. It was a story which fitted into their way of life, a story they could understand. It was heavily overacted, nothing was covered up. The characters ate and drank to excess, vomited all over the stage, blew their noses on the tablecloth, made a semblance of urinating in a corner of the room, in fact broke every rule of good behaviour. Then a cameraman crept stealthily onto the stage and the actors froze, only resuming the dialogue when filming was over. The audience loved it, they shouted and encouraged, boo'd the villains and cheered the hero, this was something they understood.

After the final curtain ,we prepared to leave but the rest of the audience stayed put, they all intended to see the second House with the dialogue in Shan. I wondered just how many of that large audience were Christians and if they appreciated the religious significance of the story. Later that night as midnight approached we were startled to hear Carols being sung by a well trained choir. It was our Chinese missionaries of the Drama Group come to sing in Christmas with us. Sadly they never again tried to repeat the success although a return visit would have been very popular.

Years later on a flight to Bangkok a charming lady befriended my small son and our conversation led to talk of the Shan States.

'The Baptist Church have a large Mission there in the north run by a Dr Lu' she said, 'have you ever met him?'.

13

Talk of Justice

There was a hesitant knock on the verandah door and out of
the dark night a young Indian boy whom we knew, stepped
into the sitting room. He looked furtive and worried as he
asked if he could speak to Takin alone. This was at 9 p.m. and
an hour later I was called to give my opinion on the problem
that was troubling the boy.

Early that morning he and his young brother had set out
into the nearby jungle in search of firewood. They found a
well worn track which led into a small clearing where, to their
horror they saw a man's hand protruding from a newly dug
patch of earth, someone had been buried alive and had been
trying to claw his way out of the rough grave. Aghast, the
boys fled, all thoughts of firewood forgotten. They had told
their father of the dreadful discovery and he, realising the full
implications of the grim discovery, had called in all male
members of their family for a consultation. All day they had
been debating what course of action they should take, should
they go to the Police and tell what the boys had seen, or keep
quiet about it, hoping that no-one had seen the boys go that
way. At last in desperate indecision they had decided to seek
the advice of the all-wise Takin from the West, little realising
that in doing so they were implicating us in the affair.

At home in England there would have been no problem, a
quick telephone call to the police and apart from answering a
few questions that would have been an end to their part in the
enquiries, but it was not so simple in Namhsan. There in the
eyes of the law one was guilty unless and until proved innocent
and anyone remotely connected with a murder would have
been locked up immediately on suspicion. Without a great deal

of luck a poor man had little chance of legal representation or
help in any form. The Inspector in charge of the Police Station
was a tough and awesome man. He would have reasoned that
it was too much of a coincidence that the boys should have
found that grave by pure chace. No, they must have heard a
whisper of the affair in the Bazaar, or perhaps more likely
around their own fireside. Boys were always into mischief and
might have thought it exciting to take a peep at the scene of
the crime, then fearful of being caught, the family was trying
to cover up the murderers tracks. This was the way the wheels
of justice turned in the minds of those people. The two boys
and all male members of their family would have been
detained for questioning, locked up in that dreadful cage until
after days of fear and trouble one of the older members of the
family would almost certainly have confessed to a crime he
had not committed, in order to save the others from further
trouble. This had been their problem and knowing the line the
law would most probably have taken they were reluctant to
report the grisly discovery. Yet as law abiding citizens they
felt that the dead man should be identified, avenged and
buried with all proper rites. They knew only too well that if
they withheld the information they could be in even greater
trouble.

I sympathised with them knowing that their fears were only
too well founded. Had anyone suddenly vanished I asked? The
boy said they had already made discreet enquiries and were
sure the victim was not a local man. They thought he could
have been a trader bringing goods to sell in town. The Dacoits
never allowed their victims to tell tales, or perhaps he had
fallen foul of the Insurgents, although those people wanted
such executions to be news and generally left the mutilated
remains on a main highway for all to see. So perhaps the
fellow had been an Insurgent or dacoit himself and rather
than waste a bullet on him as he lay dying after some battle or
ambush, his confederates had hurridley thrown his body into a
shallow grave and he had not had the strength to claw his way
out. It was no good speculating if the affair was to be kept a
secret, but could they be sure that the younger brother would
not talk about such an exciting secret? The boy drew himself
up to his full height and fiercely said that he would stake his
own life on his brother's silence. He would put such fear into

the younger boy that he would never dare to even think of that day again. So at last he went off rather grimly determined on silence and we wondered if perhaps we should have made greater efforts to persuade him otherwise. I wondered what passed between the brothers that guaranteed such complete silence, though that would be one experience they would hope never to have to live through again.

My first impression of the law as it was practised in Tawngpeng had been of shock and disbelief and I had found it very hard to sit back and condone what to me seemed an absolute travesty of justice. There had been a rather unfortunate accident involving one of our staff and he called one afternoon to tell me the results of the Court Enquiry. He had a small tea factory a few miles out of town and at weekends he would drive down there to inspect the week's production. On that fateful morning an old Palaung man had begged a lift, but his dog had refused to get into the jeep and had eventually been tied to the seat only to howl dismally as they drove down the narrow precipitous road. There was one very tight hairpin bend where the road hugged the rock face on the up-gradient and on the outer curve skirted a sheer drop to the valley below. It was at that point that a taxi driving up from Lashio had charged wildly round the bend swinging out into the oncoming jeep and the impact pushed the jeep over the precipice. Our friend was young and agile, and he managed to leap out of the vehicle before it crashed over the steep precipice but the old man was not so lucky and was thrown out fracturing his spine whilst the poor reluctant dog had no chace of escape.

We had sent a team of men with block and tackle to recover the jeep. To us it was an obvious case of careless driving on the part of the taxi driver. The old man had died of his injuries and the Judicial Minister had called our friend to an informal discussion. It was agreed that our friend had owned the jeep in which the old man had plunged to his death, so said the Minister our friend was responsible for the man's death and must compensate the widow and care for his family. I could scarcely believe what I heard. Surely he had not accepted such a miscarriage of justice. The offending taxi driver had not even been questioned. My arguments that he must appeal only distressed the poor fellow. No-one had ever done such a thing. He considered it was a correct judgement and insisted that even though it ruined him he must care for the dead man's family. Unable to get beyond his Eastern fatalism I gave up trying to change his mind, and I realised for the first time that those people saw many things through quite different eyes and they were not going to alter their ways to please me. From that day I tried to keep my thoughts to myself although many times I was to listen to their strange judgements with reluctance, but in the end without trying to interfere.

14

Festivals of the Full Moon

The Full Moon of Wazo heralded in the Buddhist Lent which lasted for three lunar months. For five days before the Full Moon everything shut down, only the Indian owned shops in the Bazaar were open for business as usual. The Palaungs in those last few days of July closed their factories, shops, houses, villages and all set out for Namhsan, the women wearing their newest costumes each weighted down with a fortune in silver and gold ornaments. The men would be dressed in smart Shan suits with turbans of bright pink or green chiffon instead of the everyday white cotton. They had all come to have a last spending spree before the three months of fasting. Their first call would be to make offerings to the Pongyi Kyaung then, religious duty done, they would flock into town buying everything which took their fancy. The restaurants and tea shops would be full of gaudily dressed women eating whilst such luxuries were allowed. The men would be seen together in large groups around the liquor, opium and gambling halls. Before returning home to three months of fasting and religious devotions they would make one last call, to pay their respects to the Sayador of the Zayangyi Pongyi Kyaung.

The next day the town would be deserted, the shops and restaurants empty. In the villages everyone would be hard at work tilling the fields, attending to work in the tea fields which they had neglected for a week or more during the festivities. Then at half time, exactly half way through the Lent period they would begin the visiting. In turn each village would be host to one of the other villages, the visitors calling on relations and visiting pagodas. At nightfall they would all join in an enormous meal of rice and spicy vegetables, little work would be done in the tea gardens for a whole week and leaf for the factories was scarce until all the visiting was over.

It was during these half time festivities that the drums began to speak, the soft insistent throbbing sounds would start up at the Namhsan Pongyi Kyaungs and after several days of continuous drumming, the throbbing sounds would suddenly cease to leave the air empty for a few brief moments before the drumming was taken up by a village on the other side of the valley. When they tired, the steady drumming would be taken over by each of the other villages in turn so that each community took part in the ritual of keeping the air filled with drum sounds, like a giant heartbeat, until the last day of Lent.

One evening early in September we saw the people of Zayangyi decorating the big shrine with flowers and that evening as darkness fell, we saw a small procession of children headed by a group of Ko Yin, young boys who had entered the Monastery for religious instruction, each carrying a lighted candle which they placed in niches in the hundreds of small shrines. As we looked back in the failing light we saw a myriad of tiny twinkling specks of flame bobbing around the dim outlines of shadowy grey as though the pagodas were lit by dancing fireflies.

On the afternoon of the last day of Lent we saw yet another procession slowly wending its way down the steps from the Pagoda. A dozen men held aloft tall poles decorated with coloured paper with a tiny umbrella on top. A white and gold silk umbrella was held over a velvet cushion, now empty. Some offering had been made and the silk umbrella told of the high rank of the donor, and a band of Musicians had been commissioned to play sweet music.

Lent would end with the Full Moon of Taddingyut and three days before this the Palaungs would go in procession to Payagyi to fetch the Mya Tha Peik Bowl from its resting place in that most holy of temples. Each fourth year a group of citizens would be selected to be hosts for the lavish ceremonies and on this occasion of the thirty-ninth Mya Tha Peik, we were to be the chosen hosts. It was a great honour for the factory, and the staff and men were determined to make it the most spectacular of ceremonies that had yet been seen in Namhsan. For a week before the Festival they spent every spare moment in fashioning a gigantic mythical golden bird†

† Shwe Hintha = mythical bird or duck.

which they constructed around a jeep. Throughout the three
days of the celebration this golden bird would carry the Mya
Tha Peik, or Begging Bowl and would be the central
attraction of a vast and colourful procession. There were set
traditions to be followed. On the first night the elders and
needy families were given dinner. A large marquee had been
erected on our tennis court, stalls and a stage were constructed
on the volleyball pitch and it was open house. All who wished
might join in the celebrations which included music, dancing,
film shows and a drama, the entertainment finishing at 3 a.m.
On the second night, all the distinguished citizens of the
district gathered to watch the drama, and it was the only
occasion I was to meet the Chinese lady, third wife of the
Sawbwa who was representing her husband.

A troupe of dancers from Mandalay performed on a small
stage under the stars. There were three types of dancing, the
Yama Zat with themes from the Indian epic Ramayana, which
involved considerable physical strain. Then the Burmese Ballet,
the Yein Pwes, group dancing which called for long training
and team work. This type of dance was performed in the old
days, to the accompaniment of the Pattala and the Saunggauk
specially for the King. The dances for the Zat Pwes, or dramas
were often individual dances performed with sheer excitement
and joy to please the audience. The dancing girls looked like
dainty china dolls in their sinuous silken tamein with filmy
white aingyi and long gauzy scarves draped across their
shoulders. Their long black hair was clasped with gold pins
and combs and decorated with fresh flowers and to emphasise
the dancing they would toss the flowing tresses with flirtatious
ease. The men who showed their agility with every gesture and
leap, were as gaudy as peacocks with brightly coloured
lungyis, vivid turbans and sparkling ropes of beads. At the first
sound of the gong those lacquered dolls leapt into action, they
bent and twisted their bodies, swaying to the throbbing music,
slender hands fluttered like brilliant butterflies or writhed
sinuously as any serpent, so long as the audience would throw
them money to show their appreciation, the dancers found the
energy to perform.

Through the night a small group of children let off fire
balloons under the skilful guidance of one of the senior staff.
These were paper parachutes tied to small cans of fire. The

heat sent the balloons soaring into the star speckled heavens looking like fairies until the paper caught fire when they would plunge down to earth in a streak of flame and I hoped that the firewatchers were on duty.

On the third day the Mya Tha Peik, a small bowl of green glass with lid, rim and stand of gold filigree, carried the Offering given by the Sawbwa, a costly emerald. The bowl was placed in a miniature gilded pagoda built on the back of the golden bird and the procession set out for the Haw and the ceremony of the blessing. The guardians of the relics followed the bird, each man wearing white robes with crimson sashes. then came huge drums and gongs carried by boys with the great instruments of brass, wood and leather slung on bamboo poles. Behind each one a third boy followed wielding huge padded drumsticks.

There were groups of women in their brightest costumes, a small orchestra, and a bicycle fitted out with a set of brass gongs which were struck automatically with hammers, worked by the movements of the bicycle. A party of violinists fiddled merrily as they walked along and a male dancer performed amazing feats of agility to the music.

The townspeople joined the procession and at 5.30 p.m. they all began the long slow trail out to Payagyi, the biggest and holiest of all the pagodas in Tawngpeng. Throughout the night there was singing, dancing, and feasting around that mother of the pagodas which glistened and sparkled, dazzling white in the lights and torches, its square outer walls topped with tiny spires. The tall square Pya-That seemed to be made of nine graduated crowns which soared heavenwards topped by the golden filigree Hti.

We joined the crowds, barefoot in the ankle deep mud, a mist crept up from the valley and a slight drizzle hung in the air but no-one noticed and the celebrations went on unhindered. I was invited to go inside the temple and found myself in a vast square hall dimly lit by tall candles which flickered, shedding strange shadows along the length of the narrow trestle tables groaning beneath their load of offerings. There were cakes and sweetmeats, fruit and vegetables such as one might find at any Harvest Festival. Then I saw that the local artists had been busy. With great skill and patience they had carved a tortoise out of a pumpkin, a helicopter cleverly made with cucumbers, there was a vegetable peacock, cars, aeroplanes, all made out of fruit or vegetables. Behind this fascinating display of artistry was a stout steel cage, the open gates displaying a large and splendid image of the Buddha in gold. On either side of it stood uniformed Police with loaded rifles, ready to guard the treasure. I left the kneeling devotees to their prayers and joined the revellers without. On a small stage built under the shadow of the temple the young daughter of the Chief of Police gave a display of Thai dancing.

A group of Palaung men were dancing to the throbbing music of an ozi. Dressed in white suits with pink sashes and turbans, they each carried a silver staff around which they wove intricate steps, bending their bodies and fluttering their free hands as they circled in silent concentration. In a far corner a drama held a small crowd spellbound and the orchestras kept up the continuous soft, throbbing beat which seemed to hypnotise the mind. Nearby I saw a small group of Palaung women gorgeously attired in their scarlet costumes, the gold and silver of their ornaments gleaming in the flickering lights. They circled sedately, fluttering their hands, bending their bodies in intricate rhythmic movements in quiet unison.

At 4.0 a.m. all these celebrations would cease and the Sawbwa would appear in their midst. Quietly they would file into the temple for the religious ceremony. By 6.0 a.m. it would all be over and the weary crowds would make their way back to the villages and once more the town would be empty, drained of its vitality until the Full Moon of Taddingyut was seen to shine. This was the night when the towns and villages, shops and factories, every humble dwelling would become a blaze of light. Hundreds of tiny paper lanterns lit by candles would sparkle and glow in the dark night like bright jewels arranged in geometric patterns filling all the windows, swaying in the trees. The small children waved sparklers but the older children made ear-splitting bangs by filling four foot lengths of bamboo with kerosene and then plunging a lighted taper through a tiny hole in the top of the bamboo. These resounding explosions rent the night air throughout the Festival of Lights reminding everyone that the long fast was over. The lights were offered to commemorate Buddha's return from the abode of Nats and Devas.

The old fashioned way of lighting was to use small cotton wicks steeped in sessamun oil in tiny earthenware bowls. The fashion for the rainbow hued paper lanterns was being replaced by lavish displays of fairy lights and wherever electricity was available coloured electric bulbs which though not so attractive were perhaps safer.

Taddingyut was purely a religious ceremony, but a month later in November at the Full Moon of Tazaungmon there was a recurrence of the festivities. The origin of the Tazaungmon festival is pre-Buddhist and traceable to old Hindu religious traditions. This was a time of offering incense, sweetmeats and lights. Buddha's mother, re-incarnated as a god, saw that her son would soon become a monk. She wanted to have a yellow robe ready for him but had only one night in which to pluck the cotton, weave the cloth, dye and sew it. In memory of this occasion robe weaving ceremonies and contests were held in many towns and villages throughout Burma. The fresh yellow robe, the Mathothingan, would be taken to clothe the Image at all main temples in lavish Kathein ceremonies. Anything given at this time was said to have special virtues. On the day of the offering, the gifts would be tied to wooden stands which symbolised the fabulous Padesa Tree, a tree which could grant your wishes. With music and dancing the KatheinKhin or displayed gifts, would be taken to the Pongyi Kyaung and presented to the monks. Afterwards there would be a feast and much merrymaking. Mezali was a very popular delicacy to offer to guests at this time. It was made from the flower buds of the Cassia Simea, first boiled then seasoned with sessamun, spices, fried garlic and groundnuts. This spectacular occasion brought the most lavish Kathein ceremony of the year when the Palaungs of Zayangyi escorted the great silver statue of the King on his annual ride through the town.

After this the people would be free to enjoy the good things of life once more. There would be weddings to celebrate, Pwés to arrange. The Pongyis would no longer be confined to their monastery but free to travel where so ever they wished once the long period of self denial was over. This was what the lights and outbursts of joy and generosity were proclaiming.

During the five days holiday we would often visit distant places of interest in the district, and on one occasion we decided to walk up the mountain to the Loi Seng Pagoda on the pilgrims' way instead of driving up the motor road. We were spurred on by the Mahadevi who had told us of her epic walk, and if she could do it so could we. We found a steep track which took us straight up to Tawngma village. Monsoon rains had worn deep ruts as the flooding waters coursed down the precipitous path. The Palaungs did not believe in walking further than necessary and their paths took the shortest way between two points. We found the village deserted but, led by the sounds of drumming and revelry, we found a Pwé in progress at the Pongyi Kyaung. Around the courtyard the balconies were festooned with flowers and hung with paper lanterns. Four tall poles stood in the centre of the courtyard each with a long slender prayer flag, the white silk painted with religious texts in gold or black lettering, the flags weighted by huge tassels of coloured wool and on top of each pole was a spiked crown of gold paper. The whole village had assembled to watch the dancing, the women in their sophisticated black velvet gowns edged with rainbow colours and pink silk turbans on their heads, heavy silver belts encircling their waists. Two men waved silk banners whilst a third man played the Krung Hom Pom, an incredible drum with a horn at least ten feet long. The wicker covered drum was fashioned like the ordinary ozi and carried by slinging a leather strap over the shoulder, but the ten foot long trumpet was curved at the end opening into a horn. The dancer tucked the long horn under his arm and as he drummed he twirled and swayed, swinging the cumbersome trumpet in rhythmic arcs while the laughing audience tried to leap out of his way. At the same time he sang, making up the verses about people and personalities of the village.

We left the village to its revels and walked on up the steep track towards the hill top where the newly restored pagoda stood resplendent amid a mass of crumbling masonry and shrines on top of the Peacock Hill. The legend says that so long as there are peacocks on that hill the Palaungs will prosper and no-one harmed any bird or animal which sought sanctuary there. Not so many years ago a young nephew of the Sawbwa, fresh from school and full of modern theories from the outside world, decided to disprove the taboo and accompanied by a friend set out to shoot partridge and silver pheasant. The two young men had climbed a bare half mile up the steep hillside when the young Prince stumbled, his loaded gun was not on safety catch and he was shot in the knee as the gun went off with the impact of his fall. They bound up the wound and the friend dashed off down the hill to get help at the village. The rescue party reached the young Prince only twenty minutes after the accident, to find him dead. From that day on no-one dared defy the Nats of Loi Seng Hill and it became a sanctuary for many species of bird and beast. Half way up the steep stepped track we came upon a small grove of trees shading a Zayat and under the trees we found a life-size tableau of a prince in old style dress, his two servants and a magnificent blue-faced horse. This was the king of the tea seed on his eternal travels.

As we reached the platform at the summit we were met by the guardian who held out a cup of water to refresh the weary devotees. The old monk lived a hermit's life there amidst the shrines and crumbling pagodas set in a sea of pink and white cosmos which nodded their heads to the perpetual breeze.

When we went by car the ManKai boys would always beg a lift. There was Aye Gyaw, Po Sein, Tun Hlaing and Aik Buint. At the top of the hill they would say in hushed trembling voices that they were going to pay their respects to the Nagá, and then vanish through a stile in the wall of the platform. Curious, I asked one day if we might accompany them, would the Nagá mind? They took us down a sheer path, down the precipitous hillside. Tiny crumbling pagodas edged the path and half way we found an ancient Zayat where devotees could rest their aching legs before continuing down to a rocky place where, in a narrow fissure between two giant moss covered boulders we saw the statue of a golden peacock; so this was the dreaded Nagá. The boys presented us and then went down on their knees to pay respects, explaining in hushed voices that the lair of the Peacock Nagá was said to run right under the hill into a deep cave, but they had never dared to explore it themselves. Back once more on the platform, we went into the big square temple. Inside, it seemed empty and cool and in the dim light we saw a gleam of gold and discovered another golden peacock, one which had been donated during H.L.B.'s time. We decided that before we left Tawngpeng for the last time we must fill the empty place in the temple with a peacock of our own. The living birds had

had become scarce on that sacred hill but the lacquer ones would fulfil the legend.

The old pagoda had been encrusted with fragments of mirror glass which caught the setting sun and sent flashes across the valley like some miniature lighthouse. Progress overtook tradition and the next time the guardians of Loi Seng had the Stupa renovated, it was given a coat of cement and decorated with painted symbols in gaudy colours, the old mirrors vanished for ever, snuffing out the flashing signals that had winked their prayer messages across the valley for centuries.

We almost missed the King's annual ride. Zan Lyn had asked permission to use the big Land Rover as he was making a personal Tazaungmon Offering of Soonkway, and the small one was waiting to fetch the midwife to a confinement.

When at last we reached the town, it was to find that the procession had already gone and we had to wait for it to return. Two hours later we dashed up to town and were just in time. A decorated jeep headed the procession blaring out modern music through loudspeakers, and we regretted the phasing out of the old fashioned orchestras. There were the usual banners, the guardians of the relics displaying for all to see the huge gold discs, a curiously shaped horn, caskets containing sacred relics and bowls of gleaming gold. Musicians followed with a variety of instruments and then women wearing the Dragon's Dress who held aloft "Trees" covered with money and other gifts. On a litter with a conical crown made of tiers of silver leaves, reposed a large silver begging bowl. Inside another litter, in the form of a huge orange cylinder decorated with streamers and flowers, sat two small children honoured by four dainty gold umbrellas like Chinese hats. Another orchestra accompanied the dancer who hopped from one foot to the other bending his body rhythmically to the music and making slight movements with his hands as he kept up with the procession. Then we saw the king riding in state within a tall slender pagoda made of gold and purple paper. The silver statue was quite large and the seated image held out the first tea seed, a blessing the Palaungs never allowed themselves to take for granted. The spire of the purple pagoda was so tall that a man with a long pole had to walk in front of it, raising the power cables which crossed the road, to allow the King to pass.

The long and colourful procession finally ended with life-size effigies of animals fashioned in paper. There was an elephant with trunk held high and several strange looking mythical beasts. My enquiries about these only brought the answer that they were traditional for the Palaungs and their significence went back to pre-Buddhist beliefs. It was one of the old customs still upkept although few would know of their true origins. Having received a blessing from the Sayadaw the King and his begging bowl were returning to their traditional resting place for another year.

At the Zayangyi Pongyi Kyaung we saw that the huge buildings of mellow wood with ornately carved roofs were crowded with visitors and there were stalls selling sweetmeats and portable one-man reataurants serving drinks and hot pasties to the devotees.

The Sao Nang was host on this occasion and she called us into her pavilion to take a dish of tea.

After this mammoth festival the people settled down to growing tea once again until the next April and another Lent ushered in the season of fasts and festivals.

15

The Seventh Clan

Each January we emerged from our isolation with two months in which to taste the delights of so-called civilisation, but the brief holidays in England only made me long for the peaceful hills of Tawngpeng and we would try to arrange our return flight to give us the minimum of time in Rangoon. We would be whisked off to grand diplomatic parties, to the Sailing Club with its green lawns and lovely island dotted waters, to the Burma Britain evenings and shows, to exhibitions of art and industry, but all the time Tawngpeng would be calling us and we would hurry back to those distant hills.

On one occasion we took the long route home by Kyaukme to save a future journey, for we had to report our return to the Immigration Office. Otherwise we might never have seen the jungle felling near Panglong, for our normal route was on the other side of the hill.

Over a vast area of several hundred acres all the giant trees lay like matchsticks drying in the sun and it was obvious that at any moment there would be a burn-off. Nearby we saw a new village built in a strange new style with long-houses. Zan Lyn told us that they belonged to Palaungs who had escaped from China and I determined to find out more about the affair.

First I had to organise an orchid hunt. The best and most beautiful flowers grew in the topmost branches of those jungle giants and it was only when the trees were felled that we could get the plants. The boys enjoyed such outings and we set out the next morning to find we were only just in time; the burn-off had already started and we could see black clad figures busy controlling the flames. The air was rent with a fusillade of ear splitting bangs as the green bamboos caught fire and exploded, warning us of the encroaching wall of flames licking through the dry trees and undergrowth with frightening swiftness. We had to make sure that retreat was not cut off or that anyone wandered too far from the party, to be ready for that sudden swirl of wind which could swiftly spread the flames in unexpected directions. The air was hot and stifling, black ash and fiery sparks stung the face, it was not a safe and pleasant spot in which to linger. This was a good orchid growing area and we collected blue vanda, the rope-like pink vanda, dendrobiums of many varieties, the Water Festival Orchid which produced great bunches of scented white and orange flowers, there were delicate pink ones with a fringed lemon yellow tongue, foxtail orchids and many others. It needed great care and patience on the part of the Malis at Namhsan to persuade these orchids to grow at the higher elevation but over the years we produced a fine show of all the many different varieties we collected and I was happy to have saved the lovely flowers from destruction in the jungle fires.

My thoughts returned to the mystery of those black-clad people, who were they and how had they come to be felling acres of the Sawbwa's forests?

I called on the Township Officer and the story he told me was rather chilling. I had seen them in town, clad in sombre black with white headdresses, the women had heavy hoops of silver on their hips and I had never before seen such a wealth of silver ornaments, even the men wore heavy silver "bullets" through their ears. I had also noticed that they were all very young, little more than children. It seemed that they were Palaungs who had been living in the border areas and after the re-alignment of the border with China they had found themselves on the other side and no longer free to cross that barrier to visit their homeland as had been their custom. At first the Chinese authorities had left them alone and they had thought that the changes mattered little.

Then official policy became more evident and sinister. Chinese officials moved into the area and guards were posted along the banks of the Shweli River which formed the border at that point. Their young women came under insistent pressure to marry Chinese men and they found that their age old customs were being slowly but surely changed, their young people openly pressurised to accept the "Little Red Book". They were an independent people and were not going to meekly allow these new masters to wipe out their culture and age old loyalties by genocide. Tawngpeng was their traditional home and they must return there before it was too late. The elders called a Council and for many days they discussed the problem. Of one thing they were certain, if they were to be destroyed as a tribe it would be their decision and by the sword.

It was eventually decided that every able-bodied man, woman and child must attempt to cross the Shweli River. They laid their plans carefully and took their time. Over many months they turned all their property and valuables into silver ornaments for their women and as this was their custom, it caused no suspicion. At the same time they were building bamboo rafts which they hid at carefully selected points along the river bank.

The night chosen for the escape was at the Black Moon and with orders that the first duty of everyone under the age of twenty was to try to get across the river to safety — heroics to be left to the older men — they slipped into the dark night in small silent groups. The old and infirm had elected to remain behind in the village in order not to hinder the escape, but they knew only too well that they would be punished for all those who got away. The Chinese Guards were alert and soon realised what was afoot. There was a bloody battle most of the blood spilled being Palaung, but they fought with the strength of desperation, their only weapons dahs, spears, bows, their aim only to delay the well armed Chinese long enough to enable their children and grandchildren to make the border. They knew they would not survive the night. The treacherous Shweli was a river no sane man would think of trying to cross on a flimsy bamboo raft at the dead of night; about a third of the total population of the village did reach the rafts only to find the Shweli as unfriendly as the Chinese guards and many perished in the swift flowing waters. Of the original party only about a hundred young people made the crossing, having escaped the bullets they found the Water Nats demanded a heavy toll.

The survivors made their way to Namhsan and presented themselves to the Sawbwa asking for his help. They asked only for land where they could live in peace and safety, to rebuild their village and shattered lives.

The Sawbwa was sympathetic, acknowledging their bravery and independent spirit. They would be a drag on none of the other Palaung communities, their wealth was to be seen adorning their womenfolk, so he gave them several hundred acres of virgin jungle and his blessing. They had no time to sit back bewailing cruel fate, expecting the world to set things right for them. They had to throw themselves into the task of felling the jungle giants, of building themselves homes and of producing food and a living from the land given to them. They wanted only to be worthy of the sacrifice so many of their people had made to give them the chance to live in freedom.

This was the story of the Seventh Clan as it was told to us and we had no reason to doubt it. The last I saw of those refugees from China was a small thriving village, surrounded by fields of vegetables and acres of hill rice. They were managing very nicely and something of a lesson to the rest of the uncaring world.

16

The Lavender Hat

It was rather a pretty hat which would have graced a garden party or wedding and when I bought it in London one cold February day, I had little idea of the impact it would have on my other world.

We often had to drive down to Lashio or Kyaukme for the day and after a four or five hour journey over hot dust laden roads I would arrive with my long hair looking like a dusty haystack and no place where I might tidy it before having to attend a local function or meet some Government official. The hat had seemed to be the answer to my problems for headscarves were too uncomfortable in the heat.

It was the very latest style, a cloche of delicate lavender coloured ribbon lace. This I thought would keep my long hair tidy and my head cool in any situation. I first tried it out on a visit to Kyaukme to see Mr Aziz, the advocate who was representing two of our Chinese workers in their appeal against deportation.

Whilst Piet and Mr Aziz attended the Court I walked down to the Bazaar. After a while I noticed that a crowd seemed to be gathering and wondered idly if they were going to an entertainment of some kind. Then with surprise I began to realise that whenever I stopped, the silent crowd halted too. It was not long before I was sure that the ever growing crowd was following me. The Bazaar shops all had open fronts and so there was no window reflection to put me wise to anything unusual. I decided to slip into the nearest tea shop where Piet joined me. But the crowd was not to be put off and at least sixty people squeezed into the tiny room. They sat on and under the tables, squatted on the floor and lined the walls while in the doorway was a squash of faces, all silent and staring at me. At last an old woman pushed her way to the front of the crowd. She pointed to my head and asked in Burmese 'What is that?'

I put my hand up to my head to find the cause of the sensation. That silly hat! As it was light as thistledown, I had forgotten I was still wearing it.

'It's a hat' I replied and she translated into Shan for the benefit of the crowd. There was a chorus of incredulous exclamations.

'Ah loo!' they all said and after a long and heated exchange, she again turned to me.

'They all say that it cannot be a hat, it's full of holes and no protection from either sun or rain.'

I laughed and assured her that it was an English hat.

'Do all English ladies wear those?' came the query and when I said they did there was another chorus of incredulity from the crowd. I could see them all visualising thousands of English women walking around with fancy fishing nets on their heads. Their minds boggled at the idea. The old woman warmed to her task of interviewer and interpreter and she began to fire questions at me which came from all corners of the room and ever more embarrassing. The crowd argued amongst themselves, some liking the strange hat, others feeling that it ought not to be allowed. I decided that the time had come to escape before they came to blows over their differences and seeing the Land Rover approaching I whisked the troublesome hat off my head and offered it to the old woman saying that as she admired it so much she might like to have it. The crowd roared, daring her to accept and she could not think up enough excuses for refusing such an embarrassing gift. I began to enjoy the exchange and got away at last amid cheers from the onlookers and still in possession of that silly hat. I wore it often after that but took good care to check that I had taken it off before venturing into any town, realising that for those people, it was the unusual which became the sensational.

17

No Place for Pets

Eastern peoples are not addicted to keeping animals as pets as we of the Western world so often are. With few exceptions animals are fed and cared for so long as they can work for their living. Because of the terrain and lack of good motor roads the mule, and to a lesser extent the pony, were valuable property. All transport depended on the mule trains to bring in supplies to the outlaying villages in Tawngpeng. There were ancient highways which cut across the hills leading straight to China in the north, India and Thailand to west and east, and large caravans could be seen hurrying purposefully along those well trodden tracks any day of the week. There was safety in numbers and the muleteers were well armed. They often had to defend their cargoes to the death when they passed through territory controlled by merciless bands of dacoits, or perhaps their profits would dwindle as they paid tolls and protection money to these war lords. The mules were big fine animals and generally well cared for although the wooden frames which carried the heavy packs would chafe and gall if the muleteer was careless. Should an animal fall sick or was injured it was a major disaster for the owner and unless it was reasonably certain that the animal would recover quickly, it would be abandoned to meet a slow lingering death as best it could.

The few ponies one saw were small wiry, rather shaggy animals and were used on the shorter runs, or occasionally for riding.

One hot, dry spell I drove up to town on three consecutive mornings and noticed a white pony standing dejectedly by the roadside. Although it was not tethered it had not moved in three days and I made enquiries and was told it had a broken leg and had been left to die there by its Chinese owner. I was always shocked by such callous treatment but this was the custom and I tried not to interfere. Although it was often difficult to subdue compassion for the suffering creatures, I told myself firmly that this time also I must leave well alone. By the fifth day I could stand it no longer, the pony lay by the roadside in the blazing sun without food or water. A pack of dogs from the town were snapping and snarling around it and two small boys pelted it with stones to see if it would get on its feet again.

I sought out Piet and told him that come what may, he must shoot it. But that was easier said than done. He consulted Mr Chang who advised a visit to the Chinese headman. Dr Peel joined the shooting party and taking the protesting muleteer with them they all set out for the Police Station to announce their intentions to the authorities. The inspector was sympathetic and agreed that the pony should be destroyed but said firmly that his men could not be ordered to shoot an animal, he did however send the sergeant to escort them to the Army Headquarters at the High School. The officer in command of the post was also sympathetic but said he had no ammunition to spare for acts of mercy but he did give his permission for Piet to use his shotgun. All private weapons had been surrendered to the Army and Piet was one of the few exceptions, but his gun was of little use to him if he had to get permission from both Police and Army each time he wished to fire it. Two soldiers who were ordered to join the Party swelled their numbers to eight. Just to shoot a harmless dying pony!

When at last they arrived with shotgun and ball to put the poor beast out of its misery they found that word had gone out on the Bazaar grapevine and every able-bodied man, woman and child in town had assembled to witness the execution, each carrying a dish, for the moment the shot was fired the muleteer slit the pony's throat and began to carve it into joints which he sold to the eager crowd. Piet retuned home sickened. It was in moments such as that we almost hated our Buddhist friends.

Namhsan was a town of unwanted dogs, and litters of puppies swelled the canine population annually without anyone attempting to stop the menace. Whilst the puppies

needed only their mothers' milk they were welcomed as toys
for the children but the moment they needed to be fed by the
household, they would be abandoned. The usual custom was
to take them up to a distant pagoda and leave them as an
offering to the shrine. Eventually they would escape from the
loosely tied sack and finding their master gone would huddle
together in some niche keeping each other warm. All the
hilltop shrines were visited regularly by devotees who left
offerings of rice so there was food of a sort and if the stronger
pups survived the cold, starvation and hungry panthers, they
might follow someone back to a village. When this happened
the puppy would be fed by that person for so long as it chose
to remain under his roof.

Bess, our Labrador, was a very determined old bitch and to
the last she would find some way of escaping detention to keep
a love tryst, later to produce a litter of Pi-puppies. The first
time this happened after our arrival I decided to let her keep
one black puppy which looked as if it might grow up to
resemble a labrador, the rest of the litter I put down, a
mistake I was made to regret.

H.L.B. had told me a rather involved story about a large
python which lived under the bungalow and consumed Bess's
annual litters of puppies. The significance of his story only
came to me when I saw the shock and horror on the faces of
my Buddist servants at the "execution" of the new-born pups.
I suddenly realised that I was going to have to think of some
story which matched H.L.B.'s or I would have a revolt on my
hands the next time Bess had a brood of unwanted puppies.

One day some clever fellow hit on the idea of depositing a
heaving sackful of puppies at our gate, I was sure I had seen
those very puppies being fondled by children in the town and
I felt more angry than I would ever have thought possible. We
drove up to the spot and without saying a word I put the sack
down in the road and released the fat wriggling puppies in
front of a small silent crowd. The captives were obviously on
familiar ground and with yelps of joy dashed across to a group
of children at one of the houses. With what I hoped was an
expressionless face I got back into the Land Rover and we
drove home. Soon after this I noticed an abandoned puppy
wandering around the Chinese Quarter, it was pitifully thin
and covered with tar from the newly mended road. There

were nasty sores on its back and already it showed signs of the mange which turned the Bazaar dogs into hideous hairless monstrosities. Its tail had been broken and drooped crookedly and it was hopping around on three legs. I had been horrified to see some of the older boys kicking it around like a football laughing at its screams, but my protests merely resulted in a sullen silence from the boys and the puppy being hurriedly removed by a younger child. Perhaps someone thought it a good idea to give that sorry little scrap to me for one morning I was to find it crouching in my garden.

The doctor fought a losing battle against local opinion and customs over these unwanted and diseased dogs and puppies. He held his own "cull" each year in the interests of health and the absence of any Vets. He was only too pleased to help me with a puppy such as that sad, broken little creature. Even so, it broke my heart. I realised that the principles of my local friends were having a deeper effect on me than I had thought. But if puppies were abandoned in such a callous way, older dogs were allowed to live on to their natural end no matter how sick, injured of diseased they might be. There were no Animal Dispensaries and no-one seemed to care nor even notice the horrors around them. What I saw in the town sickened and shocked me, dogs and bitches in the last stages of venereal tumours, their bodies one great open sore and the flesh literally shredding off their bones. No-one took any action about it and they were left free to roam the streets and spread the disease until it killed them.

During our first year the Sawbwa had presented us with an Alsatian puppy and during our absence on home leave he had escaped to roam with the town dogs, resulting in him contracting the disease. We tried every possible cure to no avail and at last the Chief Government vet in Rangoon sent us an urgent message, 'This dog is dangerous, not only to other dogs but also to human beings'. He explained that it only needed one of the flies which swarmed over everything to settle on an open cut on the human body for the incurable disease to be transmitted, and having seen the horror which stalked the town and the swarming flies, I needed little convincing. In the end we gave our beautiful HpuHpu an overdose of sleeping tablets knowing that we were committing an unforgivable crime. He had been a gift from the Sawbwa to make things worse.

When the Burmese Army moved into Tawnpeng one of their first acts was to post notices throughout the town decreeing that all stray and diseased dogs would be destroyed, and they cleaned up the town, earning my undying gratitude. I hope they continue to maintain their high standards for if it was a decision which rested with the Palaungs, the dogs and the disease would triumph to stalk the streets of Namhsan once more.

18

The Opium Run

Smuggling was big business in the Shan States, and it was so easy. With few motor roads most goods were moved by mule train over the ancient highways and tracks across the hills which were difficult, if not impossible, to patrol. If unscrupulous men slipped a few balls of opium into some packing case or bundle it was very unlikely that they would run into anyone who would ask to inspect the packages. Only when they had a tip-off was there any hope of the police catching the smugglers. The Kyemaing and his young brother who was Chief of Police in the Tawngpeng State Administration, spent many long hours chasing elusive balls of opium around the hills and occasionally they would tell us of the more spectacular hauls and the tricks the smugglers had used to conceal the drug.

It looked like serious trouble for us when several balls of opium were found in chests of tea, chests which bore our brand name. An enquiry proved that they were chests purchased by a Lashio Trader who, after selling the contents, had added to his profits by selling the empty chests to a muleteer. The chests had been refilled with locally made tea, each with a ball of opium in the centre. It was a clever ruse which under cover of our brand on the box had nearly succeeded and regulations had to be tightened up at the factory to prevent a recurrence of such an embarrassment.

The Shan Army was financed by this trade. Centred mainly on Lashio, it was whispered that a deadly rivalry and power struggle existed between the opium barons. People involved in this trade invariably met a violent end and it was commonplace to hear that yet another headless body had been found on one of the lonely hill roads.

We would walk for miles along the old roads with our dogs and would often encounter the mule trains. Many things came over the border: pottery bowls carefully packed in straw inside giant wicker baskets, bales of silk and cotton, sheets, blankets, and foodstuffs. small wooden barrels of a fiery spirit, strong as the best brandy, and giant jars of oil big enough to hide the "forty thieves" in, were slung in pairs either side of the mule just as they had been ever since trading began. Sometimes the packs would be covered with waterproof sheets and often the baskets or boxes were of such odd shapes that I wished I knew just what strange things could be inside them.

If the Caravans stopped in town for food and night's rest we knew they were honest traders. Those with guilty secrets pressed on, avoiding the town, taking a rest only when absolutely necessary and when safe from surprise attack. We discovered this fact when returning from one of our long walks with the dogs late one evening. We had walked for several miles along one of the old highways and the light was rapidly fading whilst we were still several miles out. The road suddenly curved around a clump of trees and there we came upon the sad-faced old Chinese and his two villainous sons. They had made camp in the shadows of a spiny thicket and had a lookout manned by the younger boy on top of a small bank. A huge pot of rice bubbled on a smokey fire and an inviting smell of spicy food filled the air. The old man glanced up at us and then continued to stir his pot, ignoring us, but the two youths stood in the path one in front, one behind us, dahs at the ready. A black scowl spread over the face of the older brother but the younger boy had recognised us and we knew he was friendly. We smiled a greeting and held back the "devil dogs" as they called the Alsatians. Jokingly we asked if they were going to invite us to join in their picnic as the good smell made us hungry. Slowly the scowls faded and they relaxed although the older brother still held his dah, a surly watchfulness on his face. They were waiting for the night train the younger boy told us. They often brought food to some pre-arranged spot when the business was urgent and the muleteers did not wish to waste time going into town. We asked no more and after a few pleasantries we hurried on, not anxious to be around when the visitors from China arrived. We knew that we had only been allowed to go because they felt quite certain that we would not talk in town of what we had seen. Any stranger who had been unlucky enough to walk the road at that time would probably have been cut down instantly just in case he was a police spy.

If by some chance the police had raided their camp that night we would not have been able to expect such a friendly welcome the next time we met the villainous trio. We realised that perhaps it was unwise to be out on these lonely highways at dusk and that but for the two Alsatians who seemed to strike terror into the hearts of even the toughest characters, we might easily have met a sticky end on that particular occasion.

The Palaung women whom we met on our walks would flee in terror from the dogs or cringe against a wall or tree covering their eyes with their arms and crying out 'Och, Oh, Och Oh, deng Och Oh'. At first we thought they were merely crying out in fear but eventually we learned that they were calling out a warning about the big dogs. Those two Alsatians were friendly to the point of foolishness but we decided that perhaps it was not a bad plan to keep up the myth of ferocity just in case we again bumped into our villainous friends on one of their dubious missions.

19

The Ghostly Guardians

Whether fact or fantasy the Nats, and the strange world they are supposed to inhabit, have been revered by the peoples of Burma and the Shan States since the beginning of their history. Though devout Buddhists, they somehow combine this strange worship of the Nats with their other religious beliefs and I was never able to decide where the dividing line came. It was not just that the less sophisticated peoples of the remote country districts still clung to old gods. Even in the cities I was to find pagodas which were dedicated to the spirits. In Rangoon I was taken to see the Ta Paung Zu, a strange shrine frequented by many who felt that the spirits could help them attain their desires. It was ornamented with odd little statues which would have seemed more in keeping with a Hindu Temple, and there was an uneasy air around the place. There are thirty Nats and each has its special place in the Nat hierarchy, each its festival day.

Thagya Nat, Chief of the Order of Nats sits apart on his three headed elephant but the rest are divided into five groups. All had been living people, legendary figures deified for their feats in battle, or great leaders and powerful kings. Others, perhaps after the style of some of our saints, became Nats after martyrdom or some particularly horrifying death.

The first group of seven were a part of the early legends surrounding King Duttabaung. The second group of nine came under the influence of a great conqueror whilst two Kings of the Ava Dynasty of the 15th century headed the third group. A 16th century King of Taunghoo ruled the fourth group and the last and fifth group surrounded Bayin Naung of the Ava-Pegu Dynasty whose exploits were mentioned by 17th century Portuguese explorers.

These then were the most powerful of ghosts, names to be mentioned with awe, but I was to find other guardian spirits, the guardians of places, of villages, the water Nats which presided over rivers, streams, lakes and the lives and prosperity of the people who lived and worked around them.

Near every village there would be some revered object, perhaps a large boulder, a niche in a rocky hillside or a tall tree festooned with orchids, and in or under each of those would be the abode of the Guardian Nat.

Daily offerings would be taken and placed nearby but on special occasions the whole community would gather to hold lavish ceremonies to propitiate the goodwill of their Guardian ghost.

The Palaungs believed that the spirits of their ancestors lived in the tops of the tea bushes and that when a Palaung died, the tops of those tall tea bushes would be the first resting place for his spirit and so the bushes were allowed to reach for the heavens. No matter how straggly the bush became nor how poor the yield, to prune them would bring the wrath of those guardian ancestors down on their heads and they would not chance doing that.

In ancient days when a palace or special shrine was to be built, a fearless warrior would be buried alive at each corner of the building beneath the foundations. It was thought that the spirit of each of those living corner stones would remain there to patrol the outer walls keeping out evil spirits and so ensuring the well being of the building and all those within.

As strangers in that beautiful land where in so many ways, time seemed to stand still we found that as well as having to adjust to life in a devout Buddhist community we also had to take account of those ever present Nats which loomed so large in the lives of the villagers. In general they were considered to be benign guardians of places to be treated with reverence and respect, and we soon realised that we were no exception to the rule. At times this led to odd situations, especially when friends from the Western world came to stay who scoffed at the idea of supernatural beings as fairytale nonsense. They gave offence through mere thoughtlessness, but we had to live on with their mistakes.

A party of guests set out on their own to explore the road

down to the valley below. Hot and dusty after negotiating the steep track they were overjoyed to see the sparkling lake at the bottom and they stripped and plunged into the cool clear water enjoying the unexpected pleasure of swimming and sunbathing in what they thought was an uninhabited valley. They had seen no-one, but their exploit had been observed and the villagers were outraged. The lake was the home of their Guardian Nat. A deputation of the village elders called to complain that now the Nat was offended, every possible disaster seemed to have befallen their village and the only way to make amends was for the foreigners to give a ceremony of appeasement. But the guests had departed and it took a generous donation to put things right. We made a mental note to make sure that no future guests of ours indulged in nude bathing parties or we could see our costs for appeasement ceremonies soaring. It was easy to tell when a place "belonged" to a Nat for there would be the shrine, often just an ornamental wooden box set in a tree or niche in the rocks. Sometimes a very powerful Nat would be given a large ornate house and supplied with all the accoutrements of Nat worship: a couch, a pillow, clothing, weapons, tools, all in miniature and fashioned in careful detail. In front of the shrine there would be a table for the offerings of rice, fruit, flowers, for the guardian ghost must not be neglected.

One of our favourite walks took us past a very ancient shrine on the hillside above Zayangyi. At the end of the "airstrip" the track divided at a huge banyan tree and turning left there took us to the reservoir through tea fields bounded by wild apple trees, gnarled and lichen covered with cascades of giant honeysuckle showering from their branches. Great bunches of pale gold trumpets, each flower at least nine inches in length, would fill the air with sweet scent in April; the damp areas around the waterpipe were overgrown with bright pink impatiens and a balsam with shell-pink flowers like curled shrimps. Tall spikes of blue and white lobelia edged the path and early in the season the white rhododendrons would blossom.

Sometimes we would take a track through a gloomy wood then along the ridge top to circle back again to Namhsan. The wood was empty of life, no sign of birds, bees, or butterflies, and it always made me feel uncomfortable. Overhead the thick

canopy of leaves cut out the sunlight; underfoot a deep carpet
of moss deadened footfalls and the tall smooth trunks of the
trees might almost have been pillars of grey marble in a great
silent temple. An ornate Nat House on a small platform of
moss covered rocks stood at the end of the path. Behind it I
noticed a pile of old vases and one evening my curiosity
getting the better of my dislike of the place, I lingered there to
sort through the broken crocks. I found the older vases were
well made with intricate moulding and pierced work, of a finer
glaze and finish than the later pots, but much the same design,
I had the feeling that I was being watched although I was
alone in the wood, Piet having walked on ahead. It was as
though I was surrounded by an aura of intense animosity. I
broke out into a cold sweat and told myself I was being foolish
to feel pricks of fear for no reason. Even so I would not have
considered taking away a single piece of those old broken
vases. I almost ran out of the wood and did not escape the
sense of evil until I was well away from it. Was it just
imagination? Piet made me walk that way again soon after just
to prove my fears were nonsense but I was never again able to
set foot in that little wood without the feeling that I was
surrounded by an unfriendly force and I wondered what dark
doings could have happened there. Was that why the local
people tended the shrine so carefully? Questions were evaded
and I never found out the history of the place.

A particularly powerful Nat inhabited a large rounded
boulder which took up one quarter of the factory volleyball
court. Plans to remove the troublesome rock with a small
charge of dynamite had to be abandoned when a deputation of
elders from a small settlement above on the hillside came to
ask that it should not be disturbed for they said if their
Guardian Nat was blown up disasters might befall them? The
rules of volleyball were amended to suit the situation and
everyone was happy.

There was yet another Nat which had a very considerable
influence on our leisure; this was the Water Nat at Lilu. The
Guardian of the River became our friend, his tree shaded our
beach of silver sand, we picnicked in its shade, sheltered from
sudden downpours of rain by sitting beneath the large wooden
house on stilts, and swam in the wide deep pool formed by the
bend in the river at that point. This particular Nat was greatly

revered by the people of the river villages who considered that their safety on the water, their prosperity and luck depended on the benevolence of the Guardian of the River and we were warned to be most careful to give no offence.

A narrow track led from the village, crossed the Nam Ko-ai River which joined the big river at the wide expanse of beach, then the path edged the Namtu River for about a hundred yards ending at the Nat Tree. The jungle trees. came right down to the water's edge and beneath them was an impenetrable mat of knee-high, spiny, purple-flowered mimosa pudica edged with clumps of plants with shrimp-like flowers, after the style of the beloperone. Beyond these was an impassable thorny thicket. The tree dedicated to the Nat was a leafy giant festooned with long ropes of the lovely pink vanda orchids and beneath it the large wooden shrine which was an exact replica of a Shan house, and like a dolls' house, the open front displayed the furniture and accoutrements within. A stout bamboo fence enclosed the compound which was swept daily by the fishermen who frequented the beach and none of them would set foot on a raft without first making some offering to the Nat to ensure his safety on the water and fill his traps with heavy catches of fish.

We decided we must have a boat so that we could explore the upper reaches of the river and that meant a boathouse which was to involve us even further with the Nat. The only suitable spot in which to build it was within fifty yards of the Nat Tree. The Headman shook his head doubtfully when we approached him. It would be difficult to arrange he said but he would consult the elders. They might allow a special ceremony to appease the Nat. The next time we visited the river we heard it had all been settled, we must donate two hundred kyats for an appeasement ceremony after which the villagers would build the boathouse just where we wanted it. To secure the boat we had no option but to pay up. In some subtle way this changed our status. We found the villagers were more friendly, more willing to offer help and advice and after we had built a Shan House on the opposite bank of the river, we were treated as one of the community. The house made our visits so much more enjoyable, we could change for swimming in comfort and privacy, and cook food in the lean-to kitchen at the back of the house using an iron trivet over a wood fire and on a number of occasions we spent several nights there.

It was on one of those long weekends at the time of the Water Festival that we were entertained to an evening of music, dancing and lights as the villagers came down to the river in procession at dusk each carrying a tiny coloured paper lantern swinging on a bamboo pole. An ozi beat out a throbbing rhythm to which the flickering lanterns bobbed and swayed like so many fireflies flitting along the riverbank, each of the dancers finally sticking his lantern into the sand to make an avenue of lights. Offerings were placed on the table which was lit by dozens of tiny candles stuck around its edge. Then the young boys and girls filled cups with water from the river and with shrieks of laughter they dashed around the beach sprinkling everyone with it; the solemn procession had become quite a friendly riot. The next day I crossed the river to see what the villagers had given to the Nat with such ceremony. I found the house had been completely refurbished, a tiny saffron coloured satin cushion was spread over the little wooden couch and on this lay a miniature suit of yellow silk, Shan pants, jacket and turban. The house was decorated with all the necessities of life that a Water Nat could possibly need. Carefully woven of rattan or straw each was a perfect miniature of the real thing, a sword, a belt, chains, a tiny boat, baskets, a mule, hats, flowers in profusion and enough rice to feed half a dozen Nats. The river people had paid homage in the hopes that the river would not vent its wrath on their homes during the approaching monsoon.

We became well known on the river but more often than not we had it to ourselves for the weekends were always holy days and the villagers took a rest from fishing.

After a long tiring day boating, swimming and fishing we would lock the boat in the new boathouse and then return to the shade of the Nat Tree to take some refreshment before driving home. One hot evening as we sat there sipping our tea I suddenly became aware that we were not alone. A young man wearing old-fashioned Shan dress, his hair done up in a top-knot and a dingy cloth wound around his brow, had appeared inside the Nat's enclosure and was busy sweeping and tidying up. How he got there I shall never know, for from where I sat it was impossible for anyone to have approached from the path or the river without being seen. I was puzzled and slightly uneasy for I had searched every inch of the area around the beach just to make sure there was no hidden path for at first we had to change for swimming on the beach and we had no wish to offend the modesty of the people or their Nat. We packed our things and Piet walked on ahead leaving me to give a small offering to the Nat as usual. In silence the young man waited at the gate hands outstretched to take the oranges and he smiled his thanks. I hurried down the track after Piet but still puzzled, I paused after walking only two or three yards and looked back. The Nat enclosure was empty. My oranges lay in solitary splendour on the offering table but the young man had vanished as mysteriously as he had appeared. There had not been time for him to have floated a raft and poled up river and there was no other way he could have gone. I shook myself mentally. I was not going to fall into the trap of believing in the Nats and yet I was not satisfied with the explanations I could think of. I never saw the mysterious young man again and we left soon afterwards with the question still unanswered.

20

Kingdom of the Water Nat

The boat added a new dimension to our weekend outings and we were able to explore the secret world of the Water Nat, those upper reaches of the river which seemed untouched by man's interfering ways and I always felt I must tread quietly or I might spoil the splendid peace. To build a house by the river's edge in this quiet paradise had been an inspiration, I would cook meals Shan style using an iron trivet over an open wood fire in the tiny lean-to kitchen at the rear. All firewood had to be gathered from the surrounding jungle and for water we had to paddle the boat upstream to a spring where cool fresh water gushed out of the rocks. The river water was heavily polluted with chemicals used by the Bawdwin Silver Mines at Namtu and we did not dare to drink it. As plumbing was non-existent the river served as an ever ready hot bath on our doorstep. Our lavatory was the jungle. That early morning sprint with a spade rather shocked our "civilised" guests who shook their heads over us and muttered that it was the first sign of going native, but I believe they truly envied us our jungle home.

Game was plentiful in the surrounding area and I had ideas of providing fish and fowl for supper, but I could not bring myself to shoot the lovely silver pheasant, and the fish would not bite. They would nibble my toes as I waded waist deep up and down trying my hand at casting flies without success. My efforts with a worm on a hook were equally unsuccessful and one of the local fishermen would watch my efforts with great mirth, almost falling off his perch on a large boulder overhanging the water as he rocked with laughter.

He would point to my bait and shake his head. 'You'll

never catch anything with that' he would chortle. Eventually
I persuaded him to let me into the secrets of baiting those river
fish. He dug quickly in the mud at the river's edge and
uncovered several small worms vividly striped brown and
yellow. Not that his advice helped, I still had no success but it
gave me plenty of exercise. The old hands told me that the
only sure way to catch those river fish was to throw a small
stick of dynamite into the water. Successful maybe, but it gave
an unfair advantage and did not appeal to my sporting
instincts. At the village shop I would sometimes see fish which
had been caught in this way, like huge carp, some had flesh of
an unappetising shade of yellow and others were coarse,
bony, red as any salmon.

Paddling up-stream was a very hazardous and strenuous
pastime. Because of the stong current we were not able to use
the deep water channel on our way up-river but steered a zig-
zag course between the great jagged boulders near the river
bank and as the water level dropped in the dry season it
became ever more difficult and dangerous.

Sometimes we would strain to hold the boat against the
current expecting at any moment to hear the grinding of
jagged rocks ripping a hole in our hull. Often we would be
passed by one of the villagers on a home made bamboo raft
which he could pole with surprising ease and speed round all
obstacles and we realised how much more useful this native
craft was on that rock strewn waterway. We toyed with the
idea of buying a small outboard motor, but as that would have
spoilt the one thing we most enjoyed, the peace and quiet, we
decided to forget the idea.

Beyond the curve of the river we found a different world;
there were no tracks along the river bank and the dense jungle
came almost to the water's edge. In several places we found
tiny beaches of silver sand nestling in the shelter of giant
boulders which might have been piled into those strange heaps
by the giants or dragons of the old legends as they did battle
with each other. In March the miniature blue vandas hung in
profusion in all the tree tops. In May it was the pink vandas
which twined their rope-like stems around the branches and
hung in long flowery streamers over the water. The Lagerstroemia trees also flowered in May: the Queen's Flower was
beautiful and in the hot season the great pyramids of flowers

would fade through shades of purple, mauve and all the pinks, to be scattered over the surface of the water in dense masses seeming to dance on the ripples like troupes of fairy ballerinas in their crumpled pink crepe tu-tu's. Silver Pheasant scratched busily in the undergrowth quite unmoved by our presence, monkeys played in the bushes and trees and lovely birds in rainbow hues dazzled as they darted overhead amongst the Heavenly Blue or the Sweet Pea Creeper which twined its waxy, powder-blue flowers in the bushes at the water's edge. If I looked long enough I would see the Bee Eaters, Kingfishers, Purple Sunbirds and others, each like a sparkling jewel flashing across a costly painted screen and in sombre contrast, the Great Hornbills with their grotesque yellow bills and black and white plumage. When fires broke out in the dry season and the hillsides were swept by walls of flame the Hornbills would drone overhead in great noisy flocks of thirty or more protesting at the disturbance, in their weird honking calls as they flapped to safety, their loud bellows serving to warn the small creatures on the jungle floor of the impending danger.

At certain spots along the water's edge I would see shimmering patches of colour which would rise in fluttering, jewelled clouds when disturbed: gorgeous butterflies in every shade of yellow, blue and green. These lovely insects would swarm in their thousands, gorging on the salt soaked up by the sand at each spot where some creature had urinated. My father, a keen Lepidopterist, had presented me with a butterfly net and instructions to find him some interesting specimens, but although to catch those lovely insects presented no problems, I could not be seen to kill them or I would have come up against those Buddhist Principles again so I devised a way of sedating them for a while and then if questioned I would take one out of the jar and leave it on a sunny rock. Within seconds the delicate wings would flutter into life and so my strange pastime was accepted, but I took care to collect no more than one or two specimens of each species if I could help it.

I had found some strange and exotic insects at Namhsan, odd looking beetles in gaudy colours, leaf and stick insects and others which were masters of disguise, as well as nasty lozenge-like things which inflicted painful stings. After dark the great Atlas Moth and the lovely Moon Moth would flutter around the garden but none of these made the breath taking display of the Lilu butterflies. There were great clouds of Lemon Migrants, Blue Glassy Tigers, The Painted Jezebel and amongst them swallowtails and many other species which had forsaken the shady jungle walks or village gardens for the lure of the salt seepages, The Red Helen, The Great Mormon, Paris, Hector, The Great Orange Tip, The Common Mormon and many others.

In the shallow warm pools by the river's edge lurked huge water snakes, the black and yellow banded bodies coiled like deadly springs and we had to look carefully before plunging into the water. About half a mile up-stream we found the rapids. We could see the churning white water ahead and to make matters worse the whole force of the river was suddenly squeezed into a narrow channel between two of the largest boulders I had ever seen. With a mighty roar the imprisoned waters burst through the trap to plunge into a deep wide pool full of great smooth rocks which sulked just beneath our boat, churning the racing waters into a sort of whirlpool before spreading out into the shallows. We found ourselves trapped over the hidden boulders and for what seemed an age we fought the current to manoeuvre the craft into shallower water and comparative safety. Aching with exhaustion I refused to go further by boat but the next problem was to find some safe spot in which to leave our precious boat. The force of the water would have torn it away from its mooring and in the end we had to drag it ashore and haul it into a small tree where it rested like a giant bird's nest. I had no wish to be marooned in that wild place and had the boat been swept away there would have been no possible means of returning to our house. We walked on to the head of the rapids clambering over the scattered boulders and wading through the shallow pools. We wanted to be able to say truthfully that we had been there, but I was not eager to repeat the experience.

Our house was shaded by a giant fig tree which produced an enormous crop of luscious looking fruits, juicy pink and seedy. Unlike the figs which grew in the garden at home these grew on short stems out of the main trunk of the jungle giant and in clusters along the larger branches. The ants loved them and when the over-ripe fruits fell to the ground to burst and cover everything with their succulent juice and seeds and fill the air with the tangy smell of fermentation, we had to watch our step for the giant red ants would swarm everywhere. Despite the tempting sweet succulence I never tasted those figgy fruits leaving them all to the red giants which marched through our house in relentless columns making our lives a misery with their painful bites. One problem was to protect my young son during his afternoon nap. In the end I outwitted the pests by using a rubber air mattress and inflating only the outer ring; he would sleep peacefully in the boat-like bed surrounded by a protective circle of Derris powder, the only thing I found that those red giants were afraid of.

I asked friend "Ghengis" if the figs were edible and a look of horror came over his expressive face. He clutched his stomach and with heart rending groans fell to the ground feigning death. Remembering the affair of the carrion lily when I had ignored his advice to my acute embarrassment I decided to take this warning to heart and treat the figs as a deadly poison.

The first time I slept in that jungle house was one I shall never forget. I had expected the night jungle to be a place of silence with the birds and insects asleep but not a bit of it. To begin with there was a bird with a mournful cry like a wailing banshee. We had taken two of our small Palaung friends from Mankai village with us and with pale faces and trembling voices they insisted that it was no bird but lost souls calling in the graveyard across the river. That was not a good start to my first experience of the jungle life but I busied myself cooking supper which we ate by the light of two oil lamps.

Darkness fell abruptly before 7 p.m. in the evening for we nestled in the depths of the narrow gorge with the jungle covered hills rising steeply above us and as the last glimmer of light vanished behind the ridge that jungle closed in on us with a blood-chilling variety of sounds such as one might expect to suffer in a bad dream; the jungle nights were evidently theatres of high drama. Sleep was impossible and I lay on my hard bamboo bench which served as a bed at night and listened to the clamour. It must have been around midnight when a sudden awful silence fell as though the living jungle was waiting for something with bated breath and it was then I heard a new sound. It was a familiar noise and I had heard it before, at home in England when the family cat sharpened his claws on the furniture and purred. Shaken by the realisation that this one would not be the kind of cat to fondle I listened to its steady purring for a few minutes then unable to stand the suspense any longer I crept across the tiny room to wake Piet. I suppose a good many men have had the experience of being awakened in the middle of the night by their wives and told to get up and put the cat outside, but my husband was not amused at being roused from his slumbers by a wild eyed woman brandishing a dah and demanding he should dash out into the night to chase away a maurading leopard. I returned to my uncomfortable bed to listen, the deep silence convincing me that the creature was about to attack. At any moment I thought wildly it would burst through the flimsy bamboo door and carry me off helpless and screaming, my imagination ran riot, I would put up a fight before I made a supper for that cat I decided and I waited, sleepless, with the dah across my knees.

It must have been about 3 a.m. when again I heard ominous sounds, hoarse shouts, the jangle of harness and a pounding of hooves which seemed to come from the hillside just above us. I knew of a track up there and that it was often used by dacoits when they came on pillaging forays to the surrounding villages. What if they knew of our house and came to rest there until the Ferry Service opened at dawn? I leapt to my feet, again rousing Piet telling him we must get to the boat and escape to the safety of the upper river, but by then the sounds were nearer and it had become obvious that it was a party of muleteers setting out before dawn to some distant village. They were on the other side of the river and the sounds had been deflected onto the hill above us.

By the second night I was too tired to even notice the noisy commotion without and would not have cared if half a dozen hungry leopards had been battering at the door. Jungle life was not as easy and carefree as I had imagined. To get water meant that long tiring paddle upstream and I realised how precious it could be, for to waste it or spill it would mean another trip to the freshwater spring. The firewood had to be collected and the hillside above our house proved impossible to climb. The steep slope was of loose shale and every step forward loosed an avalanche of small stones, this meant long and tiring walks to less difficult slopes, and I soon found that every minute of our day had to be carefully planned unless we were to tire ourselves out retracing our steps in search of something forgotten or lost.

The last night of that first never-to-be-forgotten weekend at our jungle house was racked by a violent storm. The winds howled around our flimsy dwelling but to my surprise it rocked a little yet remained unscathed; the Shan housebuilders had been making those same flimsy dwellings for centuries, their only materials were the bamboos, and tall grasses they made into a thatch which was surprisingly waterproof although when the fires raged around in the near vicinity the flying sparks set fire to it on a number of occasions. Luckily for us our friend Ghengis was not far away and the house survived.

We set out for home only to find the road blocked by a fallen tree uprooted by the night's storm; it had slipped down the steep hillside to land head down on the road. The rock walls rose, impassable, on our left and on our right a sheer precipice fell several hundred feet to the ravine below. We either had to reverse for several miles back to the village or set about the task of hacking our way through the mass of branches which had crumpled into a solid barrier across the road. Our only tools were a rather blunt dah and a small pruning knife but undaunted by the size of our task we took turns with the two Palaung boys to hack at the main branches, to swing on the end of those branches to keep open the cut and to push the pieces over the precipice. After an hour and a half of gruelling work we had cleared a tiny space on the precipice side of the road and Piet managed to drive the Land Rover through with only inches to spare. We had been spurred on in our task by the thought that at any moment some other vehicle would round the bend and we would have help but none came and thankfully we continued our journey home, tired, blistered but triumphant.

Not all our weekends at Lilu were enjoyable. During the monsoon season the river would rise as much as thirteen feet in a few hours, the whole beach area would be flooded, the ferry unable to operate and our boat quite useless in the raging torrent even had we been able to reach the boathouse across the swollen Nam Ko-ai River. Whole trees would be swept away in the floods to charge down river, rising and falling in the water like monstrous serpents rearing up their long necks. This flooding was always a signal for a "gathering" of the frogs. They would congregate by the tens of thousands and "sing". It was an eerie and unforgettable experience to stand at the waters edge and listen to that monstrous orchestra as it groaned and sighed filling the whole valley with weird vibrant sound which echoed across the vast shallow lake which had once been the beach. No wonder the local people dedicated those sighing sands to the Water Nat. Sometimes clouds of minute midges would swarm over the sand to add to the misery of heat and humidity, and on one such day we had retreated to the shade of the only tree on the beach. It was a stunted and mis-shapen little tree, surrounded by tall nettle-like weeds which seemed to repel the flies, and it marked the limits of the sand. Hoping to escape the attentions of the insects we had just submerged in the patch of cool vegetation when we saw three Shan men hurrying down a track from the road above. They stopped at the water's edge and stripped off all their clothing. This was surprising enough as those people were modest to the point of prudishness but I stared at them amazed and fascinated. They were tattooed from head to foot in a dark blue lacy pattern and looked as though they wore long sleeved vest and tights, only a narrow strip around the loins gleamed whitely, stark and untouched against the blue patterning on the rest of their bodies which only made the whole appearance more barbaric. Even their shaven heads seemed to be covered by a blue lace skull cap.

Much time and pain must have gone into their unusual birthday-suits, and it certainly added to their air of villainy which brought visions of Mongol Hordes to mind. They dashed into the flood waters and dragged out a huge wicker basket, a fish trap which I had missed when paddling nearby. Each man in turn thrust his arms deep into the trap and pulled out handfuls of gleaming silvery flapping fish which he would then hurl with absolute ferocity onto the rocks, time and again, until all sign of life was gone and at the same time those fierce naked painted men were chanting a wild song as they leaped and twirled their bodies like frenzied dervishes. It was a disgusting orgy of death which went on until the last of the fish was out of the basket. Then they re-set the trap and dragged it back into the water. They squatted around the pile of fish sharing out the catch equally, then they dressed, put their fish into conical wicker baskets which strapped onto the back of their waist belts, and then they hurried away up the track again. I breathed a sigh of relief, we had not been spotted by them as they passed our bed of weeds; their reactions on finding they had been observed by foreigners, one of them a woman, might not have been friendly and I kicked myself for having left the ciné camera in the Land Rover. What a sensational film it would have made! Sadly I never again saw those men and their fishy death dance although I carried the camera around the beach hopefully for many weekends after that.

One hot March morning we had arrived at the beach to find confusion everywhere. It looked as though a battle had been waged there, dozens of small craters had appeared on the grassy banks and water meadows around the Nam Ko-ai River. I saw two small girls digging furiously; suddenly they pounced on something in the hole they had dug and I saw them drop whatever they had caught into a large tin then the whole process was repeated. I went across to join them curious to know what treasure they were seeking. They took the lid off the tin and showed me their catch, milky white cicada grubs almost on the point of hatching. In just a few days time the cicadas would emerge from their burrows in great swarms and disperse into the surrounding jungle they told me. The older girl spotted another luckless insect which she dragged out of the burrow, tore off its legs then dropped the mutilated live insect into the tin. They would eat them for dinner that night she explained, if you could find the grubs before they hatched they were much tastier to eat.

A week later we arrived at the river to find that a row of tall poles had been driven into the sand at intervals along the whole length of the beach. Being interested in all new activities on our beach I went down to investigate to find that the sand was swarming with cicadas. The big hatch had begun. The cicadas were not quite ready to fly and were drying out in the hot sand. They rose up under my feet in great clouds, their shrill calls disturbing every insect along the river bank. The giant flies crashed into my face, battered my arms and legs, deafened me with noise that threatened to split the ear drums and inflicted painful scratches with the sharp spikes on their legs. I saw that the poles were covered with a sticky paste, they were giant fly-papers. The crowd of men and children would run along the sand disturbing the newly hatched cicadas which would take flight in their thousands and the unlucky ones would blunder into the poles to stick fast. Each family had marked out a section of the beach and they worked ceaselessly collecting the wretched insects as soon as the poles were covered and I saw them tear off legs and wings before dropping the still living cicadas into deep tins. The noise was unbelievable and the beach more crowded than a seaside resort on a hot summer's day, and the villagers would remain there until every last cicada had hatched. It seemed that the first showers of the year were a signal for that rather macabre harvest and I wondered that there were any cicadas left to ensure a "crop" for the following year.

We gave up all idea of having a quiet swim and returned home leaving the cicadas to their fate for it seemed that those giant flies were outside the protective principles of Buddhism.

21

Journey to Namhkam

Everybody talked of Namhkam, they said it had the most famous market in Burma where tribespeople from many different States would gather and just across the river was China. If you were lucky you would see a glittering array of colourful costumes and characters. We set out early one morning, tourists for once. The journey to Lashio took about five hours and Namhkam was almost double that travelling distance beyond Lashio. The first town of any size after Lashio was Hsenwi and a few miles short of the town Zan Lyn suddenly turned onto a stony track saying there was something interesting in the trees ahead.

The small grove was shrouded in billowing clouds of steam and we found it was another hot spring. Crystal clear water gushed out of a fissure in a wall of bright green rock and flowed into two small concrete tanks. A woman and her two children were bathing in the larger tank, splashing happily in the hot water. Below several women were doing their weekly wash. I tasted the water and found it rather bitter but without the usual sulphurous flavour. Zan Lyn said it was a famous Spa and was said to cure skin diseases. We drove on through Hsenwi, past the massive ruins of an old palace and skirted a large lake which was covered with giant lotus pads through which the huge white flowers rose stiffly above the water on long stems. The scenery became rugged and mountainous and as we rose out of the early morning mists I saw great jagged peaks rising stark and grey against the sky. Looking back across a sea of white mist I caught a glimpse of the green hills of Tawnpeng in the far distance. Ahead of us rose a great wall of sharp tooth-like peaks gaunt, grey and

inhospitable, they loomed over us forming a "divide". Once
across the Pass we found a plateau of waving grasses and
sunflowers, ahead a country of rounded hills, scorched brown
grass, deep dales and then a wooded hill section before
KutKai. We had no time to linger there except for a cup of
tea and we left down an avenue of cherry trees which took us
to the Ghat section and we could look back over that gentle
plateau towards those strange jagged peaks. The small stunted
oak-like trees were in their autumnal colours of golds and reds
but at the top of the hill we again found ourselves on bare
down-like hills where we came to MonGyn. There the road
divided, straight on for China where a few miles ahead lay the
only road bridge to cross the Shweli River. It was a desolate
spot and Zan Lyn said the Chinese guards watched all visitors
to the bridge suspiciously through binoculars from their post
on the other side.

We turned left at MonGyn and from there the road began
to twist downhill through pineapple plantations until at last
we could see the Shweli on our right and beyond it the purple
hills of Yunnan. The people working in the fields were
Kachins and the women wore the traditional handwoven red
tapestry kilts and silver decorated turbans. In Musé we
stopped for a meal at a Chinese restaurant and I noticed that
there were more Chinese people around that border town than
we were accustomed to seeing. The road ran steeply downhill
following the Shweli. In the paddy fields the rice had been cut
and small stacks built on wooden frames were dotted around
the fields. It was harvest time and small groups of people could
be seen flailing the rice whilst blindfolded bullocks circled
round trampling on the bundles of rice stalks. The river I saw
was several hundred yards wide. We saw a few canoes but no
sign of life on the Chinese side. Still the road wound steeply
down. I stared with surprise at curious round wells each with
a pagoda roof and with a long handled scoop. There seemed to
be one in every field, and then just as the light was fading we
saw Namhkam, a long straggling town with a large open
square, in the centre of which stood a pagoda surrounded by
tall poles topped with gilded crowns and fluttering from each a
long silken prayer flag. The next day was the big market we
had come so far to see. It was certainly a brilliant bustling
throng, full of Kachin women in their red kilts and silver

jewellery and Lishaw girls in black dresses weighted down with
heavy silver ornaments. The border was now closed but at one
time the tribes from the other side of the river would always
come to Namhkam for the market. The stalls were hanging
with the handwoven red Kachin bags, and flock mattresses
covered in the brightest of cotton prints. There were displays
of fruit and vegetables, flowers, jewellery and clothing. In fact
whatever you might need could be bought there.

On a small hIll overlooking the town we found Dr
Seagrave's hospital. He came to greet us, a massive old man
with a vice-like handshake. Proudly he showed us the old
hospital which was still in use and built of smooth rounded
stones which he and a few helpers had gathered from the river
bed. We were taken round the new buildings and the doctor
told us he no longer operated as his hands were too shaky. I
laughed for mine was still smarting from the handshake. The
hospital was his life's work and he hoped it would go on caring
for the people long after he had gone. We parted with a stern
warning from the doctor.

'Take care not to get caught up in local politics' he said
with some feeling.

Later a friend in Lashio told us it had been his unpleasant
duty to arrest Dr Seagrave; he often saw the doctor in Lashio
he said but could never bring himself to speak of a matter
which time refused to blot out of his memory.

Dr Seagrave had dedicated his life to the Namhkam hospital
and he died there after forty years serving the people he loved.

22

The Crooked Valley of Precious Stones

In Burma the name Mogok meant rubies and at first I did not realise that the precious valley was so close to us. In the dry season we would often walk to the hill top shrine of LoiPra and from there we looked across to MongMit which was on Tawngpeng's western border. The ruby tract was just across the valley and yet there were no precious stones in Tawngpeng. Mogok was originally the property of the Shan Sawbwa and the name of the valley, Mainkoot, is Shan meaning crooked valley. Years ago I was told, a farmer from MongMit lost his way and wandered into a deep crooked valley, there he saw crows pecking at something red which lay scattered amongst the rocks. He took some of the red pebbles and presented them to his Sawbwa. They were rubies. The hill above that precious valley was called Kyeer-Tawng, the hill where the crows call. In 1360 a Burmese king took over Mogok in exchange for twelve river settlements and the ruby tract passed out of Shan jurisdiction.

Not so many years ago one only had to walk up the hill slopes, uproot a small shrub and shake the earth from its roots to get a shower of rubies, but now all the surface stones are gone. People had been digging there for hundreds of years yet still the supply had not been exhausted. Mogok was like a jewel itself set in encircling hills above a clear lake. Driving down to the mines in the early hours you would see workers hurrying along, Shan men with tan coloured pants hitched up to their knees, white collarless shirts and on their heads the conical Shan hats which served as sunshades or umbrellas according to the weather. Women too, hurrying to work perhaps with a flat panning basket on their heads, their dress the inevitable black cotton tamein and white aingyi. The mines were all surface worked and during the dry season a rich mine owner would have pits dug, often fifty feet deep or more, down to the ruby bearing tract. In the monsoon season these rich mine owners would keep their pits open with pumps which sent streams of muddy water coursing through different channels and levels to be sifted by women who would pay small premiums for the privilege. Groups of workers, both men and women, would be employed to sift through the mud brought up from the pits and they used the flat panning baskets. In every little stream one would see groups of women walking up and down the stream bed feeling for the stones with their feet. Finding a likely spot they would scoop up a pan of mud and wash it in the clear water sorting through the residue of pebbles, with experienced eyes and fingers picking out a ruby here, a topaz there. If you walked out barefoot to join them they would smile indulgently at your excitement if you found some small stones and might allow you to keep one. Each of those hard working "miners" hoped to find a really good stone, then their fortunes would be made hopes dashed by nationalisation when all precious stones found at the jewel mines were declared to be the property of the Burma Government.

At the larger mines the work was done more professionally with all the sifted stones piled onto long wooden tables to be sorted by experts, graded for size, quality and colour. These stones, rubies, sapphires, amethyst, zircon, topaz, aqua-marine, lapis-lazuli and spinels would be cut and stored, boxful after boxful of glittering jewels, precious and semi-precious, well guarded for now sales are carefully controlled by the Government.

The red spinels though not valuable look so much like rubies that they are in great demand and are used in much of the cheaper jewellery sold throughout Burma.

Another stone for which Burma is famous is jade, found chiefly in Hong Kong Valley to the north of Mogaung. This lovely soft stone is greatly prized and becomes more scarce with demand.

Amongst the hill peoples the idea of putting their money into a bank was unthinkable; instead it was the custom to buy gold, silver and jewels to adorn the women and when times were hard these could be cashed.

The Mahadevi had some lovely jewels and she told me that once a year two women came from Mogok bringing jewels for her to see. Would I like them to call on me she asked. I would certainly be interested to see them I told her but doubted if I would be able to afford to buy any.

It was some months later on one very wet August morning that the Haw jeep drove up to disgorge the Mahadevi's personal attendant May-de-La, a senior Nun, and two elderly ladies. These two ladies were the jewel sellers and they might have been just two charming old ladies come for tea. Each carried a large wicker bag and out of these they drew dozens of paper packets, and these they opened to display sets of gold bracelets heavily encrusted with rubies or sapphires, amethysts or jade and each had matching earrings, sets of buttons and hair ornaments. They had many packets of loose stones to match the bracelets, gold combs and necklaces, and pearls as well as moonstone and topaz. These were the most popular choice of the local ladies, they told me. My dining room table suddenly looked like Aladdin's cave and I wondered how those two rather frail women dared to travel around by bus and taxi, a fortune tucked under their arms, when the hill roads were infested with the fiercest of dacoits, but they accepted the risk putting their trust in fate.

The first time I had seen any of the Mahadevi's jewels had been at a farewell luncheon she had given for H.L.B. Silently I had admired the lovely amethysts, but our friend was not so restrained and showed his approval enthusiastically. With a mischevious smile he asked Mahadevi's permission to tell me the story of her crown.

Many of the senior Sawbwas had attended the Coronation in 1937 and Tawngpeng had been very impressed by all he saw. He admired the State Crowns and decided to have a gold replica of the Queen's Crown made for Mahadevi. She had been delighted with the gift and wore it on every possible occasion for about a year. It was some time before the Sawbwa realised that the crown was no longer seen even on the more important occasions and puzzled, he asked what had become of it. Mahadevi's reply rather took him aback. She had decided that the crown really did not suit her and had exchanged it for some bracelets. At this point of the story the

Sawbwa began to laugh and Mahadevi to look rather embarrassed. She turned to me saying she was sure I would understand, for after all no woman could be expected to wear a new hat forever, and that was how she had felt about the crown. I held back a smile wondering just how many women in the world had gold crowns to tire of.

23

The Rape of the Silver Hill

Only once did I visit Namtu and found it a depressing and rather sinister place. The Land Rover blew a tyre as we drove through Bawdwin and our driver, Zan Lyn, walked on to Namtu to get help, leaving us in the stranded vehicle beneath a great rounded bare blackened hill which had been stripped of all vegetation by the polluted air. It had seemed a place of absolute desolation.

Waste products from the smelters found their way into the Namtu River and so to Lilu, turning our favourite stretch of water into an opaque grey soup fit for neither man nor beast to drink. On one occasion when the mines closed down for a week we found the change in the river almost unbelievable. The water had become clear and sparkling with every rock and pebble on the bottom easily seen as well as the shoals of fish of all sizes which normally were invisible in the murky waters.

I thought of all the people of the river villages whose diet consisted mainly of fish. Surely their health must suffer eventually as a result of all that pollution.

I found the Silver Hill a strange place. It was like a great black blot on a landscape famous for its beauty but the drab unloveliness of Bawdwin and Namtu was a result of riches not poverty.

At the turn of the century the discovery of a small mountain of rich lead-zinc ore at Bawdwin had caused quite a sensation and mining engineers sent to investigate the area were to re-discover the ancient Chinese silver mines. Deep inside the Black Hill they found forgotten galleries which extended for great distances. Silver had been extracted at Bawdwin for many centuries until in 1860 the Chinese miners† went on strike an it was that rebellion which resulted in the Chinese abandoning their search for silver and so the old mine was lost for many years.

Silver was greatly prized by the ancient Chinese and despite the distances and difficulties of transporting it they had worked the Bawdwin mines for centuries perfecting a method of extracting almost pure silver from the ore. The residue of lead and zinc they had thrown away and so over the centuries the mountain of ore had grown.

The report from the survey team was exciting: thousands of tons of high grade ore lay on the surface waiting for someone to find a use for it and it was not long before a company was formed to exploit the dumps of ore and re-open the old mine. The mines manager told us that much of the silver lay within the boundaries of Tawngpeng and that the ore was transported from the face on an underground railway system which took it to the modern plant at Namtu where it was crushed and smelted.

After the fall of the King of Burma in 1885 when the Shan Rulers had agreed to become a part of the British Empire to be administered from India, we had educated those Princes in the complexities of Western style Government. Men of the Frontier Service went to those remote kingdoms to offer help and advice until 1922 when the Shans took over the reins of Government and the new policy of peace and co-operation brought the first signs of prosperity to the Shan States.

Over the centuries the Chinese had exploited the mines taking away all the riches they extracted. Later the British and in the end the Burmese were to have control of that wealth and from the beginning the Shans had little say or share in that great Silver Bonanza.‡ We were always hearing talk of the mines being worked out but despite the rumours it has managed to carry on. Certainly it brought work to the peoples of the Shan Hills but I wonder if the story of the Shans would have been happier had they been able to have a fair share of all the riches extracted from the bowels of their black evil-

---

† The Panthays = Mohammedan Chinese Miners who rebelled in 1860 causing the eventual closure of the old Silver Mine.

‡ Lords of the Sunset = Maurice Collis — 1936. Pages 234-235 — "We owe the Shans an amende honourable."
"They trust us to do well for them, Or at least, fairly well;—"

looking hill. Would the descendants of those old Heavenly Lords still be warring with those of the Sunrise Kings as they do today in their vain search for a national identity.

24

Hill Walks

We were regular visitors to Loi Pra and Loi Seng, the two
highest of the hill top shrines, and sometimes if we were feeling
especially energetic at the end of the monsoon when the air
was washed clear of smoke and dust enabling one to see vast
distances we would drive up to the Pass on the Kyaukme road
and walk along an ancient track to Loi HsamHsip, one of the
highest hills in the district. It was one of the main roads to
Kyaukhpu, an isolated and unfriendly village where some of
the inhabitants had a rather sinister pastime as was later
proved. Sometimes on our walk we would meet a party of
Kyaukhpu Palaungs returning home after a shopping expedition. The men and young boys rode small sturdy ponies and
always passed us without a word. The women and very small
children would walk behind their menfolk, and heavy bags
supported by wide straps across the forehead, hung down their
backs. We always greeted them with smiles and a few words of
Palaung but they showed little interest beyond a surly
greeting.

They turned left down the hill to their village, but our road
led us straight on along the top of the ridge. Much of the way
was across wooded slopes and there I found many flowers and
shrubs I had not seen at the lower elevations. There was a
pretty shrub which produced bunches of tubular flowers in
white and lemon with a strong sweet scent, and just below the
Pass I found the lovely pink Kalmia, but all my efforts to
propagate them were a failure. In sheltered spots just at the
tree line I found yet another balsam, taller than those at the
lower elevations and with hard woody stems, leaves and curled
shrimp flowers of darkest crimson. Like the orchids, each

flower or shrub had its own elevation and grew nowhere else. On the highest hills I discovered a large white orchid with a lingering sweet scent. This lovely orchid seemed to thrive in the cold winds of those inhospitable hill tops. As we reached the higher slopes the vegetation seemed to shrink to dense thickets of waist high shrubs and then the bare grassy slopes of the summit. It was at the divide between the grass and shrubs that I stumbled over an eagle. It suddenly swept into the air from under my feet, some small creature in its sharp talons, and I gasped as the enormous fierce looking brown bird almost knocked me off my feet. It had a wingspan of at least six feet, its breast was softly speckled with beige and it was streamlined like a modern jet aircraft as it soared high into the air gliding on the air currents. I never tired of watching those great birds wheeling and swooping against the clear blue sky.

From the top of Loi HsamHsip on a clear day one could see to the Southern States on the one side of the ridge and to China on the other. Loi TawngKyaw was the highest point of the district, and its bare grassy slopes rose to 7,478ft. behind Aram village.

It was a challenge we could not ignore. When word of our proposed expedition got around the houseboys all asked if they could accompany us. We teased Ba Than Gyaw when he turned up on the morning of the expedition armed with a heavy dah. Was he expecting to meet bandits or bears we asked? Fortunately he was resolute and we were later to be glad he had been prepared to carry the cumbersome dah. It was a forty minute drive to Aram over a rough road and from there we had to walk. As we approached the village a small boy suddenly darted out into the street shouting as he ran ahead of us "Dah Bo, Dah Yah Bo ha eu", we had learned enough Palaung to know he was announcing that the Honourable Grandfather and Grandmother had come. For the first time I realised that we were no longer "The Foreigners", that mischievious little boy at Zayangyi had given us a new name and we were strangers no longer. Our visit seemed to please those austere, withdrawn Palaungs of Aram who welcomed us with friendly smiles. They pointed out a well beaten track beyond the village and we set out following the contours of the hill, hairpinning around the ridges, past busy Gurkha settlements and a Lishaw village. We saw large plots of vegetables and maize and above the villages small boys tended the herds of buffalo on the steep hillsides. It was after almost three hours of hard walking that we reached the towering slopes of Loi TawngKyaw and began the serious climb. It was steep and slippery. There were gaunt trees festooned with mosses and lichen, unusual creeping plants and ferns. One tree was covered with the pink pleione orchids. Then we found a barrier to our progress, a wide belt of trees beneath which the undergrowth was so lush and tall that without the much despised dah we would never have got through. A leopard roared somewhere deep in the wood and I felt a stinging sensation spread across my neck. Looking closely at the tall undergrowth I was pushing my way through, I suddenly realised that I was standing in a bed of giant nettles which towered well over my head. Once we had hacked our way through the giant undergrowth we came out into a sort of petrified forest, a hillside of dead trees their stark rotting branches hanging with ragged curtains of grey mosses. It was a weird and desolate place and then the clouds closed in around us and we reached the top in a heavy mist. We descended to more sunny spots and found a grassy knoll where we picnicked. Lured on by the desire to see what lay beyond the high ridge we walked on to find we were no wiser, in front of us rose another higher ridge and a land which seemed empty, bare and unfriendly. We retraced our steps to Aram not daring to linger too long on that bleak hill if we valued our safety.

25

The Fruit Thieves

We had a thief in the garden. Whenever the Mali advised waiting a few more days before picking the delicious green skinned bananas the thief would strike that very night. It was the same with the peaches, strawberries, pineapples, jak fruit and mayman-thi's. The best fruit would be taken just before it was really ripe. I was beginning to doubt the Mali's honesty when I caught the thief red-handed, or perhaps pawed would be a better description.

The mayman-thi trees were very tall with thick straight trunks and no low branches to make climbing easy. In September they would be laden with small round black plums which hung in bunches like grapes high in the top of the tree. Walking through the garden before breakfast one morning I was suddenly showered with plums as a small animal leapt out of the tree leaving behind a strong scent of musk in the air. It looked rather like a large fluffy tailed Siamese Sealpoint cat. Its slender body was creamy beige and it had short, chocolate-coloured legs, a slender head with curved muzzle, tiny rounded ears and, the dark mask one associates with the Siamese cats. The Palaungs called it the "honeymoon cat" because they were always to be seen in pairs and seemed to have happy, loving, playful natures. I was interested to find out more about those beautiful thieves yet although I visited Zoos in Rangoon, Bangkok and Chiengmai they had not heard of anything which remotely resembled my honeymoon cats. Eventually I received an interested reply from the curator of the London Zoo. He suggested that it might possibly be a member of the Palm Civet family but without a photograph, or better still a live specimen, it was not possible to identify it with any certainty.

I resolved to take up animal collecting seriously and when the fruit season came round again and the lovely little raiders returned once more to the garden I called in Aung Miet, Deputy Headman of Zayangyi village, who was one of our staff. He was a kind, gentle fellow, always anxious to please and a mine of information about the local flora and fauna. He was immediately full of enthusiasm for the cat project and dashed off saying that he would have one of the fruit thieves for my collection in a day or so. He assured me he could capture one without harming it. A few days later as I walked across the lawn close by the three giant mayman-thi trees I was suddenly swept off my feet, flung headlong to the ground with my ankle caught tightly in a wire noose. Aung Miet had caught something big, Yah Bo herself!

Luckily the trap had not been intended to finish off its captive. I thought of the lethal porcupine traps set by the Malis in India when the victim would either be impaled on sharpened stakes or crushed by a load of rocks and decided that I had had a lucky escape. The two Alsatians had run on ahead of me and must have missed being caught in the trap by only inches.

The laugh was certainly on me and those happy little thieves were probably having a quiet chuckle at my expense like the houseboys who had a grandstand view of the event from the kitchen window. I called off the project telling myself firmly that the lovely chocolate and cream cats were happier left to their perpetual honeymoon and the world's zoos would have to manage without them.

26

The Forgotten Princesses

The young ruler of a neighbouring state had married a European girl and we were to become good friends. We would call at the Haw whenever we drove through the town on our way to Kyaukme and sometimes she would persuade us to stay on for lunch. She was tall and good looking, her long black hair coiled in the local style, her dress always the ankle length black skirt and white aingyi as worn by most Shan women. She had two small daughters and her romance was almost like a modern fairytale. She had met the Sawbwa at University and they had fallen in love. He had warned her that it would not be easy to adjust to the simple life of a Shan lady. She would be isolated from all Western influences and culture. As his Mahadevi she would be able to take part in local affairs only as custom allowed. His was a strict Buddhist world but he had not asked her to change her religious beliefs unless she felt sincerely that she must. As the new Mahadevi she had thrown herself completely into integrating with the Shan way of life, she had become a Burmese citizen and spoke the languages fluently.

Everyone had tried to make things easy for her she said, but there had been some embarrassing moments. One morning when practising her newly aquired Shan she had asked the maid to brush her hair. There was no reaction and so she repeated the order and the girl had giggled helplessly. The Mahadevi's rebuke at what had seemed a show of insolence produced a flood of tears and the girl had dashed out of the french windows, across the lawn to a pony grazing nearby. My friend had forgotten the five tones in the Shan language: the words for hair and horse were identical except for the tones.

Seeing the maid begin to groom the pony was too much and the young Mahadevi sought out her husband who was in conference surrounded by his ministers and advisers. Her tearful story had reduced him to hearty laughter and the rest of the Council obviously thought it a very funny story. She said she was ready to board the first aeroplane bound for Europe.

As I came to know her better I asked if she had found it difficult to change her religious beliefs. I had called one morning to find her in an unhappy, depressed state of mind over her favourite cat which had been run over by a car. For three days she had personally tended the dying animal doing what little she could to relieve its agony. The battle between the principles of East and West was causing her a great deal of heart searching. At first the difference in their religious beliefs had not seemed to matter she told me, and then she saw that whenever her little daughters needed advice on even the smallest matter they would go to their father, aunts, friends, their nurse but never to their mother. She began to resent being shut out of a part of their lives and came to realise that unless she joined them in that last principle they could never be a truly united family and she had not regretted her decision. It was only when some incident such as the injured cat put her to the test that she had any doubts.

I wish I could say that my charming friend and her family had lived happily ever after as fairytale princesses do, but this was not to be. Her husband's only interest was to modernise the farming methods of his people. He had invested in new labour saving machinery, new and improved strains of fruit and was full of plans for a canning factory which he was sure would create more jobs for a growing population and ensure a future prosperity.

After General Ne Win handed back powers to the Civil Administration in 1960 the situation in the Shan States began to deteriorate. The Cession of the Sawbwas only aggravated the troubles and a vociferous majority began to call for a national identity. Conditions in the Shan States had always been made difficult by the dacoits and it was not long before these gangs banded together into small private armies and it was difficult to know which of the ambushes and atrocities were the work of dacoits out for gain or insurgents with ideals, calling for self-determination for the Shans.

There were frequent and ferocious attacks on the trains. No road was safe for travellers and any Burman caught in an ambush would be singled out, led away into the jungle never to be seen again. Inevitably the Burmese Army began to tighten control on the trouble spots.

On the last occasion I was to meet the Mahadevi and her husband she told me that it was becoming increasingly difficult to work their pineapple plantations because of insurgent activities. They could no longer visit their Summer Palace because the surrounding hills were over-run by the Shan army and to go there would only have made the Burmese suspect them of being in collusion with the rebels and they had enough troubles without that.

They had decided to live permanently in Rangoon. Already she had sent all their valued possessions and the air-conditioning plant to the Rangoon Haw. Soon they would make the move and she hoped we would call on her sometimes. Just two months after that conversation the Burmese Revolutionary Council led a coup for the second time and on March 2nd 1962 the Burmese President, Prime Minister, Chief Justice, prominent politicians and most of the Shan Government administration as well as the Shan Sawbwas were arrested in a dawn swoop. By some twist of fate the Mahadevi had chosen that very morning to drive to Rangoon with her two daughters but they got no further than the state boundary and they returned to the Haw under armed escort. Her husband had left in the early hours of that same morning to fly down to Rangoon, but they were not destined to be re-united that evening as they had planned.

During the year that followed we made many attempts to see the Mahadevi only to be turned away by armed guards at the Haw gates. I wrote to her, sent magazines and books but received no reply. When the time for our final departure came we applied to the Army Commander for permission to see her and say goodbye but once again we were met by a refusal. We did learn that our letters and books were eventually reaching her and that she was not allowed to reply. A day or so before we finally left the Shan States I received a brief message from her. She was grateful for the books and hoped I would continue to write although she would not be allowed to reply.

They were well but without the air-conditioning plant the Haw was unbearably hot and she was not allowed to use the swimming pool which remained empty in an untended garden. She was hoping to get permission to take her two daughters to Rangoon for dental treatment but so far even that had been refused. That was the last I heard from my charming friend.

Later whilst living in North Thailand I met a former Minister of the dissolved Shan Government, one of the few prominent Shans to escape the net on that fateful second day of March. He had made his home in Chiengmai and had a silver factory there, producing silverware in an exquisite blend of Burmese and Thai art. He had called to see me hoping for some news of his family, but if he had expected to find in me a strong supporter of the insurgents he must have been disappointed as my sympathies were entirely with the Palaungs who wanted no part in the troubles. He stared at me thoughtfully for a while and then, perhaps with the intention of shocking me, he said bluntly that my friend's husband was dead.

'Shot whilst resisting arrest as he was about to board his private aircraft' he told me the Burmese report had stated. 'We called it cold blooded murder' said my Shan visitor and he said he believed that the Mahadevi had not been told of her husband's death up to that time. She was still at the Haw and under close arrest; no-one had been allowed to see her.

I found his cool statement hard to accept and hoped that one day I would hear of a happier ending to the princess's life-story. Many times since that day I have written to friends asking for news of the Mahadevi but always my questions have been politely ignored. I had decided not to send any more letters to her knowing that anything posted in North Thailand, with its border so near to insurgent territory, would only heap suspicion on her and I had no wish to cause her more trouble. Regretfully I tried to put her out of my mind and hoped she would understand the neglect if ever she heard the reason, but there is still a question which troubles my conscience: as a Burmese citizen she could be detained at the General's pleasure but surely the Mahadevi and her two pretty daughters are not still locked up in that empty palace in a remote Shan State capital, forgotten princesses? Have those two sweet children grown to womanhood as prisoners in their own home without any hope of a fairytale prince to come to their rescue?

And what of the many Shan Sawbwas who were arrested on that fateful March day nearly twenty-six years ago? The ones I knew were kindly honest statesmen. but their crime it seems was having been born to rule the rebellious Shans. Will they also remain forgotten for ever by a world which talks glibly of Human Rights?.

27

A Glimpse of Buddhism

Astrologers chose the hour when Burma should leave the British Empire to become an Independent Republic. This was to be 4.20 a.m. on 4th January 1948.

Did Burma really turn back the centuries at a stroke when, under the guidance of the Prime Minister U Nu, they chose September of 1961 to declare a Theocratic State? From that time on they were to dedicate themselves to the welfare of the people both in this existence and in the innumerable others they would pass through before Neikban, the final extinction; would they ever escape from the past into the present? The Prime Minister announced that he had counted sixteen thousand problems to plague the devout in this present existence and the future held little promise of any relief. Since that time Burma gradually withdrew from the world around her, choosing to meet the future in her own quiet way.

Buddhism rules every decision made by the Burmese and Shans, their names, daily lives, where and when they build their houses, found a business or get married. The Astrologer plays almost as important a part in their lives as the Sayador.

The 2nd Anglo/Burmese war broke out in 1852, and in 1853 Mindon Min seized the Throne of Ava from his brother, King Pagan Min, after a palace revolution. King Mindon Min achieved his greatest ambition by convening the 5th Buddhist Council at Mandalay in 1854. One of the resolutions made by that council was to place a new Hti on the pinnacle of the Shwe Dragon Pagoda. It was made of gold, set with jewels and it cost an immense fortune.

After Mindon Min's death in 1878, Thibaw, son of a Shan Princess from Hsipaw State, seized the throne. In 1885

Thibaw accused the Bombay Burmah of defrauding the Burma Government over teak royalties and he imposed heavy fines on them.

This precipitated the 3rd Anglo/Burmese war and led to the defeat of King Thibaw in November 1885. In February 1886 Burma became a province of the Indian Empire.

In 1954, a century after Mindon Min's 5th Council, the 6th Buddhist Council was held in Rangoon and the Prime Minister, U Nu, realised his dream by the resolution to build a "World Peace Pagoda" known as the "Cave". This was built not far from the Inya Lake at a cost of 900,000K/- and was made as a replica of the Sarnath Cave in India, all the rocks used in its construction being brought from those Indian hills. Landscaped gardens beautify the roof of the vast artificial cave which contains portraits of the great patriarchs, but it was not as perfect as it should have been for the roof leaked and spoiled the relics and it needed a great deal of time and money to repair that great religious souvenir of World Peace.

From early childhood every important event in a Burman's life is celebrated by giving a pwé. Their devotion to religion does not spoil their enjoyment and fun and for the girls the first celebration of any significance will be an ear-boring ceremony when all relations and friends will gather to witness this first step into womanhood. The Shinpyu is perhaps the most important landmark in every boy's life and the family will save for months, sometimes years, to provide the lavish feasts and the fine clothes. In an atmosphere of supreme happiness the family will provide rich clothes for the boy to wear, an elaborately decorated car or cart to take him in procession to the Monastery where with a great deal of ceremony he will cast aside all signs of worldly riches, then with newly shaven head he will put on the saffron robes of a monk. For two weeks he will study the scriptures with many other Ko-yiens, or student monks. Some never leave but those who do return home must dedicate a week or so of each year by returning to the Kyaung and re-affirming their faith.

The Soonkway is a ceremony which is important to the Burmese as an Act of Merit and is usually given in honour of a dead relation. This is a ceremony of Feeding the Monks and may be held at the donor's house or at the Pongyi Kyaung. As the monks do not eat after mid-day the family will gather at either 5.30 a.m. or 11.00 a.m. to welcome their guests. It is the duty of the youngest member of the family to wipe the feet of each guest as he enters the house.

When all the guests are seated the oldest member of the family offers the first Soon, or offering of rice, to the candle-lit altar. Sometimes the altar would be merely a shelf with carved supports which held an image and a vase of flowers and this was in no way inferior to the rich household's elaborate carved shrine. The soft sounds of the Keezi them announce that the ceremony has begun.

The whole family would have co-operated in the preparations, in providing as lavish a meal as they could afford. There would be steaming dishes of rice, kaukswe, spicy dishes of fish or vegetables, perhaps hingo, as a special fish soup is called and typical Burmese salads, tosaya, which are made of fresh and cooked vegetables tangy with spices. Then there would be the tolec molis, nga-pi, pickled tea, sticky rice, sweetmeats, fruits in season and plain tea to drink. A great deal of trouble would have been taken over all these preparations. The Pongyis follow strict rules when eating. They must not break their food or bend low over it and they never spill their food or clatter the cutlery. They eat in complete silence broken only if the Sayador, or senior monk decides to show appreciation. When all the guests can eat no more the Sayador will say prayers and then the ceremony will be over.

We saw such a ceremony on the sunbaked terrace of a monastery, a large gathering of Pongyis sat cross-legged on the floor, their saffron robes a golden pool in the dim interior of the Zayat. A frail old lady was busy serving her guests with food and we were told that the Soonkway was in honour of the old lady's husband who had died some years before. This Act of Merit counts in retrospect and families may save for years in order to give merit to long dead relations.

Kindness, gentleness, Acts of Merit, helping those in need are a way of life. They protect and care for most small creatures and no-one would kill a fly or step on an ant. One day the headlines in the newspapers announced that the Prime Minister had ordered that all live crabs held by shopkeepers in Rangoon that week must be taken out to sea and released; this was an Act of Merit on the grand scale. To release animals or birds from captivity was a favourite way of attaining merit for the next existence and on auspicious days a rash of stalls hung with tiny wicker cages would mushroom around some of the more important shrines to be bought by many of the devotees visiting the temple, smiling girls, gentle faced old women, who would open the doors of the little cages setting the captive birds free.

They had a duty to preserve life for as long as possible even though this might cause prolonged suffering to some fatally injured animal. To my way of thinking this sometimes seemed cruel in the extreme and I often found myself tempted to interfere, I would ask myself if it could possibly be that my principles of destroying a dying, suffering animal were worse than theirs of refusing to take a life no matter what the circumstances.

Most tourists to Rangoon would pay a visit to the glorious golden Shwé Dagon which towers over the city from the midst of a veritable forest of mini pagodas, tazaungs and shrines, some just to look, some to pray, others perhaps to give water to the ancient Tree of Knowledge in the hope that it would benefit them. At the smaller Sulé Pagoda which stands in the centre of the city there was a wishing stone but only those who managed to lift the smooth worn stone would have their wishes granted. These two great golden bells were not the only shrines and places of interest which enrich the city.

A Burmese friend took us on a "pagoda crawl" and after what seemed a surfeit of shrines we came to a lovely peaceful place which I was told was a famous teaching monastery. As we entered the vast, empty, cool room a tall saffron-robed figure rose and came forward to greet us. Our friend whispered that he was a famous teacher and that when he spoke on any subject great crowds would fill the huge room to sit cross-legged on the floor, silent and attentive as the teacher paced back and forth on the long raised "cat-walk", discoursing on some point or principle from the scriptures.

The gentle, tranquil face turned in my direction. Was there anything I wished to know? He smiled as I asked about the role of women in Buddhism.

Women were in no way inferior he said, and he set out the twenty or so principles about women, their lives, education, work, and religious duties. There were five obligations a woman had towards her husband he said, and five others

which a married man must observe towards his wife. At last
the gentle voice dismissed us, the unexpected interview was
over.

'I am not sufficiently well versed in Buddhism to write at
length on the subject, but briefly, it seems that those five
obligations a wife has to her husband are to manage all
household affairs, to entertain his relations and friends, to be
faithful, and devoted, not to waste his money, and to take an
interest in everything around her. The husband should honour
his wife, respect her, love her and be faithful, give her comfort
and security and make her happy with gifts of clothes and
jewels.

I had been told that Burmese women were free from any
form of subjugation and the gentle old monk had tried to
explain that under Buddhism their women were assured of a
role, a place in a loving family whether wives, sisters, aunts or
grandmothers.

Rich devotees of the Buddhist communities will spend large
sums of money not only on the building of pagodas but also to
commission beautiful wood carvings to place in the shrines and
Zayats. Panels depicting religious texts expertly carved by
artists would always be decorated with flowers and birds, trees
which seemed to sway gracefully as though bending in a gentle
breeze.

Rural scenes were a favourite or perhaps a happy family
outing, carts and boats were popular amongst the country
people as gifts to be donated in the hope of gaining merit in an
after life. The size and cost of the gift were not important,
what mattered was the pleasure, the help given to those who
would see and use those objects. The gift of a Zayat which
would give shelter to weary travellers gained great merit for
the donor but the less costly gift of a shelf to hold a waterpot
so that those same weary travellers could quench their thirst,
or a carved panel to please and sooth tired eyes would also be
considered very meritorious.

The Burmese love to have beautiful things around them and
over the centuries the carvers of wood had become masters of
their art. Nothing was too difficult for them and the skills were
jealously passed on from father to son. No matter what the
customer asked for, from the familiar to the fantastic, it would
be undertaken without question. The apprenticeship was long

and the trainee carvers would first be taught to draw the traditional designs. Later they would learn to use an adze and to cut those designs onto the timber. The finer details, the intricate pierced work would only be attempted after many years' training. Teak was grown extensively in Burma and this beautiful wood was put to many uses. In former days all houses, monasteries and palaces were built of wood and the one outstanding feature in the architecture of those old buildings was the design of the roof. All had tall spires which were composed of a number of roofs diminishing in size, each of which had wide projecting eaves which seemed to flow upwards amid a sea of pinnacles and carvings. This type of carving was quite unlike that found in the inner sanctuaries but it was bolder in design, heavier in detail and often of a rough finish made to withstand the rigors of monsoon rains, hot sun and drying winds.

In the old days there were strict Laws of Sumptuary which governed the number of roofs a man was allowed to build over his house, for it was unthinkable that anyone, no matter how exalted, should raise more roofs over his head than the King of Burma and the old law set out just how many roofs were allowed to each official rank from the Princes down to minor ministers.

Although the old palaces have gone, the graceful flowing lines of the old style still linger on in moderation, in the design of the Pongyi Kyaungs which are still built of wood in the country districts and the Burmese love of beautiful things to decorate their own homes as well as the monasteries has ensured that the wood carvers' art has flourished.

After a long self-imposed isolation Burma is today once again opening her doors to foreigners. It will be interesting to see if the new Burmese Socialism has inflicted any drastic changes on those age old principles of Buddhism in which her citizens have been so deeply, devoutly and happily steeped over so many centuries and if any of the ancient arts have been lost in the process.

28

Chinese Celebrations

Mr Chang had persuaded us to accept the wedding invitation and, not knowing that apart from family and friends, most guests arrived only in time for the dinner in the evening, we had duly arrived at the time given on the invitation, 3.30 p.m. The ceremony was being held in the Assembly Room of the Chinese school and we found the long room decorated with flowers, the women all seated together on the left and the men on the right side. It seemed that I created a problem. Should I be segregated with the other women? Eventually I was put on the front row amongst the men but that was to be an embarrassing mistake. The bride and groom arrived to stand in front of a long white table behind which sat the Priest and elders. She wore a long white satin gown and carried a small bouquet of flowers like any Western Bride. Only her hair reflected the Eastern traditions. done in the wedding style the long black tresses flowed from a high lacquered cylinder of hair on top of her head with fresh flowers pinned behind her ear and gold combs to keep stray tendrils in place. As the religious ceremony proceeded the groups of men and women would each stand in turn to smile, nod their heads and recite lengthy passages in unison.

This was where the embarrassment began, should I remain seated or was I expected to stand up when the men did. I tried standing when my side of the room got to their feet only to see the faces of the women opposite break into huge grins and eventually helpless laughter. Those women had obviously never before seen such a funny situation and I had no idea just what I could do to be correct. In future I decided I must sit with the women.

The bridal pair signed a long scroll of red and gold which was closely inscribed with Chinese characters in black and then it was all over for us until six o'clock that evening when the main wedding feast would begin.

When we returned later that evening we found a crowd of children playing chin-lon, a game which calls for the agility of a ballet dancer and we watched for a few minutes as they circled and kicked the wicker ball from the most impossible angles. Mr Chang made a way for us through the noisy crowds and led us into a gaily decorated room where tables were set out for the guests. Eight places at each table had to be filled and to ensure the omens were lucky an empty place would be filled by someone from the crowd of relations and friends outside. By the door sat an old man with a long white beard busily painting black characters onto a long red scroll and we were told that he was recording the gifts left by well wishers. A succession of smiling boys brought in handpainted pottery bowls of steaming food, bird's nest soup, sea slugs, fishes' stomachs, spicy dishes of chicken or pork and vegetables of every variety. Everybody shared the food in the bowls all dipping in with their chopsticks and painted pottery spoons. They would offer me some special delicacy from their chopsticks and I felt such communal eating was very unhygienic but to refuse would have offended those kind people so I tucked into the feast, hoping for the best. The only thing I was never able to eat with any pleasure was the glutinous, musty flavoured ancient eggs which were a great favourite. I grew to like the noisy feasts and looked forward to the laughter, banter, the happy atmosphere and even came to accept that always the Bazaar dogs would be there snapping and snarling around one's ankles as they fought over some bone or tit-bit thrown under the table by the guests.

The newly-weds appeared carrying trays of small glasses of sweet wine which had to be downed in one quick gulp whilst the guests teased the bridegroom who countered with witty remarks but the bride remained silent and solemn-faced, her only reaction to all the banter being to spit slowly and deliberately onto the floor. A big smiling man who might have been the model for one of those portly jade figures began to circulate. He waved a large glass of rum pointing to a mark half way down the glass and challenged the guests to a drinking match. As the only female guest I was excused but none of the men could match him and he moved on to try the wager at all the other tables. Music was called for and a young man wearing a smartly-cut black suit produced a microphone insisting that each guest must sing and eventually we left them still making merry late into the evening.

It was not only the weddings which were a time for rejoicing, I was to find that death was accepted in a strangely light-hearted manner and was yet another excuse for feasting. When the mother-in-law of the Chinese Headman of Zayangyi died the whole Chinese population celebrated the funeral for a week. Aik Hti, one of our houseboys, asked for time off to cook for the occasion. Each day for a week, he said, the family of the dead woman would provide food for all comers. The old lady, dressed in her finest clothes, would lie in state in a gaily decorated coffin of heavy wood and in her honour the people of Zayangyi would gather to gamble and feast for three days and nights. On the fourth day after feeding all who came to the house that morning, the coffin would be placed on a bier shaded by a canopy of rainbow hued paper streamers and flowers and a yellow silk umbrella. I watched the approaching procession with some surprise. It was headed by four men who set a fast trotting pace as they held aloft white silk banners inscribed with black characters which told of the virtues and good deeds of the dead woman. After them came a priest dressed in baggy orange silk trousers and a voluminous smock his large black umbrella bobbing up and down as he tried to keep up with the coffin. Then came the whole of the Chinese population of the town, men, women and children all dressed in their best and brightest clothes, all chattering animatedly to the accompaniment of a party of musicians who played a rousing marching tune. As they sped away towards the Chinese cemetery on the far hillside I thought how very different it would have been at home, a solemn procession of grief stricken mourners, yet these people felt only happiness for the departed. And a week later they would all meet again to gamble and feast throughout the night as a final show of respect towards the dead woman.

Some of the Chinese families choose sites on top of the highest hills for their family burial grounds and each spring Mr Chang and his wife and children, accompanied by their relations no matter how distant the connection, would visit the family graves on Loi HsamHsip. The happy family group would spend the day there cleaning the graves offering incense, rice, fruit, to the ancestors, talking of those ancestors as though they were living members of that family party enjoying a picnic. This annual pilgrimage meant that the family would never drift apart and each one would bring up his or her own children to respect the old custom.

29

The Golden City

Amarapura was the royal capital of ancient Burma and shortly
after the second Anglo-Burmese war, Mindon Min was
proclaimed King of Burma. He decided the old city was
unlucky and sent his soothsayers to the top of the highest hill
on the horizon to divine an auspicious site for a new golden
city, The ShweMyo. They chose a spot where the clanking,
hooting and bustle of the river steamers would not spoil the
peace but near enough to the Irrawaddy to make communica-
tions easy with the widespread kingdom. It was in 1858 when
the first stone of the ShweMyo was laid and to mark the centre
of the city, the great golden spire of the Mye Nan Daw or
royal palace, rose to about two hundred feet in tier after tier of
gilded carvings. The vast rambling palace was built of teak
with three spires and beneath the central spire was the great
Audience Hall and the Lion Throne Room where the
greatness and valour of the King were symbolised by a huge
gilded throne of teak supported by two carved lions. A
Burmese friend told us that the palace had been panelled
almost entirely in glass and mirrors, glass latticework partitioned
the rooms and the lofty teak pillars which supported the roof
were covered with gaudy glass mosaics. The roof with its
diminishing tiers and pinnacles gleamed in gold and vermilion.
The new city was surrounded by twenty foot high walls of rosy
red brick, each side of the square they formed being at least a
mile in length. There were twelve gates and at intervals along
the walls were tall watch towers with ornamental ironwork
gold tipped spires. A wide moat surrounded the walls with a
bridge at each gate. The royal barges were moored near the
main gate and the King and his retinue would be rowed

around the city. King Mindon Min proclaimed his golden city to be the centre of the universe.

Of that lavish golden glass palace nothing remains; it was completely destroyed during bombing raids in 1945. Only the great outer walls with their crumbling watch towers still stand, guardians of the past, and the moat, choked with water hyacinth, looks rather like a giant strip of lilac carpet when the lovely but unloved waterweed blossoms. Ghul Mohr trees grew at the water's edge and the reflection of the flame flowers in the few remaining clear patches of water turned it to liquid fire, full of motionless fish like specimens set in ruby glass, a target for small boys who would stand there for hours with rod and line hoping to catch a free supper.

As we flew over the city we had an aerial view of the great square formed by the moat and walls which enclosed a grassy park in the centre of which towered the Independence Monument like a space rocket ready for blast-off, and I saw that the new Mandalay had been laid out with every street parallel or at right angles to the old walls.

Perhaps my expectations had been coloured by the old song but what I found there disappointed me at first. It was just another Eastern town, dusty, choked with litter and over-run with pi-dogs. There were few fine buildings apart from the rather magnificent gleaming white railway station, and in the South Quarter of the town the Arakan Pagoda, its graceful gilded spire glittering in the noonday sun. Over the years those first impressions mellowed as I learned more of King Mindon Min's golden city.

Our Agent in Mandalay was a typical Burman, tall and spare, full of charm and anxious to show us Mandalay at its best. His wife was small and plump and she always clucked over me like a fussy mother hen. She would pinch my arm and shake her head. I was too thin she would complain. If only I would stay with her for a while she would soon have me looking more as a woman should. She would lead us to a table spread with steaming bowls of rice, great dishes of kaukswe, sauces and toli-molis. On each occasion there would be some new delicacy to try and she would hover over us pressing us to try more of the exotic dishes which were not always to my taste although I would not have hurt her feelings by refusing to try them. Having been persuaded to try what looked to me

like overcooked prunes my appetite vanished when I found a
head and claws. Her husband told me they were Mandalay
sparrows. He said that at the beginning of the monsoon,
groups of trappers would set up fine mesh nets in the paddy
fields then boys would beat gongs to drive great flocks of the
tiny birds into the nets and they would be caught by the
thousand. They were considered to be a great delicacy by the
Burmese and the demand could never be met.

It was the end of November and the hosts for the
Tazaungdaing Kathein that year were to be the traders of the
Bazaar Quarter. For a whole year they would have saved to
buy gifts to present to the monks and for the lavish
entertainments which were also a part of the festival. The
celebrations continued for three days up to the Full Moon of
Tazaungmon and on that first Sunday evening our agent and
his family took us to the most fantastic display of generosity I
have ever seen. Motor vehicles were quite useless in the crush
and so we joined the crowds which thronged the streets. The
whole of the Bazaar area had been cordoned off and every
street was brilliantly lit. Lining each side of the streets and
alleyways were stalls and "trees" as the bamboo frames for
displaying the gifts were called. There were stalls piled high
with silver bowls, bundles of yellow robes, clothing and
sandals, gaily coloured blankets, medicines, toothbrushes,
chamberpots, dozens of "trees" groaning under a wealth of
paper money and stalls with enough food to feed an army.
One street was full of wooden beds complete with mattresses,
blankets, sheets, mosquito nets and bedside lamps. The gifts
represented a vast fortune and each year similar generosity
would be shown. But that was not all, at each intersection of
roads there was an entertainment, perhaps a drama, dancers,
jugglers or an orchestra, comedians or puppet shows. We
stopped to watch a puppet show and it was quite unlike
anything I had seen before. A sudden clashing of gongs and
cymbals announced that the show was about to begin and
after the third roll of drums the curtain drew back on one of
the traditional marionette plays with themes which have
remained unchanged for centuries. We saw the beginning of
the world, then its destruction, followed by its re-creation by
fantastic looking Nats. The animal puppets then appeared to
take their place in the scheme of things, horses trotted across

the stage followed by plodding elephants, fierce tigers troublesome monkeys and giant birds which ruled the skies. Then traditionally the king and his ministers would appear to strut across the stage in their old world costumes, grand and regal although some of the court officials seemed quite ridiculous. The court jester was a great favourite but the villains, bullies, rogues and simpering court hangers-on were booed mercilessly. Perhaps the most important characters in each play were the prince and princess. With their songs, dances, love making, they symbolised happiness and hope which sometimes ended in tragedy. The height of the puppets varied from two to three feet and each would have up to sixty strings. In exaggerated accents the controllers spoke their parts to a great deal of noise and encouragement from the crowd. There were cheers for the heroes, boos for the villains as the wildly cavorting little marionettes marched on and off the stage, fought battles, danced, sang, set the world to rights to the delight of the crowd jostling good naturedly and enjoying every minute. They knew each story by heart and would let the puppet controllers know their disapproval if the traditional set pattern was not adhered to. It was open house everywhere, you just walked through whichever open door took your fancy, to be welcomed and offered every kind of refreshment. At one house dimly lit with coloured candles we were given a cup of Ovaltine and biscuits. Another offered us a feast of pickled tea, spices and sweetmeats. Again later we were pressed to try the sticky rice which was a local delicacy. A special rice was put into short lengths of green bamboo and then steamed. When the rice was cooked the bamboo would be split open and the solid cylinder of hot sticky rice would be eaten as a sweetmeat without sauces or any other food to help it down. The favourite food of our host's young daughter was Kaukswe and she consumed a huge bowlful although after all the sweetmeats I had been pressed into sampling, I had no appetite left.

The festivities lasted most of the night and the following day. After the Full Moon everything would be taken to the Pongyi Kyaung in a great colourful procession where the gifts would be blessed by the Sayador and then distributed amongst the Pongyis at a solemn religious ceremony.

The Arakan Pagoda in the South Quarter of the town was next on our host's sightseeing list, a huge square building of dull gold with a lofty spire. We left our shoes at one of the four entrances and walked down a corridor lined with shops and stalls selling flowers, sweetmeats, pictures, carvings, books, offerings for the shrine and souvenirs to catch the eye of the tourists. In the very heart of the temple sat a giant image surrounded by offerings, flowers and a forest of tiny lighted candles which spread a soft glow over the kneeling devotees and the air was heavy with the scent of the burning wax.

We were led into a tiny courtyard lined with bells of every size from great bronze giants to small ones about a foot high. Our host seized a stick and hit them with great rapidity one after another setting up a deafening clanging and vibration which hurt the ears. This was to send a prayer winging heavenwards he told us. He pointed to a door at the far end of the courtyard and took us into a large room crammed with relics rescued from the old palace at the time of the fire. There was a huge crystal bed with four glittering glass posts. It stood in dusty splendour in the middle of the room, once a favourite of Queen Supayalat. Around it was an array of gold vases, toys, dolls, watches, a frilled Victorian basket and many other small objects of little but historical value, the playthings of royal children and pampered wives.

We turned our interest to the Mandalay Hill. We had two hours to spare in the morning before our appointment with the dentist, a pleasant young Indian who talked to us of his early training in London, and of motor racing. He followed the fortunes of the top racing drivers with avid interest. Our visit to the hill was no leisurely tour. It rose a sheer 500 ft from the flat plain and at its foot was a forest of 739 small decaying pagodas all arranged in neat rows. These were Mindon Min's Kuthodaw or Royal Merit and each had contained a marble slab engraved with Buddhist Scriptures.

Two giant Chinthays with blood red tongues and jaws kept eternal guard at the foot of the stairs which led the devout up to a series of platforms each with shrines, tableaux and images. Half way up the hill we found a forty foot high golden image its gilded finger pointing to the spot where King Mindon Min was to build his palace. On another terrace a ghastly tableau depicted the revelation and inevitable decay after death. At the top of one flight of steps an old monk sat cross-legged, a small bell shaped gong in his hand and a plain wooden bowl beside him. If one dropped a coin into the bowl he would ring out a prayer on his gong and few passed by without the clear tones of the old man's spinning bell sending its message heavenwards. We had no time to linger and our legs ached after hurrying up the hundreds of steep steps to the top terrace to find that the views were worth the effort although I felt that only the most devout would face the climb a second time.

That night we were invited to a party by our dentist and his wife. It was as though I had been transported back to India. The moonlight garden was illuminated with hundreds of paper lanterns and silk saris rustled as guests strolled amongst the moon-silvered flowers enjoying the scented air or sampling a selection of Indian delicacies from the buffet laid out on a long table.

The next day we visited the blending plant, a Government venture for blending and marketing locally made teas. It was run by a portly smiling Burman who showed us round demonstrating all the latest labour saving machinery. There was a party at his house that night which showed us yet another face of Mandalay. We might have been stepping inside a disco with dim lighting and a crush of young people dancing to modern music. I was handed a microphone and told to sing something: each guest was expected to contribute to the entertainment. Amongst the guests I saw one of the Tawngpeng Princes and was told that the girl with him was his new second wife. He was head over heels in love with the beautiful young girl to the great amusement of the other guests and I learned that although polygamy was practised only by a dwindling minority, those who did were accepted with admiration by the rest.

Mandalay was one of the main mango growing areas and our drivers would often bring me large baskets of the delicious fruits. I was to find there were many varieties, some tasting like peaches and cream others with a decided flavour of turpentine. It was the same with the bananas: there were delicious green-skinned ones, huge crimson ones with a peachy flavour and miniature golden ones like a bite of honey, then the country bananas, fat and overripe, so full of hard black seeds they were almost inedible. In July it was the pineapple season. Old women and young boys would sit by the roadside near the plantations displaying baskets of fruits for sale to passers-by and the stalls in the Bazaar would be piled high with ripe orange-gold fruits. the season was short and the profits small.

In the old days I was told there had been many strange customs and one which was remembered by some with anger and others as a source of great amusement was Thieves' Night. This had taken place at the Full Moon of Tazaungmon in November and practical jokers would take the opportunity to "steal" some large article, usually furniture, from a friend and take it to one of the main streets or squares.

On the following morning pandemonium would reign with roads almost blocked by great piles of furniture and bric-a-brac and groups of irate owners frantically searching for their lost property. Understandably the disruption was unpopular with most people and would not be tolerated by the authorities today, but Thieves' Night is not forgotten my friends assured me.

We were driven out to the Ava Bridge which was completed in 1954 for both road and rail traffic and its ten spans tamed the Irrawaddy for after that the people did not need to risk their lives in tiny boats. Across the river a high rounded hill rose up behind the bridge. Sagaing was the only high ground for miles around and we saw that it was dotted with a rash of little white pagodas, each of great antiquity and interest. The Oo Min Thronze was one of the better known ones and in a cave in the hillside sat thirty stone Buddhas each in its niche and although over the years the images have increased to more than sixty the old name is unchanged. Walking on up the hill path one passed a large water tank, or pool, guarded at each corner by Nǎgǎ, or Dragon Spirits and beyond this many other pagodas ending with one which was poised at the end of the ridge. One had to admire both the view and the lovely soft colours of the ceramic tiles with which the platform floor was laid.

The Pagoda of the Elephants had been split asunder during an earthquake and this revealed a cache of valuable jewels and gold which had been buried inside the stupa. The treasure was put on display amongst the ruins. No-one would have risked the dire consequences of removing it, and the patrons of that Pagoda announced that they intended to rebuild it and restore the treasure to its hiding place.

Some of Burma's finest silverware was produced on Sagaing

lovely bowls and dishes, ornaments and household utensils. All these articles would be decorated in traditional style, some engraved with geometric patterns, others with more ornate designs. The expressive figures dancing around the bowls or posturing on the boxes were heavy, often erotic, and perhaps reflected their origins in Hindu art and religion. We returned to Mandalay to buy some lacquerware, another thriving industry which had survived the centuries without changing its methods very much. The shops were full of objects large and small to attract the tourist, the housewife or devotee looking for some gift to offer to the temple. The Tamin-Tsa-Oot, or Alms Bowl, with spired lid was to be found in black or vermilion decorated with gold, there were panels depicting religious texts, bowls, dishes, cigarette boxes, trinket boxes and frivolous objects such as owls in all sizes from miniatures to giants. Then there were the peacocks which also came in all sizes, great eye-catching golden birds with spread tails decorated with coloured glass which could be made to order.

The lacquer is actually a varnish which from earliest times had been made from wood oil; this oil is tapped from the trunk of a large tree, the Burmese Varnish Tree, with a tongue-twisting botanical name — Melanorrhoea usitatissima. The black oily sap, called thittsi by the lacquermakers, is coloured by the addition of vermilion or yellow to the oil. The method of making these articles has changed little and usually the "form" of the object required is woven out of thin strips of bamboo, this is coated with the thittsi and when dry it will be covered with a special paste. Three kinds of paste were used by the old lacquermakers. One was made of burnt bones, another most commonly used was of burnt rice husks or sawdust whilst another version was made of cow dung and mud. When these pastes had hardened, been ground to give a smooth finish and the final coats of thittsi gilded and decorated, only an expert could tell the difference between them although the cheaper versions crack easily and are not a good buy. Formerly Pagan and Nyoungoo were the chief centres of the lacquerware industry. The Burmese Varnish Tree was grown extensively in N.W.Burma and around Manipur but in more recent years large plantations of the Tung Tree (Aleurites fordii), were being cultivated for the "drying" oil which was extracted from the kernels of the nuts for use in the manufacture of paint, varnish and for making linoleum. This was also used locally for lighting and by the lacquer industry.

We had seen a lot of Mandalay in just a few days but the long journey home was not without interest. As we left the Golden City we sped by fruit orchards and paddy fields, then came a belt of grotesque rocky hills, empty and arid. The intense heat which radiated from the rock walls felt as though someone had left a fan heater at maximum. The air was stifling as we wound our way up the sixteen and a half miles of tortuous twisting road with its twenty-two hairpin bends. The only living creature I saw there was a hideous vulture which was perched ominously on a small tree overhanging a burning gulch, a little tree of breathtaking beauty, its leafless stems and branches thickly encrusted with "pea" flowers of a delicate magenta shade. Suddenly the desolate landscape was behind us and the plateau ahead seemed very welcoming by comparison, green and lush with well cultivated fields full of brightly coloured asters, or Maymyo Pán, of strawberries and vegetables of every kind.

At the outskirts of the town we came to a giant archway which welcomed the visitors to Maymyo, the Hill Station which had been made popular by Colonel May as a cool resort for British troops many years ago.

I found it a place of faded charm, the lovely old houses had a neglected air, shabby with peeling paint but with gardens which were well tended and full of English cottage garden flowers. Once there had been a large British community but now most of them had gone. Horse drawn Victorias still plied the streets and the scent of the tall Blue Gum Trees which lined all the outer roads hung heavy in the nostrils. At 3519 ft elevation the town had a pleasant cool climate but with the departure of the British and the invention of air-conditioning the need for its quiet cool lanes diminished. The Botanical Gardens did not share the apparent neglect the town had suffered and the wide sweeping lawns of coarse grass were clipped and tidy, the borders full of flowers. There were mature specimen trees of many varieties, an Orchid House which hung thickly with exotic blooms and a Summer House where visitors could rest a while and perhaps buy some of the rose bushes grown specially in pots.

We were to visit Mandalay and Maymyo on a number of occasions and always there was something new to learn about the Golden City and a feeling of relaxation in Maymyo's tree lined walks, but on each occasion the outstanding feature which impressed me above all else on the journey was the Gokteik Gorge. It was a long, deep fissure in the earth which, when seen overhead from an aircraft, formed a great slash dividing the countryside for miles. The road hairpinned down for seven miles to the darkly shaded little river at the bottom of the gorge. The atmosphere there seemed airless and I felt that I was standing at the bottom of a deep pit. The road ahead of us was so steep, the bends so tight and the gradient so sheer that some lorries had to reverse before they could negotiate the worst of the bends. Across the narrow gorge the road seemed to be a mere stone's throw away as it snaked its tortuous climb up the opposite cliff face avoiding the worst of the hazards and I marvelled at the spectacular rock formations which overhung the road in a perilous fashion, streaks of rust and ochre splashed across the cliff face like some monster mural and the towering limestone walls were covered with a ragged "wig" of shrubs and trees which somehow managed to find a flimsy foothold, their roots seeming to writhe agonisingly as they contorted themselves into every crack and crevice. At the narrowest point of the gorge a delicate and spindly looking bridge had been erected to take a single track railway line across. I never tried it but my friend Mrs Hansen, told me that the train would suddenly emerge out of the dark entrance tunnel into the bright sunlight and at a snail's pace would begin to cross the gorge. With all the bridge's supporting structure beneath the train it was easy for the traveller to imagine that he or she was floating slowly across, but to look out of the window could be equally sensational for the bottom of the gorge was at least eight hundred feet below at its deepest point. Built in the early 1900's the bridge was said to be 2,260 ft long and it was supported by fifteen steel trestles. There had been a number of attacks on the railway line by the Shan Army and several sections of track on either side had been damaged on a number of occasions, but fortunately the bridge itself had survived. During the war years it had been partially dismantled, to be rebuilt again at the end of hostilities.

After the spectacle of the Gokteik the scenery as we made for Kyaukme seemed decidedly dull except when the wild sunflowers bloomed and then every uncultivated patch of land would sprout with the tall plants which dotted the flat countryside with drifting gold. We had the choice of two roads to Tawngpeng, the one by Haikham took us straight up into the mountains with quite spectacular scenery, particularly as one reached the last section and neared the Pass. The other way ran through the low country skirting the hills to take us to Hsipaw and the river at Moté where there was another Flying Ferry built to the same design as the one at Lilu. After that we were on our home territory once more, and with almost two hundred miles of narrow twisting roads behind us, it was easy to understand why the Burmese King in his Golden City had seemed to be a world away from Tawngpeng and its tea growers and why even today there is a gulf which divides the hill people and those of the plains as effectively as the Gokteik must have divided the land before modern engineering spanned it.

30

The Lair of the Ghostly Blacksmith

Eastern bazaars held a great fascination for me as there was always something new to see and Mandalay was no exception. There seemed to be quite a stir at the far end of the Zyegyo and above the usual hustle and bustle I could hear music and, curiosity aroused, I went across to see what the excited crowd was gathering to watch. The four musicians sat in a line along the edge of a square of dingy carpet; they were dressed in brightly coloured lungyis and each had a gaudy pink scarf wound turban-like around his head. Even the smallest of orchestras would carry the Pattala or Burmese Xylophone, a melodious instrument made of twenty-four bamboo slats set in a semi-circular, carved, wooden soundbox, and the father of this family of musicians was seated behind such an instrument accompanied by his sons, one playing a bamboo flute, another fiddling merrily on a Tah-yaw, a curious instrument, half violin, half trumpet, and the youngest son tapped out the rhythm on the Pat-saing or set of drums.

A plump smiling woman had arranged three large wicker baskets in front of the musicians. Once she had danced at their shows but now she beckoned to her pretty young daughter. The slender girl was dressed in a clinging yellow tamein and filmy white aingyi and standing in the centre of the carpet facing the baskets she began to sway to the throbbing music. As the pace quickened she leaned over one of the baskets and removed the lid, dancing slowly, kicking aside the hem of her overlong skirt, she rocked her body, swaying from the hips she sometimes bent over backwards arched like a bow, her arms bent stiffly whilst her twitching fingers stabbed the air writhing like the serpents she was charming, her bones so supple she seemed to press the backs of her hands along the forearms.

Lured by the music a large cobra rose slowly from the basket, hood spread as though ready to strike. It stared at the swaying girl and I was not sure whether it was the dancer or the reptile that was hypnotised until suddenly she picked up the deadly reptile, stroking it and allowing its forked tongue to flick over her face, then gently she wrapped it across her shoulders and turned to the next basket. As its fourteen foot occupant began to slither across the carpet there was a gasp of horror from her audience and, laughing delightedly, she picked it up offering it to her audience.

This dainty laughing girl was a child of Mount Popa and in no danger from the snakes she handled with careless ease. The people of the two villages on that revered mountain are said to have an unusual affinity with the Nats and cobras which live on its fertile slopes and each year they develop an immunity to the snake venom which lasts for exactly ninety days.

An old man standing near to me began to tell me what he knew of Popa. It was a magical place, he told me, and the home of powerful Nats. It was to Mount Popa that the former Prime Minister, U Nu, would retreat for long periods each year to meditate on the trials and troubles of his people. The old man continued his story, telling me that on the day the safe period begins the Snake Charmers will go up to the top of the mountain and at a secret place known only to themselves they gather in front of a deep fissure in the rocks. The musicians would begin to play soft rhythmic music and a young girl would step forward to dance in honour of the Snakes and Nats of the Mountain.

The silent crowd would watch anxiously until, with a sigh of relief, they saw a large snake was being lured out of its rocky lair by the music. Head erect, poised as though to strike it would watch the swaying girl and not until she had kissed the reptile three times would the Nats be appeased. The girl, said my new friend, would be quite unharmed and after that, with the annual tribute to the great snakes of the mountain accepted, the Snake Charmers of Popa would know it was safe to catch the cobras they needed for their shows. Often they would travel many miles giving their shows wherever they found people willing to watch but before the ninety days immunity ended they would be back on their mountain and the snakes released amongst the rocks and flowers.

Mount Popa lies just south west of Mandalay and is still considered to be the home of powerful Nats. It is an isolated volcanic peak which, according to tradition, rose from the plains during an earthquake in 442 BC and was to become the centre of the iron and steel industry.

It rises to a great height out of the hot dusty plains of Myingyan, near Kyaukpadaung, and there is a deep crater at the summit which, said my self appointed guide, is almost a mile across. Below the rocky crater the slopes are lush and green with flowering trees and shrubs throughout the year because the mountain so often has its head in the clouds causing moisture to condense and so keeping Popa's streams flowing all the year round. The surrounding countryside is brown and dusty for most of the year and the contrast of the green hill rising up out of the parched plain is so great that there is little wonder Popa has the reputation of being a magical place.

It is the legendary home of Maung Tin De, the Ghostly Blacksmith who was said to wield a giant hammer in each hand, his anvil roaring like thunder would set the sparks spewing forth from the crater on top of the mountain.

In the early seventeenth century some Portugese travellers were arrested and deported to Shwebo, not far from Mount Popa. They were smiths by trade and eventually persuaded their captors to allow them to ply their trade and to teach their skills to the local people. From that time on Shwebo, Popa and Sagaing have been the main centres of metalwork industries in Burma. The Taupwadi Quarter of Mandalay is still an important centre for the manufacture of Hti's, those gilded "umbrellas" which adorn the tops of most of the larger pagodas. The method of making these has changed little over the years. First the design is drawn onto thin sheet metal, cut out with shears then finished in all its delicate detail by a Master Hti-Maker. Traditionally they are built up of five, seven or nine concentric circles which diminish in size, each one connected to the central vane by spokes like those of an umbrella. Seen at close quarters they look like woven tinsel but when set upon the top of a pagoda they look like filigree gold lace. The early Hti's were simple, made like the flat open umbrellas which were always the symbol of regal dignity but over the years the styles have become more lavish and ornamental looking more like great lacy parasols or perhaps a fantastic tiered crown. There are other artists in metal who make ornamental or household articles, often inlaying these simple everyday tools and utensils with intricate designs done in silver-wire. The ornate pierced screens which ornament the inner shrines are as delicate as old lace and could easily be mistaken for gilded draperies rather than cold sheet iron.

These ancient crafts have changed little over the centuries, each group or guild guarding its secrets jealously with long apprenticeships. So long as there are pagodas to beautify these arts will continue to flourish.

31

Ambush

The May Man bus was grinding its way slowly uphill on the daily journey from Lashio to Namtu. Jungle covered banks rose steeply on either side of the road obscuring the view as the bus approached Mile 22 on the Mansam road. It was hot and dusty and the passengers nodded sleepily until a series of loud reports and the wildly lurching bus jerked them out of their day dreams. A bearded Italian priest from the Mission at Namtu was one of the passengers and for a second he thought that a tyre had burst, then with horror and disbelief he saw that the woman in the seat opposite had fallen forward, blood spurting from her throat.

A man in front had collapsed onto the floor in a widening pool of blood and the driver lay across his wheel. The priest's immediate reaction was to dive under his seat. The bus careered wildly out of control since its driver had been the main target for the marksmen and it crashed with a shattering of glass and scream of tortured metal as it ploughed into the bank. The priest became aware that a dozen or more masked men bristling with rifles and dahs were ordering the passengers out into the road.

This was a typical ambush, an all too common occurence on those hill roads. The bus driver was already dead and the dacoits were dragging the two injured passengers out of the vehicles then the terrified passengers were searched, everything of value being taken. The priest had only his breviary and that too was thrown on top of the pile of loot. The injured woman was told to hand over her rings, bracelets and earrings but she was dying and fumbled weakly, too slow for one villainous looking fellow who turned on her with his dah cruelly slashing off her ears and fingers to take the jewels showing no pity although she was still conscious, they were impatient to be gone.

With the same cold impatience the dacoit turned to the injured man, a Karen known to everyone as Lloyd. He was a staunch Baptist, who had joined the British Forces during the war years. For some years he had been manager of the bank in Lashio and was admired and respected by everyone and we knew him well. Through no fault of his own he lay dying in the hot dusty road and the horrified passengers saw the dacoit, dah raised, intent on hacking the helpless man to pieces.

'Why waste time on a dying man?' he shouted.

Without any apparent thought for his own safety the priest grabbed the dah throwing it aside and turning to face the dacoit leader he quietly told him to allow the injured man to die in peace. The priest knelt beside the dying man and, their differing religious beliefs set aside, he comforted the stranger with a prayer. Rather shamefacedly the dacoit leader came forward to restrain his men. The priest's courage had impressed him and he apologised for his companions saying they were over excited. Pointing to the breviary lying on top of the pile of loot the priest asked sternly.

'Are you a Christian? What will you do with that?' Without saying a word the leader handed back the breviary to its owner.

This was a typical occurrence, the more blood spilled, the more terrified the victims, the better the dacoits liked it and it was almost impossible to find witnesses. Only when they became careless were they likely to be caught for the web of terror was their safety net.

Shocked and saddened, everyone in Lashio was talking about the tragedy, for Lloyd had been popular, his kindness and good deeds were on everyone's lips and all were agog with stories of the priest's heroism.

Once a year priests from the Catholic Mission and School at Namtu would visit Tawnpang walking to outlying villages where a few Catholic families lived. The Italian had called to see us shortly after the ambush and as usual he was accompanied by a flock of admirers and followers from the town. It was he who told me of the worsening situation and dangers for the people living in the outlying settlements and in a quiet voice without excuses or recriminations he went on to give me the gruesome details of the ambush at Mile 22.

After he had left the full implications of the ambush hit me hard. I had been closing my eyes to the dangers faced each time we took to those jungle roads. With a sinking feeling I realised that tomorrow they might all be discussing my butchered remains and I was afraid.

Piet suggested that I should go down to Maymyo for a while but that would have been running away and I had always believed in facing problems.

Shortly afterwards we had walked to the top of Loi HsamHsip and I had sat there in the warm sun looking down on the enchanted garden. Above me the eagles wheeled effortlessly against the blue sky. In the distance I could hear the tinkling of mule bells and somewhere a shepherd boy called to his flock. Was I going to allow myself to be driven away from that lovely place by a few evil men I pondered? On the slopes far below me I could see Palaung women looking like poppies swaying and drifting amongst the tea bushes as they plucked the leaf.

They could not run away. They had to carry on working and care for their families yet they seemed to accept all the horrors, the terror that was yet to come, without fear. They believed with absolute fatalism that death was pre-ordained and they would enjoy evey moment of their lives whilst they could. I resolved to try to be like those daughters of the dragon, there was too much to enjoy around me to waste such precious time as I would have there on brooding over ambushes and death. It was as though a great weight had been lifted from my shoulders and the world suddenly seemed a brighter more exciting place.

In the years that followed we had a number of narrow escapes and I often felt that some kind fate must guide us, or was it perhaps Thusan-ti?

32

The Rebellion

Tawngpeng had always been a land of peace, its rulers just and citizens law abiding but perhaps it was inevitable that the serpent should put in an appearance in the end as in that first garden.

We would hear of unpleasant incidents. Murder which had been unheard of in former days became an everyday event. Armed bands roamed the once peaceful hills spreading terror in their wake. At first we had thought it all the work of the local dacoity, and so the full scale rebellion crept up on us quite without our realising what was happening. After the cession of the Sawbwas many Shans began openly to express their separatist views and the age-old antagonism between the peoples of the hills and plains did not help the situation. The new Burmese Revolutionary Council showed little interest or sympathy towards the Shan desire for Devolution and when unrest became open revolt they took firm measures to stamp out the Devolutionist movement. The centuries old conflict between the Heavenly Lords and the Sunrise Kings was not far beneath the surface of fragile peace.

After all the unrest in the district, the Burmese Army set up a permanent post in Namhsan to try to control the situation. The commanding officer was a charming Colonel, a man of tact and understanding who quietly but firmly maintained order behind a friendly approach. His men were encouraged to join in the local feasts and ceremonies and some married local girls. On the surface all was well.

Returning from leave at the end of March we drove up from Mandalay to find change everywhere. We could scarcely believe what we saw. Every village had been "spring cleaned" during our two months' absence. Fences were painted white, and there were no signs of the usual untidy litter or stray dogs, but strangest of all I saw that in every restaurant and tea shop white clad figures, their faces hidden behind white masks, were preparing or serving the food. Such sparkling cleanliness was almost unbelievable. We were not left for long to wonder on the changes. The Colonel called to greet us on our return. He had a liking for English afternoon teas and would invariably drop-in around 4 p.m. When I mentioned the astonishing and welcome changes he looked pleased. It had been done on his orders he said and he expounded his plans to improve the health of the village people.

Soon after this we again saw the charming Colonel. He was reviewing the local militia in Manhsam village. We were returning from Lashio with a large shipment of cash and had no wish to advertise our whereabouts but we could not resist lingering a while to watch the unusual ceremony in Manhsam village square. There had been a call-in of all arms in the Shan States and we had seen army lorries piled high with ancient muzzle loader guns. The villagers had been encouraged to form a Home Guard and we saw our friend the Colonel reviewing the ranks of farmers and shopkeepers who stood smartly to attention shouldering their cross-bows, long bows and spears alongside the cream of the Burmese Army attending the Review bristling with all the latest in modern weaponry. It made a strange picture of contrasts but we realised that no matter how brave, the villagers had little chance of defending themselves against the well equipped Shan army.

Shortly after this the Colonel returned to arrange a tour for General Aung Gyi, Minister for Trade in the Central Government at that time. The General wanted to see conditions for himself and our tea factory was high on his itinerary. He had refused an invitation to come down to the bungalow for drinks saying he was too busy for social engagements, and I decided that perhaps his reputation for disliking Western pursuits in general and Western women in particular was correct after all.

The Colonel had arranged a party that evening in the mess and we arrived to find all the prominent citizens of Namhsan there as well as the Sawbwa and Mahadevi. I think perhaps the General felt it had been a mistake to include two women in what should have been an all male affair and his disapproval showed. He sat apart silent and scowling surrounded by senior officers. The mess had been decorated with paper streamers and bunches of balloons, the army cook had surpassed himself for as well as the usual local delicacies the buffet table groaned beneath a spread of short eats which would have done credit to any of the diplomatic parties in Rangoon.

One of the visitors, a senior officer, began to talk volubly to me regretting the passing of the British influence and I caught the disapproving eye of the V.I.P. guest. I had a feeling that unless he was more careful the pleasant man talking to me would find himself in deep trouble. I made my excuses and joined Mahadevi feeling it safer to indulge in "girl chatter" and noticed that the visitor's scowl relaxed.

The irrepressible Colonel began to organise games, determined that the party should be a success and I found myself partnering the Sawbwa in a balloon tennis match against the General and Mahadevi which ended in a decisive victory for the visiting team. The ice was broken and everyone began to enjoy the evening, whatever weighty problem had been on General Aung Gyi's mind was banished temporarily. Mahadevi and I left the party early leaving the men to their talking.

Shortly after his visit the General fell into disfavour for his moderate views and he fled to seek sanctuary in a monastery, free only by virtue of the yellow robe.

The Colonel was eventually recalled to Rangoon and after his departure events in Tawngpeng took a more sinister turn under the harsh rule of a dictatorial Major who set at nought all the good work done by his predecessor.

The full horror of the growing insurgency was only fully brought home to us when the victims were people we knew, friends, children.

It was at 7.30 p.m. one mid December evening that the quiet little village of Manhsam was taken over by a party of thirty or so men wearing green military style uniforms and an impressive display of modern weapons. The villagers were ordered indoors and armed guards took up positions along the street whilst the main body of rebels surrounded the village shop. This belonged to a Shan, brother-in-law to one of our staff who came the next day to tell us of Manhsam's night of terror. The rebels bound the shopkeeper's hands behind his back, took his keys and opened the safe only to find it was empty so they vented their disappointment on the unfortunate shopkeeper and on his wife whose screams for help were soon silenced with a gun butt.

The villagers were unarmed apart from the Nehbaing who had been allowed to keep his gun, an ancient muzzle loader. And when the old Nehbaing saw his friend the shopkeeper led out into the street, arms bound, and shot down by a hail of bullets, the old headman fired his ancient gun. Fortunately the rebels thought they were under attack by the Burmese Army and they left in a hurry taking everything of value they could carry, food, blankets, cigarettes, sweets and money. Such incidents were to become an everyday affair; rumours were rife and murmurings that the Shan Government was giving its support to the rebellion brought the Head of State on an extensive tour to refute the rumours. The recently elected Head of State was the Sawbwa of MongMit, who then held the post of Burma's Foreign Minister and he came to ask for local support for the Central Government. All households were ordered to send a representative to hear him speak and those people were angry and not afraid to speak out about their grievances.

That night there was a dinner held in his honour at the Haw and we arrived there to find most of the prominent citizens already assembled and ready to start the arguments again; feelings were running high and they wanted answers. The guest of honour made a late appearance and it was obvious that he had not expected to find a woman amongst the guests. He explained that he had walked to a distant pagoda to unwind and seek guidance after the tensions of the day. To have included foreigners, one of them a woman, amongst the guests had been a clever move by the Tawngpeng Sawbwa. By so doing he had forestalled the troublemakers and with politics forbidden, the evening became an enjoyable social occasion.

The MongMit Sawbwa had been educated in England and had married an English girl against his father's wishes only to be recalled to MongMit to face a father who refused to recognise any foreigner as a daughter-in-law. The timely death of the old Sawbwa resolved the affair and the young Prince sent for his English bride and took her to his Haw in the remote hills of MongMit near the Valley of Precious Stones. He might have passed for an Englishman anywhere. He was clever, charming, an intelligent Statesman, and yet his career was doomed, for he, along with so many other prominent Shans was to be detained at the order of the Revolutionary Council. There were many events which led up to that fateful coup, and perhaps there were faults to be found on both sides.

Seeing the situation realistically as the Burmese Authorities must have done it was necessary to keep a strict control on illegal immigrants who had slipped over the border unnoticed and to be fair they had to be firm.

Frequent midnight raids by parties of Immigration Officers with support by the Burmese Army had made the townspeople feel insecure. Who next would be bundled into a lorry in the middle of the night never to be seen again? The immigration raiding parties would descend upon one quarter of the town an hour or so before dawn and they would search each house and lodging. Any foreigner who had a Foreigners' Registration Certificate which was questionable in even the most minor detail, anyone who aroused the slightest suspicion or doubt would be bundled into an army lorry and driven off into the night. Deportation was a nightmarish word on everybody's lips and inevitably the legal immigrants were often put to a great deal of trouble. Horrifying rumours about the terrible fate awaiting any Chinese who were handed back over the border set the Bazaar agog. So-called eye-witnesses would tell of the Shweli River running red with blood and of headless bodies to be seen floating down the river every day. Much of this was probably an exaggeration but for the large immigrant population in the district the possible truth behind the stories only aggravated the uneasy situation. Many people were of mixed parentage and the new strict policy on immigration was to cause much hardship when a husband, father or even a wife was summarily arrested for deportation leaving behind a family with no wish to be uprooted and sent to a strange and unwelcoming land.

When an Immigration Post was set up in the town the officers were far from popular and brought the quiet peace-loving Palaungs to the point where even the mildest incident could have sparked off a bloody revolt.

The officers became embroiled in a quarrel between two local men at the Annual Pwé and we were told that they took one of the quarrelsome Palaungs behind the opium tent and shot him. The infuriated Palaungs forgot their gentle ways and marched on the Immigration Post surrounding it for several days. The besieged officers were eventually rescued by the Army and it was many months before any of them could be persuaded to man the post again.

But it was not only the Immigration Officers who were stirring up trouble. The Major in command of the Army Post had enlisted the step-son of one of our drivers to help him seek out local trouble makers. He was a handsome youth and the power put into his hands rather went to his head; he drove around the district with his armed escort and began to settle old scores. Anyone who displeased him was likely to be taken in for questioning no matter how flimsy the evidence. His wings were eventually clipped after a midnight fracas at the Police Station. The patience of the police was wearing thin and one of them, perhaps unwisely, had punched him on the nose. I was later given the details by Dr Peel who had been called out in the middle of the night to witness the confrontation the Major intended to have with the Police Station Officer. The infuriated and insulted P.S.O. was tired of seeing his officers made to look foolish and of having his orders countermanded by a local lad with a gun and the good wishes of the Major. He was fearful that the incident would end in a shoot-out said the doctor, but in the end good sense prevailed and the Major and his men withdrew.

The Major added to his growing unpopularity when he asked one of the Senior Nehbaing for his young daughter and one day in October the pretty vivacious schoolgirl had duly been installed as his mistress in a large house near the Haw, home of a friend of ours who had been ordered to vacate it at a moment's notice. She was a pretty charming child and one of my special friends. Her father's house nestled at the foot of the Loi Seng Hill and whenever we visited the shrine there she and her brother would run out waving, asking if they could accompany us.

As the Headman's daughter she held a good position in the social hierarchy and perhaps the Major thought the alliance would strengthen his position. I found it hard to condone the affair. Had he merely wanted a mistress there were older girls in the town who might have been approached or better still he could have sent for his wife and family. That way would not have resulted in so much ill feeling. Local opinion was that Aik Pok had taken co-operation with the Burmese Army beyond the bounds of duty and he was eventually to pay for the mistake with his life. The Shan Army had put a price on Aik Pok's head and for a number of years he went in fear for his life, never daring to travel far without an armed escort. In the end however the Shans caught up with him. He had begun to feel that the threats were idle talk and he became careless. Setting out one morning to visit his wife and family in Tawngma he was met by a party of insurgents just a mile beyond the town. It was useless for him to plead with his captors that he had only carried out the Burmese policies for the good of his people. He had shown that he was prepared to give more than other men, His young daughter. He was summarily tried and executed on the spot, hacked to pieces and left a pitiful heap in the middle of the road as a warning to others.

But to return to the Major. Regardless of local opinion he called the Nehbaing from each Circuit to a meeting where they were told that he expected more co-operation from them. To show he meant business they were all thrown into the town lock-up. There they remained in that dreadful bare wooden cage for almost a month, their only comfort a blanket. Their families forbidden to see them or provide food and clothing. Appeals to the Shan Government were of no avail. Meanwhile the already inflamed situation was rapidly getting beyond the point of control. It was at this juncture that we were drawn into the affair. It was my birthday and all the happenings quite spoiled it for me.

The factory was in full production. Growers from outlaying villages would bring the plucked leaf in huge sacks by pack bullock or pony to the weighment sheds at vantage points around the district where it would be checked by the Leaf Collection Officer before being loaded onto lorries and transported to the factory. Speed was essential or the quality of the leaf would suffer. On that October morning the weighment was in full swing at Bankok village when an Army jeep drove up. The Leaf Collector was seized, his hands tied behind his

back with rope taken from one of the bullocks and then he was
bundled into the jeep and driven off without a word of
explanation.

Everyone at the factory knew that someting had gone wrong
when the Leaf lorry failed to arrive on schedule. If there was
no leaf the machines would soon grind to a halt. It was then
that the news of the arrest came through and Piet drove over
to the Army Headquarters to try to sort out the affair. He was
told that the man had been taken for questioning after reports
that he had been involved in insurgent activities. Assurances
that the accusations were false, that we could produce
evidence that the man had been in the Rangoon Hospital at
the time of the incidents in which he was supposed to have
taken an active part were brushed aside. Piet was told that the
man's family had been informed of the arrest and then politely
dismissed. We could only hope that good sense would prevail.
That same afternoon I received a visit from our Leaf
Collector's mother and uncle. Tearfully she said the Bazaar
was full of rumours that her son had been arrested and as he
had not arrived home for his mid-day meal she feared the
worst.

I felt angry that this charming old lady should have been so
distressed. She had proof of her son's innocence she said but
unless something was done immediately he would probably be
lost to his family for ever like so many of the prominent Shans
who had vanished in that way. All members of the ruling
family were watched with suspicion. They could trust no-one
in the town with such a message. Would I go and see her
younger son who was visiting Lashio at that time. Alas for my
good intentions of keeping out of local politics, but as we had
already arranged to go to Lashio the next morning I agreed
that if I met her son I would tell him of his brother's arrest.
He would know what to do after that, said the old lady.

Such a request put us in a difficult position, Piet had to
consider the Bombay Burmah first and his impartiality was
essential, but we had to do something and decided that I
might get away with a small indiscretion if passing on such a
message could be so labelled. We set out early the next
morning with the Land Rover piled high with boxes, baggage
and golf clubs. We were taking the baby and Tan Yin to keep
an eye on him, so the vehicle looked as if we were going away

for a month rather than an overnight stop.

There was a large Army Post at Man Sam Village which lay just beyond the river, and a "gate" had been set up there as part of the new security measures.

All vehicles passing through the gate were being searched for arms and it was when I saw the sergeant emptying my new golf clubs out into the middle of the road that I protested about such careless handling. This apparently was regarded as a suspicious action. Piet was immediately escorted across to the Guard House and the rest of our party ordered to stand in the middle of the road under heavy guard whilst a careful search of everything in the vehicle was made. Had word of my secret mission reached the Major at Namhsan I wondered?

A young Lieutenant came down from the Guard Room to supervise the search. He strutted around me, looking me over with studied insult in his manner as he gave orders for my suitcase to be emptied out into the dust and dirt of the road. I was more angry than afraid. Previously we had been treated with courtesy and respect wherever we had travelled throughout Burma but this was something new and I did not like the tone of it. I stared at him coldly when he asked me where I had hidden the opium we were smuggling. So that was to be his line! It was worse than I had thought. I told him we were the very last people to become involved in anything of that nature. He noticed that the driver had just finished repacking my suitcase whereupon my tormentor ordered the sergeant to have all my clothes emptied out into the road once more.

He stood over me gently swinging his revolver waiting for my reaction and I felt a wave of icy fury sweep over me. Giving him a look I hoped expressed my contempt I slowly turned my back on him and stared icily at the far horizon. I have never before or since seen a man in such a temper. He screamed at me, literally stamping with rage. Out of the corner of my eye I saw him raise his revolver to my head and I am certain that had I made any sudden or aggressive move at that moment, he would have shot me.

Luckily I was frozen with anger, my face fixed on distant horizons and, realising that he was not intimidating me, he turned to stamp and rage at his men.

Slowly, I turned to take the baby from his nanny who was white faced and shaking. They had all been standing in the hot sun for about fifteen minutes and young Jamie had been struggling to get hold of one of the rifles, blissfully unaware of the danger. Ignoring the ill-tempered Lieutenant, I walked slowly past the line of guards and requested the flask of lime juice as the baby was dying of thirst in the hot sun. The Lieutenant looked as though he would burst and then, perhaps realising that he was beginning to look rather foolish in front of his men, he stormed back into the camp. Piet was released and we were allowed to load up our baggage and depart. It was not a moment too soon for me; my legs felt weak and I was shaking. It was not an encounter I was anxious to repeat.

We heard afterwards that the Lieutenant had an unpleasant habit of singling out women at the "gate" and subjecting them to the treatment I had just endured. He would have them on their knees begging for mercy we were told before he would let them past the gate but on this occasion he had made a misjudgement in trying out such tactics on a Western woman who was not so easily reduced to tears.

We arrived in Lashio to find that the old lady's son had already left for Rangoon. We could only hope that it would not be too late by the time he received the news of his brother's arrest.

The incident at Man Sam had given me an excuse to call on the highest judicial authority in Lashio and to complain bitterly of my treatment at the hands of that ill-tempered Lieutenant. Needless to say the conversation turned to Namhsan. We were asked for our opinion on the situation there. The story of our friend's arrest was only one incident in a long chain of unfortunate events which could spark off serious trouble unless the Government took steps to cool the rapidly worsening situation. Perhaps our opinions were passed on to the right people. There was certainly a lot of activity in high places soon afterwards and our friend was released after sixty hours of questioning. He was lucky. Many others had no loyal family or friends who might help prove their innocence.

Soon after this event a Senior Officer was sent to Namshan to take over command. he was charming, tactful and worked hard to win the support of the people. He called mammoth meetings, introducing all the prominent local citizens who spoke urging co-operation with the Government. Democracy was the ultimate aim of the Government policy but the

Palaungs must help to achieve this. The Nehbaings were all released from detention, the Major returned his temporary "wife" to her parents to be sent back to school and once again life in Namhsan settled down to a more leisured pace. The Shan Army still made their rounds extracting donations from the villagers at gun-point. The Burmese Army were never far behind but the Shans were elusive and indistinguishable amongst the local people who gave information reluctantly knowing they would suffer death or worse as a result. And the Palaungs wearied of the warmongering, they wanted only to be left in peace to enjoy their festivals.

The Chinese Border Commission had been operating from Lashio to settle various disputed sections of the Sino-Burmese Border areas. The large party of Chinese Officials had taken over the Circuit House, casual visitors were turned away and we had the greatest difficulty in finding anywhere to stay on our monthly appointments to meet cash shipments from Rangoon. Sometimes we would stay at the Tawngpeng Haw in Lashio, but that was eventually occupied by helicopter pilots operating with the army.

We would try our luck at the P.W.D.Bungalow but we were only allowed to stay there on the understanding that if a government official arrived unexpectedly we would have to vacate our rooms even though it was at a moment's notice.

This was exactly what had happened one September evening; we were comfortably settled and preparing to go into town for dinner when the Gurkha Dewan descended on us excitedly brandishing a telegram. A senior official would be arriving at midnight he informed us and we must leave at once. We had no option but to comply. We had one last hope of a comfortable night with a roof over our heads. There was a private Rest House on the airfield and we had permission to use it in an emergency. We called on the Burmese officer in command of the airfield and with some reluctance he eventually agreed that we could stay at the Rest House on condition that we agreed to be in bed and lights out by 10 p.m. An early night seemed a small hardship compared with our only other alternative which would have been the Land Rover.

As we drove into Lashio for an early dinner the night seemed strangely dark although there was a full moon. It was then that we saw a dark shadow consuming the rapidly shrinking crescent: a total eclipse was well under way. Zan Lyn drove us through the Chinese Quarter of the town to see the festivities. The Chinese, he said, believe that an eclipse is the result of a dragon eating the moon. They prepare sumptuous feasts, give offerings to the dragon, make as much noise as possible to frighten it away, and when the first thread of silver is seen again, the feasting begins.

The dark outline of each house seemed to shimmer as the brilliance within burst through the open doors and windows to show us how each housewife had been busy. Beyond the open doors we could see tables piled high with dishes of food, sweetmeats, fruits and bottles of every shape and size. Tiny lighted candles had been stuck along the pavement edges and each house was festooned with a myriad of glowing mini moons, paper lanterns which swayed to the night breeze. The excited revellers rushed up and down the pavement shouting, banging gongs and drums to the background of the steady staccato explosions of the endless firecrackers. As the first shining crescent re-appeared in the black velvet of the star spangled heavens a great cry went up from the excited crowd and we drove away towards the airfield with their cheers ringing in our ears.

Zan Lyn had been instructed to signal a code with the lights as we approached the airfield gates for unless the correct signal was given the Duty Guards would fire at the approaching vehicle. We were only just in time and had scarcely time to make preparations for bed when without warning every light was extinguished. For perhaps half an hour all was quiet and peaceful. It was too early for sleep and so I was wide awake when the invaders began their stealthy intrusion. A shoe bumped across the room then some small object fell with a clatter from the dressing table. I was beginning to wonder if perhaps the Rest House ghosts were on the prowl when my mosquito net began to undulate above my head. Then I heard the patter of soft feet as something raced back and forth across my bedhead until I could stand the suspense no longer. I took the torch from under my pillow and flashed the beam around the room to find a pack of the largest rats I had ever seen busily gnawing everything they could sink their teeth into. I leapt out of bed and began to hurl shoes at every rat I managed to pinpoint in the torch beam.

'Horrible beasts, I'll teach you to bounce on my mosquito net' I shrieked, and the rats skipped nimbly out of reach, concerned only with their search for something to gnaw, but across the airfield the noisy commotion and flashing lights had alerted the Night Guard. I heard shouts, the clank of rifles and pounding of heavy boots and within seconds we were surrounded. An angry voice demanded to know what was going on inside and on being told by Piet that I was merely throwing shoes at the rats, the voice was stilled into a deep disbelieving silence. After a whispered consultation the voice out of the night said rather firmly that whatever it was I must stop doing it at once. His men were rather edgy, said the voice, after a dispatch warning them that the insurgents were about to attack the airfield. Well! I crept back into bed deciding fatalistically that if I was not destined to be eaten alive by giant rats, I was obviously going to be riddled with bullets in the forthcoming battle and I might as well get some sleep whilst I had the chance.

I awoke the next morning to an airfield shrouded in mist with no sign of any dark doings of battle. We had been lucky we were told later. There had been an affray at a bridge about three miles north of the airfield and luckily for us the rebels had been routed. As for the rats, they took a subtle form of revenge: they ate my petticoat and Piet's shoelaces. After breakfast we drove across to the Guard House to report that we were going into town for an hour or so and I noticed that the Morning Guard gave me some rather odd sidelong glances and that they were questioning Zan Lyn rather closely. He got back into the Land Rover and doubled up over the driving wheel almost choking with laughter. The Morning Guard had heard of the fracas at the Rest House and wanted to know if all English people had such odd bedtime habits, or had it merely been a matrimonial disagreement?

Our last two years in Tawngpeng were a mixture of high drama and tragedy. My diary of events began to read like some fantastic "Who dunnit" serial. At the time it was difficult to decide whether the atrocities and outrages were the work of the Shan army or the dacoits. Certainly the latter were not slow to make use of the situation.

A prominent citizen of Lashio was travelling to Hsipaw on a

lonely stretch of jungle road when he was stopped by a small band of armed men who claimed to be members of the Shan Army. After being relieved of all his valuables and money by way of a "donation" he was told, he was allowed to drive on only to be stopped again about three miles on by another armed band who also said they were the Shan Army, and that they were collecting donations for the funds. The outburst of fury which followed his rather lame explanation that he had already donated everything he possessed to their friends down the road convinced the poor man that his last moments had come, but fortunately their anger was directed at their rivals.

'Those men are dacoits and they are giving the Shan Army a bad name' said the leader of the armed band, and with apologies for having delayed their intended victim, they set off at the double down a jungle track intent on waylaying and wiping out the dacoits.

On a hillside about seven miles from Namhsan nestled the tiny village of NamLim and one April afternoon a party of about thirty men who claimed to be the Shan Army took over the little village. They demanded food and money, but the villagers were slow to co-operate and so, thinking that the spokesman must be the Headman, the rebels tied him to a tree, stuffed kerosene soaked rags into his mouth and set them alight. By that time the genuine Headman had been identified and in order to encourage others to co-operate more readily, he also was bound hand and foot, with ropes soaked in kerosene, suspended from a tree and set on fire. Although badly burned the Headman survived his ordeal but the other man died, a burnt offering to the cult of terror and if the villagers showed little resistance after that who could blame them?

A few short weeks after this incident the Tawngpeng Sawbwa and the Sao Nang were driving towards Hsipaw when they were ambushed by a large party of masked men. Their armed escort was hopelessly outnumbered and they had no option but to obey their captors. They were driven down a rough track to a small clearing in the jungle where at gunpoint they were relieved of money and valuables. One of the masked men turned to the Sao Nang his greedy eyes on the diamond buttons fastening her blouse. With a sudden swift slash of his dah he had hacked off the front of her blouse. She spoke to me shortly afterwards about the affair. It had been a terrible moment in her life she said, never before had she been so close to death and it was some weeks before she recovered from the ordeal.

About this time most of the prominent citizens in Namhsan began to receive anonymous letters threatening attack by the insurgents. The growers called a meeting when the rumours spread through the town that the factory was to be the next target. They were only too well aware that their prosperity depended to a great extent on the continued operation of our factory. Who else could buy such large quantities of tea leaf?

Slowly the pattern of action by the Shan Army became more obvious. They had to keep on the move if they were to avoid surprise attack by the Burmese. We kept track of their movements from reports of villages they had occupied. The empty Leaf Collection Sheds spoke only too plainly when the growers were silent and we concluded that generally they kept to a well defined circle covering a wide area. They would move into a village asking for "donations" and food and although sometimes they would then move on, more usually they would rest in that village for a day or so. Over the weeks each village in their territory would be occupied. Should the villagers seem reluctant to offer hospitality they would use their terror weapon without pity or mercy. One May morning such a party walked into a village not far from Manhsam and finding the people slow to offer help the rebels took hostages: an elderly man and his wife. That night the whole population from the elders to the smallest baby were ordered to assemble in the square. The old woman was brought forward with her hands bound behind her back and she was told to kneel at her husband's feet. Then the rebels began to dismember the old man, prolonging the moment of death as long as possible. They turned on the terrified old woman and slashed the ropes which bound her with dahs still dripping with her husband's blood setting her free. They had no need to ask again for co-operation.

There followed a series of daring raids on all the villages in the near vicinity of Namhsan. At midnight late in July the people of ManKang were rudely awakened to find a large band of masked men had taken over their village. The raiders seemed to have a good local knowledge and knew which households had hidden gold and jewels. They also knew that the tea growers had just been paid for their leaf and the large sums of money should still be in the village. If the incident was reported they would make a return raid and execute all the elders, threatened the leader of the masked raiders and the terrified villagers stayed locked in their houses, afraid to trust anyone. By pure chance a party of police made a routine call there early on the following morning and so were able to pick up the trail before it grew cold.

At the beginning of August the masked robbers struck again; this time at Hokyet, Tawngma and LahPai. At midnight they had descended on the tiny village of LaiPai, and they beat the villagers because they had very little money. What had they done with the proceeds of their rice transporting business asked the masked villains? They moved on to Hokyet and ransacked the whole village taking at least K30,000/- in money and valuables. We had visited Hokyet the following day and were given the full story by the owner of the teashop.

The whole family had been aroused in the early hours by a loud battering at the door and expecting to see a late traveller in need of shelter they had unbarred the door. Half a dozen masked men had burst into the shop and demanded gold and jewels. When the man and his wife both pleaded that they were poor people and had nothing of value, the raiders produced a long list which set out every piece of jewellery the wife had been seen to wear during the previous six months. The masked raiders had been doing their homework. The woman was seized and her arms were bound across a wooden table, then she was given ten seconds to disclose the secret hiding place before they would cut off both her hands. She knew it was no idle threat and tearfully disclosed the safe place where all their worldly wealth was hidden. The little daughter had sobbed bitterly as she saw her favourite bracelets and earrings handed over and the leader suddenly thrust them into the childs hands saying he did not rob small children. Now these trinkets were the only thing of value they had left, the woman told me and tears poured down her cheeks as she told us the story. She whispered sadly that perhaps one day her husband would forgive her, after all a wife without hands would have been of little use in their business.

The masked robbers boasted that Tawngma Village was

next on their list, but during the second week of August it was the unfortunate villagers of LahPai who found their houses being looted. It happened at mid-day when all able-bodied men and women were out in the tea fields plucking or weeding. Only the oldest inhabitants had been left at home to look after the small children, and they were no match for the masked raiders who took everything they could carry, pots and pans, blankets and clothing as well as money and jewellery.

After this last raid the Nehbaing of Tawngma mounted a round the clock guard on the three access roads to his village. All the local villages were now enclosed by high palisades which gave some protection after dark. These were made of split bamboo and the sharpened tips had first been dipped into the midden, anyone trying to scale those palisades would get some nasty poisonous scratches. Throughout the day and the long night hours thirty men stood guard at each of the gates; they were armed with crossbows, longbows and bamboo spears which they would not have hesitated to use with deadly accuracy. The Nehbaing had been issued with a Sten gun by the Army but he could guard only one of the gates.

We met the Nehbaing in town one morning and he looked haggard and worn after so many nights waiting for something to happen, for the leader of the masked robbers had sent him a challenge. No matter what the people of Tawngma did they would be taken. A village a day was the robbers' motto. One night, he said, they had heard the sound of footsteps and saw flashing lights on the road just below the main gate. For two weeks the men had stood guard all night long, silent, watching and waiting for such a sound. Someone had shouted a challenge saying they would shoot unless the intruders revealed themselves but there had been no reply so to make sure they loosed a volley of crossbow bolts sweeping a wide area either side of the track. They had heard a sudden sharp scream said the Nehbaing, a scuffle, dragging footsteps and then silence. The men on guard dared not desert their posts to investigate but with renewed vigilance they waited out the night. At dawn a party was sent out to search the area and they discovered a thin trail of blood going down the hill path but although they searched the surrounding undergrowth they found no body; perhaps the wounded man had friends who had carried him away. All were convinced that they had foiled an attack, for no honest men would have been out there in the dead of night, said the Nehbaing. After that scare they had doubled the guard and the night watches would go on until the raiders were caught.

Meanwhile the police had been quietly watching and gathering information. A man living in an isolated cottage near Payagyi suddenly had large sums of money to spend on the gambling tables at the Pwé yet he had no means of livelihood. The police started to ask questions. They raided his cottage to find a rifle, a Sten gun and plenty of ammunition. He was arrested for holding illegal arms but at dawn on the following morning when he was taken out of the lock-up for the morning ablutions the suspect took to his heels and fled down the hillside. The guard fired and the Police Station Writer seeing the fleeing prisoner had also seized a rifle. The phrase 'Shot whilst resisting arrest' was heard all too often in those days but that time the police were sorry to have lost a valuable suspect. Then the unexpected happened. A woman recognised a jewelled necklace which the masked robbers had taken from her; it was adorning a pretty young miss from Kyaukhpyu village. Kyaukhpyu nestled on a small ridge under the shadow of Loi HsamHsip, one of the highest hills in the district. It was an isolated and unfriendly village and not an easy place to reach. The woman had reported her suspicions to the police and an armed party was sent to investigate the claim. They found the village of Kyaukhpyu almost deserted with all but three of the men away on business so the three were arrested on suspicion, to be taken to Namhsan for questioning. The prisoners knew the precipitous tracks better than their captors and at a blind corner they made a bid for freedom but the police did not intend to allow their suspects to get away easily and so they were shot down before they could reach safe cover. Before dying one of the men confessed, giving the police all the information they needed. During a successful raid on the robber village almost all of the masked raiders surrendered and a search uncovered chests of loot, jewels and piles of gold. Some of the young men of Kyaukpyu had hit upon this easy way to get rich. They knew the district, had access to all the nearby villages at festival times when they were able to note which women wore valuable jewelled ornaments and they had enjoyed terrorising their neighbours.

They had become careless with success, never expecting that the jewels would be recognised months later by their former owners. They had counted on getting away with their misdeeds by using the cover of the Shan Army which had taken the blame for most of the atrocities. The unmasking of the robbers of Kyaukhpyu was a great relief to the whole district and good for police morale but there was still the constant threat of the Shan Army forever in the background.

The people of Namhsan were afraid. At night everyone bolted and barred their houses and shops and at dusk it seemed to become a ghost town. Gates were set up at each of the access roads and after 6 p.m. no-one was allowed through. The traders, shopkeepers, businessmen of Namhsan flocked to the factory hoping to hand in their money in return for cheques on the Rangoon Banks. To keep large sums of cash in the house was asking for trouble they all said. Speculation was increased after live rifle bullets were found amongst leaf which was being fed into the machines in our factory. One of the workers spotted the ammunition just as it was about to go through the cutters and later that same day a Sten gun bullet was discovered in the drier. Not only would these have wrecked the tea machinery had they not been found in time but they also resulted in a lot of tiresome questions by the Township officer and the police who were anxious to know how live ammunition came to be hidden in the leaf sacks. Whether the intention had been to cause trouble for the growers or the company or point evidence to a secret arms cache in one of the villages was a question that seemed to have no answer.

The threat of an attack on the factory was considered to be a serious possibility and this unsettled our houseboys. It always happened that whenever I announced the impending arrival of guests one of the boys would immediately take to his bed, or perhaps ask for leave to attend a wedding or a funeral. When Franz came up for his annual visit combining business with a welcome break from the sultry heat of Rangoon, it was Aik Siye who sent a message saying that he was too ill to come to work. He had a fever and would be off work for a day or so, declared Yu Hsung. It was too bad, I thought and handed a thermometer to Piet asking him to go personally and check the boy's temperature. If he really did have a fever he was to be sent to the hospital for treatment and if not he must be told to report for work next day. Piet had knocked on the door of the house shared by the two houseboys and a faint voice called him in.

He opened the door and stopped in his tracks staring with amazement at the empty room. Every article of furniture had vanished and there was no sign of Aik Siye. From somewhere above his head a faint voice said 'Good Morning' and he looked up, scarcely able to believe what he saw. Beds, table, chairs, all had been suspended by ropes from the ceiling beams and Aik Siye was peering down at him over the edge of a wildly swaying bed. The boy explained that as the factory was under threat of attack and as the insurgents usually fired on the houses at waist level to wound and kill as many people as possible, he and Yu Hsung had devised the mid-air arrangement of their rooms thinking they might have a better chance of escaping injury that way. We laughed at their ingenuity and Aik Siye was forgiven. It was not just a silly game, there was a terrible truth behind their folly.

That same month a large party of insurgents attacked Hsenwi. They had stormed into the town at about 10.30 p.m. converging from three directions and surrounding the Police Post. Two of the police officers managed to get away to alert the nearest Army Post whilst the others defended what they could against the larger force. The Shans took the jail releasing all the prisoners and setting fire to the buildings. Then they attacked the Immigration Office. Not content with their haul of arms and ammunition they began to hunt down the Immigration Officers and so were still in the town when the Burmese Army arrived on the scene and for four hours the battle raged before the Shans withdrew.

Lashio was the next town to be caught unawares. A large party of rebels surrounded the Treasury at mid-day and got away with one LakhKyats in a daring raid under the noses of the Army Battalion nearby. The Shans had vanished with their loot before the troops could even be alerted.

We had become a little blasé about all the battles and attacks. It was not that we took unnecessary risks, we just went about our normal business as usual and as a result often found ourselves quite unintentionally at the scene of some incident. By this time the Gurkhas of the hill villages beyond Aram had all fled from their farms after repeated murderous attacks and constant rustling of their cattle. When a village had suffered an attack, the headman and elders would ride into Namhsan to report the incident and I would often see parties of horsemen, sometimes twenty or more, galloping into town to make their report. The ponies were small and wiry and although the Palaungs used leather saddles they rode without stirrups holding their legs stiffly forward, their feet almost scraping the ground. The grim faced riders with drooping moustaches, turbanned heads, bare tattooed chests and flapping baggy pants made me think of the Mongol hordes. Things had changed little over the centuries it seemed.

We often visited the hilltop shrine of LoiPra, one of the highest and most important of the pagodas, and again Lady Luck smiled on us and we missed serious trouble by just a few minutes. The track up to the pagoda divided and that day we took the longer, easier way around the hill. The track was bounded by a thick hedge of buddleia, the thick gnarled trunks of the stunted bushes showing their great age. In December we would see the first of the sweet scented flowers, great spikes of waxy blossoms in soft shades of purple, pink, apricot and pale yellow through to pure white. Left to nature they had produced a spectacular display of colour which would have done credit to the best of botanists or gardeners.

Higher up the hill, just below the summit at around 7000 ft where little but coarse wiry grass flourished, thickets of spiny leaved Mahonia clung to the windswept hillside, their stems bent almost parallel to the steep slopes. In February the beautiful pale yellow flower sprays clouded the air with the heavy scent of lily of the valley and I would always make a point of visiting LoiPra at that time to gather a few flowers. Just below the summit of the hill a lone tree struggled to survive. The hollow rotting trunk was wreathed in moss and lichen and each year I expected to find that the few remaining branches had given up the struggle. In December however that monstrous ruin would be transformed into a fairytale tree as if in honour of Christmas. As if by magic a sheet of lilac pink blossoms would burst through the grey matted cloak and a search under the mossy cloak revealed its secret, the whole trunk was encrusted with tiny bulblets of the pleione orchid. There was small wonder that the Palaungs preserved the old tree so carefully.

We had visited the LoiPra Shrine on many occasions usually to find it deserted and an air of neglect around the place but on one January afternoon we had driven in that direction to see the cherry blossom and had decided to walk up to the shrine. On reaching the Zayat which stood in a sheltered spot below the pagoda we were surprised to see signs of very recent occupation. A fire still burned smokily; there was a litter of abandoned clothing, sandals and baskets of food. It looked as though whoever had been enjoying the giant picnic had just left in a great hurry. We could see no-one and took little notice of the sounds of gunfire which seemed to come from the other side of the hill. We must have spent an hour or more there enjoying the apparent peace of the lonely Shrine and looking out onto the jewelled hills of Mongmit which lay beyond the next ridge surrounded by valleys painted green with new rice. On our return to Namhsan we were met by an irate P.S.O. We would get him into trouble one day, he complained to us. It seemed that a party of about seventy insurgents had taken over the LoiPra Zayat sometime during the previous week. They had been observed by devotees visiting the shrine and someone had talked. The information had eventually reached the Burmese Army who had mounted a surprise attack on the very day we had decided to go up to LoiPra. The Shans were vigilant and their scouts had spotted the advancing Burmese in time for their whole party to slip away hurriedly, avoiding a confrontation they were not ready for. As we had seen, their departure had been so sudden they had no time to gather up their belongings and they had fled over the hills with the Burmese Army in hot pursuit. I wondered what might have happened had we chanced to arrive at the Zayat a little earlier? The P.S.O. insisted that we must consult him before setting out on any more of our long walks, then at least he would know where to search for the pieces — if we failed to return home, he added meaningfully.

Piet had bought a tent and was planning to spend a weekend holiday walking across the high ridge from Loi TawngKyaw visiting a series of small isolated villages there and eventually finding a track which would lead down to Lilu. I was not keen on the project because those hills were the territory of a vicious band of dacoits and often we would hear of attacks on traders who had dared to use those ancient highways. The P.S.O. advised us not to risk the dangers and it was when our plan eventually reached the ears of the Army Commander that we were forbidden to go to any distant place without first obtaining permission from the authorities. From then on our movements were restricted to short walks around Namhsan until the situation became less dangerous.

It was in April that the Corporation's manager decided to come up from Rangoon for a short visit and he was to bring a secret delivery of cash: more than two LakhKyats which would be sealed in two large kerosene tins. The journey from Lashio was without incident until they were within forty miles of home. Rounding a hairpin bend in the road not far from Panglong they found themselves in the middle of an ambush. At least thirty men of the Shan Army were ransacking the Mayman Express Bus and angry at not finding the money they had been tipped off would be on board the bus, they set it on fire. If the money was too well hidden for them to find they were making sure that no one else would ever find it. Several other vehicles had blundered into the ambush to be searched and the occupants relieved of all valuables. There was no escape. Zan Lyn had a gun at his head and the passenger was told to remain seated whilst the baggage was searched. Our guest had a camera on his knee and was tempted to snap the scene but fortunately, perhaps, he changed his mind. The insurgents were nervous and angry and might have reacted with violence. Just as the searchers began to examine the kerosene tins a whistle blew somewhere nearby and immediately all the green-uniformed men melted away into the jungle. They had been within seconds of finding a fortune. It had been a nerve wracking experience for those concerned which ended without loss or tragedy but inevitably the story slipped out. There were spies and informers everywhere and the cover we had so carefully built up over the years was common knowledge. We knew that our days there were numbered.

About two months after this incident Zan Lyn drove down to Lashio to meet the weekly plane and pick up the mail bag and stores as usual but he failed to return at the appointed time. Thinking that the aircraft had been delayed we did not worry unduly. It was the time of the first "flush" of leaf and the factory was working around the clock, everyone was busy. Piet would not return home until 3.00 or 4.00 a.m. and I would be left entirely alone in the bungalow for most of the night. I was awakened in the early hours by shouts, a loud battering on one door then another, excited voices were followed by heavy footsteps tramping around the house. I sat up in bed.

'This is it, we're under attack, don't panic' I told myself as I struggled into a housecoat.

Then I heard someone calling my name and with relief I recognised Zan Lyn's voice. I opened the doors to find not only Zan Lyn but the Tawngma Nehbaing, a turbanned Indian and a taxi driver, all dishevelled and black with bruises. They shouted excitedly and it took some time to make out their story. It seemed that Zan Lyn had met the plane as usual, loaded the mail bags, box of stores and a new ice box for cold stores, then collected his passengers, (which was strictly against the rules), and then set out for Namhsan.

At Mile Six he had rounded the hairpin bend to find eight masked men standing in the road, rifles raised to fire if he resisted. With a gun at his head Zan Lyn was made to drive down a jungle track for about a mile where, in a small clearing, they were ordered out of the vehicle and put under guard whilst the dacoits unloaded the crated ice box and smashed it open with their dahs. Their jubilant shouts as the lid was forced open faded to silence when they saw the contents, not the money they expected to find but butter, bacon, cheese, fish and a leg of lamb. Their spies had been watching our Land Rover from the moment the information about the cash shipments had been leaked and the sight of that gleaming new crate with its stout hasp and staple and heavy padlocks had convinced them that it contained a fortune. The spy had dashed off ahead of Zan Lyn to alert his confederates at Mile Six and they had been waiting for him. Their disappointment was vent on Zan Lyn and his companions who were tied to trees and beaten. The dacoits fell upon the mail bags and stores, scattering everything. They slashed the tyres, the door panels, threw the distributor cap over the precipice and did as much damage as they could before disappearing into the jungle with their disappointing loot; butter and fish for nothing else pleased them. They stubbed out their cheroots in the prime Stilton, loosened the knots binding their prisoners and vanished. The three men freed themselves and feeling that they had been lucky to escape with their lives they made their way back to the main road where a friendly passing vehicle took them on to Ee Nai.

The villagers of Ee Nai helped them to drag the stranded vehicle out of the jungle and pushed it to Ee Nai where it was left in the egg woman's garden. Once more their luck held as a taxi drove into the village bringing passengers from Lashio and the driver agreed to drive on with them to Namhsan. It was an adventure he never wished to live through again, said Zan Lyn, but luckily neither lives nor cash had been lost. The next day a rescue party was sent down to repair the damage and get the stranded vehicle home. Those two ambushes were to spell the end of our time in Thusan-ti's enchanted garden.

They set off a chain reaction throughout the Corporation. The factory was ordered to close and it was not until after deputations from the growers had persuaded the Government to allow cash to be sent for the payroll under armed escort to the Namhsan Treasury that eventually the factory re-opened for limited production and it was something of a relief not to have to undertake those long hazardous journeys sitting on a box containing a fortune knowing that each bend in the road might conceal a band of merciless dacoits or perhaps insurgents who would stop at nothing to get their hands on it. We knew that our time in that lovely place was drawing to a close. Eventually it became almost impossible for a foreign company to operate in Burma and the tea factory was soon to close, bringing hard times for the Palaungs. The small local factories would continue producing tea but could not increase their output to process all the leaf which formerly we had bought. In the end a local co-operative was formed and after much negotiation and many false starts the old factory was at last re-opened. Our friends wrote to tell us and we wished them success.

33

Diplomatic Incidents

Tawngpeng's remoteness and reputation of beauty gave it high priority on the visiting list for V.I.P.'s who would be allowed to make a tour of Upper Burma and the Shan States if accompanied by an official escort of senior Army Officers and men. Unfortunately the department in Rangoon which arranged these tours seldom thought to let anyone know that a dozen or more guests would be arriving for lunch and sometimes possibly staying on for several days. Telegrams would be dispatched only to arrive after the guests they announced had departed. But I kept a large storeroom well stocked with tinned foods just in case somebody turned up unannounced for there was no cold store or butcher's shop around the corner to dash off to in such an emergency.

One April morning the Sawbwa and Mahadevi called on us with the news that they had been notified of an impending official visit by the Commissioner General for S.E. Asia. The Commissioner and party were scheduled to arrive at our bungalow at 10.30 a.m. for a rest before we escorted them to the Haw at midday for the luncheon at 1.00 p.m. Mahadevi was delighted, the guest was very popular in Burma and no expense was to be spared for the State Banquet. Already she had sent for her cook from the Rangoon Haw; he was a good 'English cook' she said and she was planning an English menu in honour of the principal guest. She read out a long list of dignitaries who were to be invited to meet the Commissioner and her pleasure in anticipating the event was bubbling over.

A few days before the visitors were due the Mahadevi called on me again. She was bitterly disappointed having just heard that the Commissioner had been recalled to London. However the lunch was still on as his Adviser was coming in the Commissioner's place.

'It is not the same' said the disappointed Mahadevi 'but I shall show our guest that our hospitality is not lacking for no matter who comes, he represents your Queen'.

The day arrived; first 10.30 a.m. then midday passed and there was no sign of the guests and their escort. As there was no telephone we could not contact the Haw to enquire if the party had mistakenly driven there first. By 1 p.m. we were beginning to feel that something was badly wrong and leaving instructions that, should the guests arrive they were to be escorted to the Haw without delay, we drove to the palace with more speed than caution.

The Sawbwa met us at the entrance a worried frown on his usually smiling face. Where were the guests he wanted to know? No-one knew quite what to do. A large assembly of important local dignitaries and visitors from as far away as Rangoon all sat in embarrassed silence in the grand reception hall. The conversation centred on the fate of the missing V.I.P.'s. Had they been ambushed or was it merely a breakdown? The Sawbwa dashed out onto the terrace at intervals to scan the approach road with binoculars. There had been no word of any change of plans and it was becoming obvious that Mahadevi felt she had been publicly humiliated. It was then that I realised the distinguished Burmese Judge seated at Mahadevi's right hand was spreading anti-British progaganda which seemed to be deliberately calculated to fan the flames of her anger and disappointment. I moved to her left and tried to tactfully counter his jibes, to make excuses for the missing guests which sounded feeble even to my ears. At 3.30 p.m. Mahadevi suddenly rose to her feet turning to me as the only other woman present.

'I think we can wait no longer' she said icily and I followed as she swept majestically down the long room past the silent men, embarrassed for her sake. Throughout the lunch I tried to keep up amusing chatter, to talk of anything but the missing guests but Mahadevi felt that all her efforts had been in vain and she and the Sawbwa did not take kindly to being publicly humiliated.

The next morning at precisely 10.30 a.m. I heard a bellow from the hillside above. Piet had just spotted our missing guests who were arriving exactly twenty four hours late. As they walked into the bungalow all smiles and no apology or word of explanation about the delay, I felt a sudden wave of anger sweep over me. No matter who these people were, I was going to see that Mahadevi got a much needed apology. With a bright smile and what I hoped was a casual air of welcome I said.

'How nice to see you. What a shame you missed the delicious luncheon Mahadevi laid on for you yesterday'. I saw their faces fall. The Adviser had not been told they were behind schedule and the Burmese Colonel in charge of the escort was quite unrepentant. There had been so much to show the guests he said, that he had extended the tour. It had not occurred to him to radio a message through to the Haw and so save a tactless slight on their hosts. Piet had hurriedly sent a note to Mahadevi warning her of the impending visitors and her reply made me smile.

'They can have lunch at the Kaukswé Shop in town' she had written and it seemed the tardy guests would get a cool reception. The Adviser took me aside and expressing his concern over the affair asked if there was any chance he might be able to buy a box of chocolates in Namhsan as a small peace offering for Mahadevi. He was lucky. Much to his surprise I was able to direct him to Thomas's shop in the Bazaar where he could be sure to find the perfect gift for a ruffled lady: a tin of Cadbury's Milk Tray. Whether it was the chocolates or the charming Adviser I never knew but Mahadevi forgave them and at a moment's notice arranged a simple lunch for them. This lack of consideration on the part of the Burmese may have played a large part in Mahadevi's decision to close the Haw and take up residence in Rangoon. After having been deprived of his expense account it was not surprising that the Sawbwa was not happy to have his home used as a free country hotel by large parties of officials, often for a stay of several days.

We were to experience a few headaches over V.I.P.'s and I remember one incident in particular. We had returned home earlier than usual one Sunday from an expedition to Lilu. The rains were almost over and it had been hot and sticky by the river with the misery of the swarming sand flies and we hurried back to the cool hills. We found the house deserted, the houseboys had all gone up to town and the Malis had taken an unofficial holiday. A telegram lay on Piet's desk and he drove up to the factory to de-code it whilst I opened the deserted kitchens in search of tea. A few minutes later the Land Rover screamed to a halt by the kitchen door and Piet charged in waving the telegram frantically.

'What are we going to do about this' he cried and read out the de-coded message from the British Embassy. It informed us that an Ambassador who had recently arrived from the New World, accompanied by the man who was Supreme Commander of the Burmese Air Force at that time, and a full escort would be arriving for lunch on August 26th perhaps to stay for a few days. Well it was then 6 p.m. on the evening of August 26th which put us in a quandry. What if our guests had turned up for lunch? By now they would be rather hungry, and what if they were about to arrive for dinner? Piet drove up to town to make a few discreet enquiries.

Had anyone seen foreigners, or strangers in town? He dared not mention names or give true identities, but he drew a blank so perhaps this party would arrive a day late without notifying us we thought. We had to be very careful. One word that such high ranking officers were in the area might have brought the Shan Army to Namhsan and ambush was an ever present danger. There were always strangers in town, and rumour often reported that some were spies or informers ready to make use of those careless remarks. I had learned to choose my words with care. As each day passed the mystery deepened, we dispatched coded enquiries to Rangoon, listened carefully to the local radio in case there was news of an ambush, and after an anxious week the explanations came with apologies. It seemed that on meeting the newly arrived Ambassador, our friend had praised the beauties of Namhsan so ecstatically that on presenting his credentials the new arrival had asked for permission to visit us. His request was received sympathetically and he was invited to join a party travelling to the Northern States. On hearing of the impending visitation our friend kindly thought to warn us knowing it was unlikely that we would hear through official channels. With typical Burmese diplomacy the V.I.P. was escorted to Namsam, an attractive beauty spot in the South Shan States and several hundred miles south of our troubled hills. Wisely the Burmese

Government were not going to risk allowing important foreign visitors to chance their lives in the prolonged guerilla war which dragged on in the Northern Hills, and we laughed with relief at the clever manoeuvre which had kept the missing guest happily out of danger.

34

Small Friends and Farewells

I have left my special friends until the last. It was the children who gave me so much pleasure, children from all the different racial groups who treated the garden as their own. The teamaker's children, the engineer's pretty daughters and the two young sons of the chief clerk who came to practise their English; there were many others and I loved them all. I had only to let my young friends know if I wanted something to have them produce it on their next visit. When the raspberry season came around the children kept me supplied with baskets full of the delicious yellow fruits as long as there were any shan-si-thi to pick. Not all of them were models of good behaviour though. There was the 'J.D.', quite the naughtiest small boy I knew. It was after I caught him trying to drown the layke in the fishpond that I named him 'Juvenile Delinquent of the Year'.

The layke was a curious tortoise which two of the factory workers had found and given to me. The Palaungs thought it was rather special and everybody made a point of calling to see it. It had a large triangular armourplated head which, instead of retracting into the carapace like a normal tortoise, tucked tightly into the neck of the shell like the last piece in a jig-saw. Unfortunately it did not survive the attentions of the 'J.D.'

Our weekends by the river were a great attraction for the Mankai children. The five small boys always seemed to know which days we would be driving down to our jungle house and they would be waiting for us, Aye Kyaw, Po Sein, Htun Hlaing, Aik Kyan and Aik Buint looked so grown-up with long baggy pants, trilby hats and in their mouths the long cheroots which all Palaungs smoked from an early age. We enjoyed their company and they were a great help with the boat and with practice they became good swimmers. Sometimes small girls from the village would join us and it always intrigued me to see them take to the water.

They would first soak their long cotton skirt in the water, then wrap it tightly around the waist before flapping air under the wet cloth to make a quick and easy safety device, a giant air bubble which rose up over their backs and acted like water-wings. Certainly they needed some safety precautions if they were not strong swimmers for the currents were strong and dangerous.

Some of the Chinese children became my special friends. They always made the excuse that they came to see their brother who worked for me, and after a polite greeting they would ask shyly if they could see the goldfish. Their mother was a widow. She and her ten children lived in a tumbledown wooden shack on the outskirts of the town.

She was typical old-style Chinese in her faded blue cotton trousers and smock, her still jet black hair scraped tightly into a knot on top of her head and she tottered around on tiny crippled stumps which should have been feet. At least her daughters had been spared the pain and disfigurement of bound feet. She grew vegetables in her tiny garden but it must have been a struggle to feed and clothe her large family. Her eldest daughter had married a muleteer and they lived nearby in a fine new wooden house. Their next door neighbour was another muleteer, less prosperous than the old lady's son-in-law. Yah Hto's home was a tiny thatched bamboo hut. She was about ten years old, a tall thin child and not pretty like most of the other Chinese children but her pale pinched face had an elfin charm and her dark slant eyes missed nothing. She would come to the garden most days bringing her two year old sister and two mischevious young brothers whom she kept in order with fierce authority. Jamie was still a small baby and all the young friends I had made over the years would come each day to play with him. It was not just that they all thought that I was very unkind to leave him in his play-pen in the middle of the lawn. It was like a cage they all said and felt that they must come to watch over him and comfort him for no local child was ever left alone for so much as a minute, but there was also another reason: Jamie's ash blonde hair. It was considered to be very lucky to touch a fair haired person and everyone wanted to touch him, hold him and play with him.

One morning I was rather startled to hear my young son shouting to his playmates, shouting something which sounded remarkably like swearing. Wondering wherever he could have picked up such language I went outside to find two Chinese boys chasing one another around the lawn as they quarrelled over a ball.

'Bu gè, bu gè' shouted one of the boys as his older brother tried to snatch the ball, 'I will not give it', and Jamie was trying hard to climb out of the play-pen to join in the fun as he imitated the words and accent. I could see myself having a lot of explaining to do on his behalf the next time we went home on leave unless he learned some English.

Victor, the Mali, always took every opportunity to entertain Jamie and on fine days he would gallop around the lawn with Jamie in his push chair until both were exhausted and Jamie's taste for speed grew. Bahadur would entertain him in a gentler manner on monsoon days. He would be sure to find some work to do in whichever room the play-pen had been put and I would hear the Indian boy talking endlessly in a quiet gentle voice as he fielded the soft toys Jamie threw to him.

We had bought a small tape recorder and our young friends had never before encountered such magic. We recorded their chatter and then played it back to them but at first they were quite frightened, how could their voices have got into the little box, then after we explained how it worked their delight with the new toy was endless and they would use it with all the self confidence of well trained actors.

Sometimes Yah Hto would dance to please me. With all the grace and agility I might have expected of a trained ballerina she would bend and sway, pirouette her slender little body with an inborn rhythm. She had a great thirst for knowledge of my world asking endless questions trying to visualise a way of life so very different from anything she had known. I asked if she and her little sister Ah Whan would like to see some colour slides of London and our home in England and she was back within the hour saying her mother would allow them to stay for the night.

That was more than I had intended but seeing the disappointment on her face I agreed to let them stay. It would be an interesting experiment I thought. How would they cope with the sudden switch to our way of life?

The excitement of those two little girls knew no bounds, they arrived at about 6.30 p.m. and I told them that first they must have a bath before dinner. Yah Hto had come to taste the English way of life to the full and if that meant having a bath she was ready to comply, not so little Ah Whan. The moment she saw the gleaming white bath of steaming water she began to scream, kick, bite. It had just been a trap she howled, she was sure they would be boiled alive and eaten for dinner by those barbaric English. I picked up the screaming child and put her firmly into the warm water giving her one of Jamie's bath toys and a look of amazement spread over her face. It was nicer than she had expected and no-one was going to get her out of that bath. I left the two little girls splashing and soaping each other but what a performance it was to get Ah Whan out of the bath! At last Yah Hto persuaded her with stories of a strange water machine in the next room and for another half hour they studied the mysteries of the lavatory. Their stories of the marvels they had experienced at bath time were spread around the school and for weeks afterwards I had a continual stream of children calling and asking if I would allow them to see the "water machines".

At dinner Ah Whan sat in Jamie's high chair and munched her way purposefully through everything that was put before her. Yah Hto sat beside me and as the soup was brought in she whispered.

'What do I do?' pointing to the array of cutlery.

'Just follow me' I said and with side-long glances at me from time to time she behaved with complete self assurance as though she had been doing this all her life. Her greatest thrill was to sit at the long polished table instead of squatting on the floor and to be served the food by a man, for in her world the women ate only what was left when the men had finished their meal. We showed them colour slides of people and places in many countries and they marvelled, especially at the snow scenes. The world was a much bigger place than they had ever imagined.

Both children slept in camp beds near Jamie's cot. They

were accustomed to sleeping on the floor in a corner of the one room shared by the whole family and would never have dared to spend the night in one of our large bedrooms on their own.

When I had asked their mother if the two little girls could stay for the night she had readily agreed and then had called after me 'She will wet the bed', but Ah Whan was on her best behaviour and she explained solemnly the next morning that she had remembered my instructions about using the chamber-pot and had wakened up especially to be able to use it.

At home they curled up in a blanket without taking off their day clothes and they thought it very funny that we should have special clothes to wear in bed. I gave Yah Hto a pink silk nightdress which she thought was very fine and Ah Whan was so tiny for her two and a half years that Jamie's pyjamas fitted her perfectly. Both girls slept soundly, quite un-awed by their new surroundings and in the morning I gave them a snack of biscuits and milk and they set off home to resume their normal lives again. If I had found their reactions interesting to watch they had enjoyed every minute of the experiment and could scarcely wait to be invited again.

I wondered if was I being kind to give them a glimpse of a way of life they could never hope to achieve. Their world was a windowless bamboo hut where a wood fire burned in the centre of the one room with the smoke curling up through a hole in the thatched roof. The muleteer, his wife and five children shared the one tiny room, its bare earth floor covered with a few rush mats and the only furniture a small low table. In a lean-to at the back of the house lived their four mules and a flock of ducks and chickens which spent more time inside the house than out. They had a small plot of garden where the mother grew vegetables to feed her growing family and there they kept their two pigs. I had never seen animals kept in that way before. They looked most uncomfortable in a cage on stilts which was scarcely big enough for them to turn around in and the floor was made of slatted bamboo which may have kept the sty clean but must have made all movements hazardous indeed for the pigs.

Yah Hto and her family had none of the so called necessities of life. They had no tap in or near their house and all water had to be collected from a spring. Cooking was done on a trivet over the log fire in the centre of the one room of the house. Life was hard, a long struggle to exist and yet they were happy, all that is except Yah Hto who had become obsessed with a desire to live in England. Gently I tried to reason with her. She was too old to change her way of life, to forget her parents, brothers and sister and she might be very unhappy in that other bustling noisy world. Ah Whan was still young enough to make the change and adjust to an alien culture. Would they let me take her I asked? But the father would have none of it and perhaps it was as well. He took Yah Hto with him on one of his trips to China. She was gone for a week, walking with the men who set a fast pace she found hard to keep up with and doing her part helping with the cooking.

She was Chinese, her father told her and she should be proud of it. He took her to see the land of her ancestors. This was her heritage he told her and what more could she want? The ways of the West were not for her. When I saw Yah Hto again I felt sorry for her, her pale face was blistered and she looked thinner than ever but she did not ask again to accompany us to England although we remained good friends as before. When the time came for us to leave Namhsan Yah Hto brought a gift for Jamie it was a length of purple silk velvet, to make him a coat she said and it must have cost her family the price of a week's food.

When at last the day of our departure arrived I found that our friends had been secretly making gifts and I was deeply touched by the time, and thought they had put into their presents. There were pillowcases, cushion covers, tablecloths, all beautifully embroidered, Shan bags and handwoven tameins, knitted Fair Isle coats, hats and socks for Jamie. The children of the High School brought me a powder blue satin parasol and the Chinese School children came with a small tapestry picture of the "Copper Bull" in Peking. ManKwé and her sisters arrived with a giant tin of Nice biscuits and a deputation headed by the Headman of Zayangyi presented me with a monster jar of pickled Ta Fu, they knew I liked the stuff and thought it would come in useful on the journey. The staff and workers came down to the garden to make their farewell presentation and we listened to their plans for an uncertain future. One said he was returning to Karen Country to start a chicken farm, another had grandiose plans for opening a restaurant. One said he intended to use his redundancy pay to start a business in jewellery. Would I be his first customer he asked, and he produced an amethyst. It was large and well cut and a lovely clear colour and it posed a problem, if I bought it I would be unable to take it home with me for there were strict laws forbidding anything of value to be taken out of the country. I had been refused permission to send used postage stamps to a friend so there was little doubt that I would not be allowed to take anything as valuable as that jewel with me. I could not refuse to help him and so in the end I bought it as a farewell gift for Tan Yin who had worked for me over the years quietly and without question.

The gifts and good wishes were endless but as I was busy packing and crating our belongings ready for shipment to India I had little time to dwell on sad partings. First we were going to North Thailand where Piet was to survey the hill areas for the Thai Government. The hill tribes in the remote areas of North Thailand grew the opium poppy and there was a scheme to try to persuade them to grow tea instead. It was a new and interesting country and I was looking forward to living there.

On that last morning I got through all the official farewells with my mind fixed firmly on future travels. The head clerk and his family had come to pay their final respects and present Jamie with their gift. The factory workers and staff who had been retained gathered at the garden gates. They faced an uncertain future with our going. Then Tan Yin brought me her gift, a tablecloth she had embroidered. The quiet solemn faced girl who had never shown any spark of emotion during all the years she had worked for me fell weeping at my feet soaking me with her tears and I was lost, my intentions of saying a cool and unemotional "Goodbye" to all those kind people deserted me in that moment.

I left with a heavy heart and misty eyes and my last glimpse of that lovely place was of the hillsides adrift with pink cherry blossom just as they had been on the day I had arrived so many years before. Seeing those gentle hills fade into the purple shadows I realised that there nothing would ever change; Thusan-ti would still weave the magic tapestry of time as she had always done sheltering her children from the noisy exchanges between the War Lords, the Politicians, the Power

Seekers who in the end would leave little to show for their passing and I was glad that for a brief interlude I had been privileged to share the quiet happiness of the Palaungs. I only hoped that their trust in the fabled Dragon Grandmother would not be in vain.

EPILOGUE

We still receive occasional news of our friends in Tawngpeng and, despite the years which have slipped by, it seems that little has changed since we left in December 1962.

At first one of the Chinese boys would write, in excellent English, giving us news of his family and friends. Then he left school and took a job. After that we heard no more. Letters from Palaung friends each brought their share of unhappy tidings. The factory was not working; the Palaungs were in great difficulties; some even faced starvation, for tea was their only means of making a living. It took several years of negotiation and representation to the authorities before the factory was re-opened for limited production under a five member committee. The "tea boom" was over for the Palaungs, and their prosperity declining.

In 1967 we heard that all shops and businesses throughout Burma had been nationalised. In Namhsan sixty shops had been taken over and many of the Indian traders were re-patriated at short notice. One old friend wrote saying simply, 'Your Company now no longer exists in Burma'. We consoled ourselves that at least the Bombay Burmah had left behind a record that was something to be proud of, having contributed in no small way to Burma's prosperity.

The Sawbwa had corresponded with us regularly until his last illness, and always spoke of his love of the plantations and farms of his home state. Like the rest of the old Heavenly Lords he had been stripped of his lands, revenues and, in the end, his titles. He died in August 1975 after a long illness. His body was burned at a ceremony in Rangoon and his ashes buried at

241

Payagyi with his forebears. The travelling Sawbwa had come to rest with his ancestors in Thusan-ti's garden. Recently we heard that the Haw is now used as a hospital.

Still each of the few letters we received contained little good news. There were too many dacoities and kidnappings; the family of one of the drivers was being cared for by friends after their father was shot when he inadvertently drove his lorry into the crossfire during an encounter between the Government Forces and the Shan Army. The engineer had been kidnapped whilst returning home to Namhsan and it had been many months before he was released. These were hazards to be faced by all who dared set forth on those hill roads. Because of continuing insurgent activity many of the inhabitants of the more isolated villages had moved to the comparative safety of the town whilst those who could afford to uproot their families had left Namhsan to start new lives in Mandalay or Rangoon. But not all the atrocities were the work of the insurgents. The body of one of our former workers had been found with head and hands cut off and it was thought that he had fallen foul of one of the powerful opium smuggling gangs who would eliminate anyone who crossed their path or interfered with their traffic.

Uncle, Dr Peel, Zan Lyn, each had passed on towards his Neikban. Then came a silence of several years. We received a few cards at Christmas but no news of old friends as Burma sank deeper into her self-imposed isolation. Now it seems that once again she is opening her doors to foreigners and so perhaps we will hear what changes have taken place behind that lacquered curtain.

I would like to think that despite all their troubles those kind, gentle people of the Shan Hills whom I came to admire so much still have a future amongst their festivals and fables.

NOTES

Butterflies of Tawngpeng

The variety of insects was considerable including moths such as the great Atlas Moth and beetles of all sizes and colours as vivid as the butterflies. There were Leaf and Stick insects, mimics of all kinds and others which inflicted painful stings. But the butterflies were beautiful, each variety having its own "insurance policy". These safeguards were simple, some were poisonous, others had a very nasty taste or smell whilst a third group mimicked those the birds avoided either in colouring or flight.

The Common Rose is mimicked by several species and it was some time before I realised that the specimen I had caught was in fact the female of the Common Mormon so closely did it resemble the original.

The following butterflies were caught in Tawngpeng by the author and are a part of a small collection.

PAPILLONIDAE — The Swallowtails
Not all of these lovely insects possess "tails" but they are all large and eye-catching. They have a powerful, erratic flight the fore-wings being used for propulsion and the hind-wings, like the flaps of an aircraft, control the steering and evenness of their flight.

	Wingspan
The Red Helen — Papilio Helenus	$4''$ to $5''$
Papilio Hector	$3^1/_2''$ to $4^3/_4''$
Papilio Polymnestor	$5^1/_2''$ to $6''$
The Paris Butterfly	$4''$ to $5''$
The Common Mormon Papilio Polytes	$3^1/_4''$ to $4^1/_8''$
The Great Mormon — Papilio Memnon	$4^1/_4''$ to $6^1/_2''$

	Wingspan		
The Lime Butterfly — Papilio Demolens	3¼″	to	4″
Papilio Agamemnon	3½″	to	4″
The Common Bluebottle — Graphium Sarpedon	3¼″	to	3¾″

PIERIDAE — The Whites and Sulphurs
The colouring of these medium sized butterflies is always variations of white, yellow or orange. Often they are plain white on the upper sides of the wings with the vivid reds and oranges on the underside. Almost all of them have black veining or edging to the wings. They are one of the species with a swarming instinct and have been known to migrate over considerable distances.

	Wingspan		
The Great Orange Tip — Hebomoia Gluacipe	2½″	to	4″
The Lemon Migrant — Catsopillia Pomona	2″	to	3″
The Common Grass Yellow — Eurema Hecabe	1″	to	1½″
The Painted Jezebel — Delias Hyparete	2½″	to	3″
The Malayan Jezebel — Delias Ninas	2″	to	3″
The Chocolate Albatross — Appias Lycida	2½″	to	3″

DANAIDAE — The Milkweed Butterflies, Tigers and Crows.
These medium sized, highly coloured butterflies have a particularly nasty taste and fly around openly as though knowing they are safe from attack by birds and other predators. They are unable to use their forelegs for walking. Their colouring is quite distinctive with much veining and lining of the wings.

	Wingspan		
The Blue Glassy Tiger — Danus Vulgaris	3″	to	4″
The Large Chocolate Tiger — Danus Sita	3″	to	4″
The Black Veined Tiger — Danus Melanippus	3″	to	4″
The Striped Blue Crow — Euploea Mulciber	3½″	to	4″

NYMPHALIDAE
This large family of sun loving butterflies has no common factor in their shape, size or colour schemes although, like the Milkweed Butterflies, they are unable to use their forelegs for walking.

	Wingspan		
The Great Egg Fly — Neptis Heliodore	1¾″	to	2″

	Wingspan		
The Clipper — Parthenos Gambrisius	4″	to	4½″
The Autumn Leaf — Doleschalla Bisaltide	2½″	to	3″
Kalima Inachus	4″	to	4¾″
Argyrinis Childreni	3″	to	3½″
Esnipe Cycnus	3½″	to	3¾″
Euthalia Lepidea	2″	to	3″
The Burmese Lascar — Neptis Heliodore	1½″		

The Flowers of Tawngpeng

Throughout the year Tawngpeng was carpeted with flowers. The shrubs and trees brightened the thickets and forests with lovely blossoms and their branches were often thick with orchids. The Palaungs loved flowers and every household would have its show of flowers and orchids. Their gardens, often merely a few old kerosene tins filled with earth, would be carefully tended. The flowers were a part of their heritage and the villagers would preserve even half dead trees if there were orchids growing on the dying branches.

My garden was full of flowering shrubs introduced by former occupants. Poinsettias flourished amongst cascades of bougainvillea and allamanda, bignonia, holmoscoldia and oleander, and the roses and lilies bloomed amongst the English cottage garden annuals. The Bauhinia common to Burma is the variety B. monandra. In September I would see the purple flowered variety in blossom at the lower elevations but the lovely tree which grew in profusion in the sunny valleys was a small well shaped tree which in March would put on a mantle of large white orchid-like flowers. These heavily scented blossoms were greatly prized by the local people.

The Buddleia grew on the higher hills in sheltered sunny spots just below 7000 ft elevation. Many of the bushes were of considerable age with thick lichen covered trunks. They flowered over several weeks in December. The scented flower sprays were heavier and more waxy than the B. davidii and came in many colour variations of mauves, pinks, apricot and white. There were several varieties of Cassia common to Burma, the C. nodosa which formed a boundary and windbreak to my garden were tall and well shaped trees which flowered in March with whorls of deep pink scented flowers followed by dark cylindrical pods at least 18″ in length. The Burmese Pink Cassia, C. renigera, is a much smaller tree with large scented flowers and pods about one foot in length. The Yellow Cassia was one of the showy flowering trees of the lower elevations but I did know of one specimen which grew on a hillside above the Lilu road not far from HoKyet.

The flowering Cherries were a feature of the district. They were tall well shaped trees and from November to January the bare branches would be thickly encrusted with single flowers in a variety of shades of pink. Later followed the small black cherries which were extremely bitter to taste.

The "Fire Bush" was a name I gave to the small shrubs which grew everywhere on the hot plain of YayOh and this bore a close resemblance to the Red Bell Bush of India. The lovely Ghul Mohurs thrived at all the lower elevations but I did not find any growing above Panglong.

The Honeysuckle I found grew in amongst the thickets and apple trees above Zayangyi. The giant scented flowers were a pale gold like the honeysuckle of the English hedgerows but each single flower grew to about nine inches in length and the plant was heavier and stronger in growth than the ones at home.

The Jacaranda flourished everywhere and the elevation seemed to make little difference to its growth and habit. The Lagerstroemia of the hot dry plains of Burma is the white flowered one, L. tormentosa, which blossoms twice a year, in April and October, but those I found growing in the deep river valleys of Tawngpeng produced large panicles of pink or mauve crepe flowers.

The Mahonias grew only on the highest hills just below 7000 ft elevation and the heavy sprays of pale yellow strongly scented flowers were similar to M. bealei. The Persian Lilac or Bead Tree is indigenous to Burma and parts of North India. It is a tall stately tree of the sheltered forests of the lower hills and valleys and the bunches of lilac coloured flowers bear a remarkable resemblance to their namesake both in appearance and scent.

The Pieris was one of the commonest of the shrubs in the scrub jungle around Namhsan. A small spreading bush of seven or eight feet in height, it would have bracts of pink and red young leaves for a greater part of the year followed by sprays of "lily of the valley" flowers in January.

The Rhododendron flowered in February and grew to a large shrub or small tree. The large scented flowers were almost pure white and grew singly or in small loose bunches. Unfortunately Rhododendrons were favoured by the local people as a source of fuel and became more difficult to find each year. Of the fruit trees, apples grew everywhere and were small and tart but cooked well. The peaches in my garden were the white fleshed variety and produced enormous crops of large fruits. The may man thi's were unusual and these plums much prized. They grew tall, slender and straight trunked producing large bunches of round stoned sweet black plums which looked like large bunches of grapes. The yellow raspberries grew everywhere on the hills around Namhsan. The thorny spreading briars were similar to the loganberry in appearance and habit producing large bunches of sweet juicy deep gold fruits. The orchids were the most sought after of all Tawngpengs lovely flowers and I collected 27 different varieties. Each one grew only at a certain elevation and would not be found outside it. It took a great deal of care and attention to make them all flourish in my garden.

Month	Flowers in Season	Fruit in Season	Vegetables in Season
Jan.	Cherries, Pieris	Strawberries, Apples Oranges, Limes Bananas	All vegetables scarce
Feb.	Rhododendron, White Ginger, Mahonia, Pieris Orchid	Strawberries, Bananas	All vegetables scarce
March	Amherstia, Brownea Pink Cassia, White Bauhinia, Persian Lilac Blue Vandas, Jacaranda Streptocarpus, Fire Bush	Strawberries, Limes Papaya, Yellow Raspberries, Bananas (scarce)	Potatoes, Carrots Swede, Cauliflower Leeks, Peas, Beans Chilis, Spinach Cabbage
April	Water Festival Orchid Roses, Holmoscoldia Poinsettia, Giant Honeysuckle, Blue Shower	Yellow Raspberries Strawberries, Papaya Bananas (scarce)	Spinach, Carrots, Leeks Cabbage, Sprouts Tomatoes, Potatoes
May	Lagerstroemia, Roses Yellow Cassia, Ghul Mohur, Pink Vanda Carrion Lily Orchids (most varieties)	Mango, Plums, Peaches Lychees, Strawberries Lemons, Limes, Bananas	Potatoes, Brinjalls Cucumber, Beans, Sprouts Asparagus, Sweet Corn

Month	Flowers in Season	Fruit in Season	Vegetables in Season
June.	Roses, Gloriosa Superba, Heavenly Blue, Pink Balsam	Mango, Grapes Strawberries, Plums Pineapples, Bananas	Peppers, Brinjalls Cauliflowers, Cucumber Potatoes
July.	Roses, Tecoma Blue Vanda	Peaches, Plums, Limes Pineapples, Grapes Bananas	Peppers, Brinjalls Cucumber, Mushrooms
Aug.	Peacock Trees Kalmia, Scarlet Gingers Torenia	Lemons, Limes Pineapples, Pears Peaches, Custard Apples Bananas	Mushrooms, Beans Carrots, Peppers Cauliflower, Cucumber
Sept.	Purple Bauhinia	May-man-thi, Sweet Limes Apples, Custard Apples Ginger, Limes, Lemons Guava, Plums, Pomelo Jak Fruit, Bananas	Cucumber, Pumpkin Chinese Parsley
Oct.	Blue Wax Pea, Cherries Hydrangea, Blue Lobelia Snow Creeper, White Orchids, Green Clematis	Apples, Avocado Strawberries, Custard Apples, Oranges, Limes Lemons, Sweet Limes Pomelo, Melons, Bananas	Cauliflower, Carrots Parsnips, Tomatoes Pumpkin
Nov.	Cherries, Sunflowers	Strawberries, Guava Pineapples, Apples, Sweet Limes, Oranges, Pomelo Grapefruit, Bananas	Cauliflower, Carrots Beans, Broccoli Peppers
Dec.	Cherries, Buddleia Pleione Orchid	Strawberries, Papaya Grapefruit, Pineapples Sweet Limes, Oranges Apples, Guava, Bananas	Cauliflower, Carrots Beans, Peas, Celery Onions, Pumpkin, Chilis Roselle

The Wild Life of Tawngpeng and N.S.S.

The wild animals of Tawngpeng and the neighbouring Shan States were shy and seldom ventured into the cultivated tea fields. The rarest of these were the subject of a survey in 1960 in the hopes that publicity might save them from extinction. These were the Clouded Leopard, (Neofelis nebulosa), the Mishmi Takin, (burdorcas taxicolor), the Two Horned Rhinoceros, (rhinoceros sumatrensis), the Banteng, (bibos sondaicus), the Malay Tapir (tapirus indicus) and the Brow Antlered Deer, (cervis eldi).

There must have been many others which were not included on that list and I would hear rather than see them. The ordinary leopards were fairly common but the "cats" which I saw most frequently were the smaller ones.

Leopard Cats were fairly common in the jungles around Lilu. Bear Cats would raid my beehives. They were about the size of a small terrier dog with bear-like head and huge paws almost like hands.

The Honeymoon Cats were around all the time, raiding the fruit trees in my garden. They had silky beige coloured fur with chocolate mask and ears, legs and fluffy brush-like tail. We would have an occasional glimpse of the Black Bear on the hills or in the deeper valleys and in the thicker jungle around Lilu we saw small packs of the Wild Red Dog, one of Asia's fiercest animals. There were no elephants in Tawngpeng although an odd one would sometimes stray over the border from MongMit and cause damage in the outlying tea gardens.

Deer were plentiful and although I often heard them barking in the scrub jungle below the bungalow I never had a clear sighting.

Birds of Tawngpeng and the North Shan States

Birds were plentiful in Tawngpeng, some plain, others unforgettable for their beauty of plumage and colour or their strange appearance. Even my untrained eye could not fail to notice some of the more exotic birds and I later regretted that I had not taken more note of others.

The Green Peacock — Pavo muticus spiciferous — is the sacred bird of Tawngpeng. Not so many years ago the forests were full of those lovely birds but with the advent of the motor roads and the diminishing forests they had become a rarity. I was told that only about ten pairs of the "Daung" remain on the Payagyi Hill where once there had been great flocks.

The Silver Pheasant — Lophura nycthemerus ripponi — was quite common. I bought a "Yit" from some children who had it squashed into a tiny wicker bird-cage but it was equally unhappy in the large pen I had prepared for it in my garden and so one day I decided to release it. Wildly scratching claws and jabbing beak stilled as I hooded it and the lovely silver bird rested quietly in my arms. I carried it some distance into the jungle where I hoped there might be others. These lovely birds were to be seen from the river up to the hills around Namhsan. The Lady Amherst and the Mrs Hume Pheasants were also resident in the North Shan States.

Partridges were plentiful and three sub-species of Arborophilia are resident in the North Shan States, also the Chinese Francolin the Painted Quail and Black Breasted Quail.

The Red Junglefowl — Gallus gallus spadiceus — is of the same family as the Peacocks and Pheasants and is quite common over a wide area.

The Woodcock — Scolopacinae rusticola — is a migrant up to elevations of around 8000 ft. and three sub-species of Snipe are also regular migrants.

The great birds of the highest hill tops were the Eagles, huge brown gliders. The one which almost knocked me off my feet had a brown breast spotted and marked with soft beige and a wingspan of at least six feet. This close up was all too brief for a definite identification but they were most likely to be The Greater Spotted Eagle which is migrant to the North Shan States.

Another bird which held a special place in the lives of Tawngpeng's tea growers was the Cuckoo and not one of the growers would allow a single leaf to be plucked until this migratory bird had been heard to call over the Loi Seng Hill. Both the European and the Indian Cuckoo visited Burma and our Cuckoos would arrive with the first showers and vanish with the end of the rainy season.

Treepies and Magpies were plentiful in the higher open forests and yet another bird with unpleasant habits could not go unnoticed as we drove down the road to Lilu. Just beyond the last village we would come upon the gruesome larders of the Shrikes: bushes with bodies of birds and other small creatures impaled on every spike and thorn.

As we neared the river we would often see the Crested Serpent Eagles — Spilornis cheela burmanicus — and in the great forest trees of the river regions the Great Hornbills — Buceros bicornis cavatus — honked and bellowed making it impossible not to see them. Only once did we see a specimen of this monstrous black and white bird away from the river, it sat on a small tree near HoKyet. The "Yaung-yin" seldom strayed to the higher hills usually making its home below 4000 ft elevation.

In the region around the river and its villages we would see Sunbirds, Kingfishers and others I decided must be Bee Eaters. These and many other lovely birds were also to be found at some of the higher elevations I was told. Beyond the river across the hot dry plains and scrub jungle the birds put on a cloak of even brighter colours with great flocks of green Parakeets, the Hoopoe and the dazzling Scarlet Minivet, the dainty Paradise Flycatchers and the beautiful Fairy Bluebird. There were many others outstanding enough to be identified, the Greater Racket Tailed Drongo, the Rollers and Trogons and the Greater Coucal which seemed to be quite common in some places. On each occasion I travelled along those jungle roads there was always the interesting possibility that I might see a new bird which would be more beautiful than all the rest.

GLOSSARY

NAMES, TITLES, PALAUNG & SHAN WORDS

Da-Bo	Honourable Grandfather. (Palaung)
Da-Yah-Bo	Honourable Grandmother. (Palaung)
Deng	Large or big (Palaung)
Haw	Palace (Palaung and Shan)
Ka-Tur	Tribe of Palaung
Khun	Tribe of Kentung
Kyemaing	Heir Apparent Palaung (pronounced Ch-maing)
Lishaw	Minority tribe widely scattered in N.S.S.
Lilu	Village and Ferry over Namtu River
Loi	Mountain (Palaung)
Loi Lung	Land of Mountains, Palaung name for Tawngpeng
Mahadevi	Great Queen, Chief wife of a ruling Sawbwa
Mani Saytu Min	Legendary Burmese King who gave the first Tea Seed to the Palaungs
Mi-Ka-Gyo	Are you well? Palaung greeting
Min Shwé Thi	First Palaung Sawbwa
Mya-Tha-Peik	Begging Bowl and Ceremony surrounding it
Myosa	Minor Lord (Palaung and Shan)
Năgă	Dragon Spirit (pronounced Nĕ-găr)
Namhsan	Capital of Tawngpeng
Nam Ko-ai	River flowing into Namtu at Lilu
Nam-Tu	River and town, headquarters of Silver Mines
Nang-Nang	Little Princess (pronounced Nung-Nung)
Nĕh	Province
Nĕbaing	Provincial governor
Oĕh-Oh	Dog (Palaung)
Ohm-Yah	Trembling Waters (Palaung name for Namhsan)
Pan-Jan	Marriage Arranger (Palaung)

Pak-Ké-Gyi	The Great Pak-Ke or Teacher of Palaung Customs
Palay	Minority tribe widely scattered in N.S.S.
Nang-Shwé-Ke	Daughter of the Dragon Grandmother
Sao	Prince (pronounced Saw)
Sao-Nang	Princess
Sawbwa	Heavenly Lord. Hereditary Ruler of a Kingdom in N.S.S.
Sawbwagyi	Highness. Term of address
Sé-Lan	Legendary home of the Palaungs
Shwé-pi	First Flush of Tea Leaf (pronounced shway-pea)
Thunsan-ti	Dragon Grandmother (pronounced Thus-an-dee)
Thugyi	Village Headman (pronounced Doogee)
Tik	Circle or District. One hundredth part of a Něh
Tik-Thugyi	Circle Headman
Vai-Ra-Liang	Older Sister — Assistant to the Great Pak-ke
Vai-Ra-Pya	Older Brother — Assistant to the Great Pak-ke (Palaung)
Padaung	Tribe famous for Giraffe-Necked Women
Udibwa	The Egg Prince of Palaung Legends
Yim	Black (Palaung) — Name of Bess's puppy
Zayangyi	Old Quarter of Namhsan
Zayat	Rest Hut for travellers

PLACE NAMES

Aram	Village — Tawngpeng
Bawdwin	The Silver Hill
Bankok	Village — Tawngpeng
Hokyet	Village — Tawngpeng (pronounced Ho-kit)
Hsenwi	Capital of Hsenwi State (pronounced Sen-we)
Hsipaw	Capital of Hsipaw State (pronounced Dee-paw)
Hong-Kong Valley	Jade Mines
Konhai	Village — Tawngpeng
KutKai	Small town on route to Namhkam
Kyaukhpu	Village — Tawngpeng (pronounced Chop-pew)
Kyaukme	Town — Administrative centre for Government Departments
Kyeer-tawng	Hill where the crows call — Ruby Mines
Lah-Pai	Village — Tawngpeng
Lilu	Village and Ferry crossing Nam-Tu River
Loi Hsamsip	Named Hill

Loi Pra	Named Hill with Pagoda
Loi Seng	Holy Hill with pagodas and temples
Loi Tawng-Kyaw	Highest Hill in the district
Mainkoot	Crooked Valley (Shan) — Mogok Ruby Mines
Man-Kai	Village — Tawngpeng
Man-Lom	Village — Tawngpeng
MayMyo	Hill Resort for Mandalay
Mogok	Capital of MongMit State
Musé	Border Town
Namhkam	Border Town
Namhsan	Capital — Tawngpeng State (Modern name for Ohm-Yah)
Na-peng	Fishing village near Lilu
Omason	Village — Tawngpeng
Panglong	Village — Tawngpeng
Payagyi	The principal temple — Tawngpeng
Saram	A village (Palaung)
Sé-Tu	Village at Payagyi
Se-Ton-Hung	Village at Tawngpeng
Tawngma	Village at Tawngpeng
Yay-Oh	Plains village

RELIGIOUS FESTIVALS

Mya-Tha-Peik	Festival of the Begging Bowl
Tadding-gyut	Festival of Lights
Tazaungmon	Robe weaving Ceremonies
Thingyan	Water Festival (pronounced Din-jăn)
Wazo	Festival for beginning of Lent

DRAMA AND BALLET

Anyein Pwé	Modern amusing plays
Yama-Zat	Traditional dancing
Yein Pwé	Burmese Ballet and Opera
Yoke-Thay	Puppet Shows
Zat Pwé	Traditional plays

MUSICAL INSTRUMENTS

Hnĕh	Clarinet

Keezi	Altar gong
Kyi-waing	Set of Gongs
Krung-hom-hpom	Palaung drum
Mowng	Big gong
Ozi	Burmese drum
Pah-lway	Flute
Pattala	Xylophone
Pat-mah	Big drum
Pat-Saing	Set of drums
Saung-gauk	Burmese Harp
Tah-boh	Trumpet
Tah-yaw	Violin

WILDLIFE

Daung-bo	Peacock
Daung-ma	Peahen
Kya-thit	Leopard
Kyan-thudaw	Malay Tapir
Layke	Tortoise or Turtle
Lin-yŏn	Eagle
Tak-Htoo	Large house Lizard
Thamin	Brow-Antlered Deer
Tharmin	Takin
Thit-kyoung	Clouded Leopard
Tsaing	Banteng — Wild cattle
Wet-kyan	Two Horned Rhinoceros
Yaung-Yin	Hornbill
Yit	Pheasant

BURMESE NAMES AND PLACES

Arakan	Mandalay Pagoda
Ava	Bridge over Irrawaddy River
Amarapura	The old capital of Burma
Aingyi	Blouse
Bayin Naung	Head of the fifth group of Nats
Bein	Opium
Dah	Short sword or chopping knife
Duttabaung	Burmese King deified as a Nat
Chinthay	Mythical lion-like beast
Gaungbaung	Turban-like headdress

Hpu-Hpu	White-repetition emphasises eg. Snow White
Hingo	A fish soup
Hti	Umbrella — ornamental top of a pagoda (prounouced Tee)
Gokteik	Gorge between Maymyo and Hsipaw
Kadaw	Homage
Kaukswe	Burmese noodles
Kathein Khin	Displayed Gifts
Kathein	Festival and Procession of Gifts
Ko yin	Probationer Monk
La-hpet	Tea — the plant
La-hpet-hso	Wet Tea or Pickled Tea
La-hpet-yé	Tea — the drink (pronounced La-pay-yay)
Ley-gon-gyin	Four Animals — a gambling game
Lungyi	Man's skirt
May-man-thi	Cherry plums
Maymyo-pan	Asters
Me-Daw	Queen Mother
Mindon Min	King of Burma 1853-78
Mye-Nan-Daw	Royal Palace at Mandalay
Nat	Spirit Deity
Neikban	Nirvana — the final extinction (pronounced Nĕ-ban)
Nga-pi	Fish paste
Oo-Min-Thronze	Pagoda on Sagaing Hill
Păn	Flower (pronounced Bun)
Păya	Pagoda
Pópa	Holy Hill of the cobras
Pongyi	Monk
Pongyi-Kyaung	Monastery
Pyà-That	Spired roof
Pwé	Festival
Sagaing Hill near Mandalay	Seat of the Silver industry
Sanghas	The Order of Monks
Sayador	Abbot
Shan-si-thi	Yellow raspberries
Shwebo	District west of Mandalay

Shwé Dagon	Burmas holiest pagoda — Rangoon
Shwé Hintha	Mythical Bird or Duck
Shwé Myo	The Golden City — Mandalay
Shwé-pi	The first flush of tea leaf
Singaturra	Hill on which Shwé Dagon stands
Soonkway	Ceremony of feeding the Monks
To-fu-cyauk	Local delicacy made from beans
Tagya-Nat	Chief of the Order of Nats
Tamin	Food — generally rice
Tamin-tsa-oot	Alms bowl with tapering lid
Tawng	Hill
Taungoo	16th century King who founded Ava-Pegu Dynasty
Taupawadi	A district of Mandalay — (iron and steel)
Tazaung	A chapel or place of worship at a shrine
Zeygyo	The Grand Market at Mandalay

AUTHORS NOTES AND ACKNOWLEDGEMENTS

In the beginning Piet and I were accepted by the Palaungs as any strangers in their midst would have been, with courtesy and politeness. It was only after some years, when they had judged us to be good friends that they began to speak openly of their customs, festivals and legends. I am greatly indebted to the late Sawbwa and others of his family for their help in understanding the customs and language and for the loan of the old books. These had been compiled from ancient records and made clear to me many of the things that had puzzled me during my first two years in Tawngpeng.

The retiring manager passed on to me many of the interesting facts he had learned about the wildlife, and the local customs. So many of the local inhabitants, who included Palaungs, Shans, Karens, Kachins, Burmese, Chinese and Indians, kept me supplied with a great deal of information about the costumes and customs of Tawngpeng as well as the wildlife, flora and fauna. Perhaps their knowledge of these things was sometimes tinged more with tradition than truth though this often added to the interest.

The Nation Newspaper and its Supplements were a constant source of information on every aspect of Burmese and Shan life, arts and crafts, and the religious festivals which I might otherwise have missed or misunderstood.

Our Lashio and Mandalay agents showed us so many aspects of their home towns which I am sure we would never have discovered for ourselves, and it was the same in Rangoon when Burmese friends took us to so many places of interest in their city which the ordinary tourist might never have seen.

My brother deserves thanks for giving up so much of his

time to reading my work. His advice was invaluable and he helped me to identify many new flowers.

We owe a great many people thanks for their hospitality over the years, especially Kit and Nina who not only put us up each year but also introduced us to so many interesting and varied entertainments in Rangoon.

The butterflies were my father's great interest. He set up the small collection which I still have in my possession and he must have spent many hours working on them.

Most important of all was Piet's contribution. He endured, encouraged and helped with all my botanical expeditions and taught me a great deal about tea. It was at his suggestion that I began to keep a diary of facts which became the foundation of this book.

Having no wish to cause more trouble for those kind gentle people of Tawngpeng than circumstances and insurgency have already done, it was only after hearing of the death of the Sawbwa of Tawngpeng that I decided the time had come when I could begin to write about them. For this reason all personal names given are ficticious.

I do not claim to be an expert botanist nor zoologist but merely an interested amateur and I am open to correction on the identity of all flora and fauna.

BIBLIOGRAPHY

Palaung — English Dictionary — Compiled from old records and loaned to me by Maha Thray Sithu Sao Hkun Pan Sein.

History of the Palaung Peoples — Compiled from old records and loaned to me by Sao Khun Hsuk of Chiengmai.

Tawngpeng Calling — U Khin Maung — 1949 — Printed at the Hanthawaddy Press, Rangoon. Copy given to me by Sao Hkun Ohn.

Butterflies of India — Chas. B. Antram F.E.S. — 1924. Thacker Spink and Co., Calcutta and Simla.

Common Malayan Butterflies — R. Morrel — 1960. Malayan Nature Handbooks. Longmans.

Snakes of Malaya — M.F.W. Tweedie MA.C.M.Z.S. — 1957. Government Printing Office, Singapore.

The Birds of Burma — Bertram E. Smythies. Revised Ed. 1958. Oliver and Boyd.

Tropical Gardening and Planting — H.F. Macmillan F.L.S. A.H.R.H.S. 1961 — Macmillan.

Flowering Trees and Shrubs in India — D.V. Cowen — 1952. Thacker and Co. Ltd. — Bombay.

Lords of the Sunset — Maurice Collis — 1936. Faber and Faber.

Encyclopedia Americana. International Edition — 1949. New York.

The Pagoda War — Lord Dufferin and the Fall of Ava — A.T.Q. Stewart — 1972 — Faber and Faber.

Hariot, Lady Dufferin — "Our Viceregal Life in India". 1889.

The Pacification of Burma — C.E. Crosthwaite — 1907. London.

Elementary Handbook of the Burmese Language — 1939 by Taw Sein Ko C.I.E. I.S.O. K.H.I. M.L.C. American Baptist Mission Press — Rangoon.

Burma Wildlife Survey — 1960.

Elephant Bill — Lt. Col. J.H. Williams O.B.E. — 1950.

Bundoola — Lt. Col. J.H. Williams O.B.E. Rupert Hart Davis.

The Nation Newspaper and Supplements — Rangoon.

Burmese Music and Dancing — U Tha Myat.

Woodcarving of Burma — Harry L. Tilly —

from Government Printing Press Burma — 1903

Iron and Steel Work — E.N. Bell I.C.S. —

from Government Printing Press Burma — 1907

Japanned Ware of Ava — Major Burney

Journal of the Asiatic Society of Bengal 1932.

Golden Earth — Norman Lewis — Jonathan Cape.